TRACKING '

MW01154691

A reconnaissance mission to discover
what our fathers did in World War II

Melaney Welch Moisan

TRACKING THE 101ST CAVALRY

A reconnaissance mission to discover what our fathers did in World War II

Wheat Field Press

Cover and book design:
Melaney Welch Moisan

Maps on pages 14, 124, 137, 204,
215, 220, 229, and 235 are reprinted
from *Wingfoot: the official history
of the 101st Cavalry* and were drawn
by Captain Crozier Wood.

Wheat Field Press
PO Box 20237
Keizer, OR 97307
www.wingfoot101.us

To purchase additional
copies of this book:
www.lulu.com; search for "Moisan"

ISBN 978-0-615-25040-3

To my father and all the other men who served
with the 101st Cavalry in World War II.
Knowing you has enriched my life
more than you can imagine.

To my husband and children.
You still have time to ask.

Table of Contents

Maps

Fathers leave footprints

deep in the earth before us,

footprints we follow, running,

always behind, trying to catch

the man who strides on

ahead of us, shaping our path.

But his footprints fade faster

than we can run.

—mwm

Introduction

It all started as one little idea playing around in the back of my mind. For years I tried to get details about my father's World War II service, but I gave up when I learned his records had been destroyed by fire in the 1970s.

Then one night in 2002, as I watched *Band of Brothers*, the television miniseries based on Stephen Ambrose's book, my idea was born. I watched the veterans of Easy Company talk about their experiences and wondered how hard it would be to find men who had served in the 101st Cavalry with my father. Maybe I could even find someone who knew him well, someone who had been a friend.

My father hadn't talked much about the war when he was alive, and he died before I was curious enough to force the issue. Talking to men he served with wouldn't be the same as hearing it from him, but it would be better than nothing. Surely someone could be found who remembered him.

Although I thought about it a lot, I didn't do anything until the fall of 2004, when I finally put my idea into action. A decade earlier, tracking down men who served with my father would have been difficult, if not impossible, but by 2004 I had come to believe that all the information I could ever want was available on the internet.

I started with a simple search for "101st Cavalry." That few minutes on the computer started me down a path I'm still wandering along; it has been an incredible journey.

When I began, I wanted to learn a little something about my father and what he did in the war; I discovered much more. For one thing, I learned I wasn't alone. I found a community of people on the web, all seeking answers to what their fathers did in the war. And they weren't all the children of American veterans; some were the children of Polish prisoners of war, German soldiers, and Holocaust survivors whose fathers had briefly crossed paths with the 101st Cavalry sometime between February and May 1945.

I found a lot of men whose experiences in World War II deserve to be told. Some of them have held their stories in for a long time, never sharing them, not even with their families, just the way my father kept silent about the war.

Some of their stories are no more than snippets – snapshot memories saves for more than 60 years:

> We came upon a group of about 100 German soldiers with horses and wagons under a tree at an intersection. We took the Germans as prisoners, and I often wonder what happened to their horses.

> We were relieving the 63rd Infantry and this tank just came crashing out the side of a house. Every gun in the corps starting firing at once to destroy that tank – it's called a 'corps serenade.' That was something. You just have to hear it – it was really something.

We saw those Hitler baby factories. The pure Aryan girls would go there and have babies. They were all gone, but the high chairs and little tables were all still there.

My electrician was Charles "Moose" Mehlich. He was a phone company maintenance man from New York, and he was called Moose because of his nose. He was shot through his nose sideways and when he came back, he looked like a new man. He had the nicest nose.

Our radio operator got shot in the rear end through a canteen and after that, every time he had too much to drink, he'd drop his trousers and say "Want to see my hemstitch?" He was so proud of that.

❧ ❧

After 60 years, memory is an imperfect thing. Some memories come back as if the events happened yesterday, and others have been lost forever.

Many men claim they can't remember anything special about the war: "Just one day the same as the next," one man told me, "us trying to kill them and them trying to kill us."

Others say they just don't want to remember; they've tried hard to forget.

I've tried to fit these imperfect memories into the official record of the 101st Cavalry as closely as possible. This hasn't always been easy. No matter how clear a man's memory of an event may be, it is rare that he also remembers the place where it occurred or the date.

But that hasn't been the hardest thing I've had to deal with over the past four years. By far the most difficult is the growing realization that this generation of veterans is leaving us faster than we can collect their remarkable stories. I missed the opportunity to talk to Alvin Romero and Louis Peele and Alec Sleptiza and Nathan Granat. By the time I found them, it was too late.

According to estimates by the Department of Veterans Affairs, approximately 1,000 World War II veterans die every day. As their number dwindles, those of us who still have the opportunity need to ask our fathers and grandfathers to share their memories now. Soon it will be too late.

Germany 2006

March in Germany looks more like winter than spring. In the countryside, everything is brown. Brittle autumn leaves still cling to skeletal trees and only the occasional crocus hints that the seasons are about to change. Flowerboxes and gardens are barren, and ice is in a slow retreat on lakes and rivers. Germany is not at its best in March. But in 1945, my father crossed the Saar River and drove his jeep into World War II in March, so that's when I would go.

I'd never been interested in visiting Germany, but as I learned more about my father's service in the war, I began to toy with the idea. Listening to veterans talk about villages where they fought, a river they forded, or a hill where someone died, I knew I needed a stronger sense of place to understand their stories better. I needed to go to Germany. When my father went, he hadn't been exactly eager to go either. We would have at least that much in common.

I didn't speak German, and I didn't have enough time to learn, so I drafted my youngest son, Ted, as my traveling companion. He had minored in German in college and had recently bicycled 800 miles around Germany. He knew the country; he knew the language. Taking him seemed like a good investment. He agreed. Even so, when I told him that it was a pilgrimage of sorts, he was skeptical. He wasn't sure he could offer much support in that area, as he didn't really believe in pilgrimages.

On the first day of our trip, he wrote as much in his journal.

> I told my mother from the start that I thought her journey was doomed or, at best, quixotic. I don't think the things that she and others like her are looking for can be found in the places where they look. Even if they could be found, I'm not sure anybody would recognize them.
>
> I mean to say that it makes almost zero sense to me to be going to Germany at all, since what changed the life of my grandfather and the lives of his comrades-in-arms, what made him and them stronger or weaker and made them sometimes alien in their own country and to their own families — these are not points on a map or features of the terrain or buildings or factories or even the camps.
>
> What changed these men, I can only suspect, were changes that happened in their hearts and minds. In, for example, the relationship between two people who have had to depend on each other through the most hopeless suffering …
> I wanted to tell my mother that if she's serious about following her father and seeing what he saw, she should enlist in the Army. I think for our purposes, she would be more likely to find

what she's looking for in the mountains of Afghanistan than in the German Alps.

He had a point. To understand fully my father's wartime experience, I would need to push and pull a comrade through the rigors of boot camp, cover his back and thank God he's covering mine during dark nights far from home. And I'd have to hold what is left of my friend in my arms while his blood soaks my shirt and covers my face. Only then would I know exactly what my father and others like him went through. The silence of our fathers about their wartime experiences may have been their attempt to protect us from such understanding.

I knew that one trip to Germany wasn't going to provide this kind of awareness. But it would give me the opportunity to see what the men of the 101st saw: the landscape, the villages, the people. I would have context for the stories they told me.

Place also provides a visceral connection to past events. People have described it to me as a chill they can feel at the site of a Civil War battlefield or a physical reaction that brings them to tears at Arlington Cemetery. I once experienced that feeling in Montana near the Little Bighorn River on a rolling plain dotted with markers honoring Custer's soldiers and Sioux warriors.

Ted and I used the daily reports written during the war and hand-drawn maps as our guidebooks. Those directed us to villages along the back roads where I hoped to find history, just not the typical history tourists sought in Germany. Our initial objectives, to use the military phrase I had come to know so well, were similar to those of the 101st Cavalry in 1945: reconnoiter Schaffhausen, Hostenbach, Geislautern, Wehrden; take Hill 283; and cross the Saar River. We would then move quick-

The Saar River as it flows through Saarbrucken

ly east and south, across Germany toward Austria. It took the 101st Cavalry almost 80 days; we had only six.

Saarbrucken, where we spent our first two nights, is the midsize capital city of Saarland, Germany's smallest state. The city is located just east of the Saar River, a tributary of the Moselle River that flows down through Germany and France from the Vosges Mountains. For centuries the area was a tennis ball in play between France and Germany.

The Saarbrucken we saw was split by the Saar River, with the old town on one side and newer buildings on the other. The new town center has a pedestrian mall filled with department stores, restaurants, and shops selling cell phones and iPods.

Eugene Tharp remembered Saarbrucken in 1945.

"We walked right down the main street of Saarbrucken," he said, "and the town had been leveled on both sides." According to the caption written on a photo in the National Archives, nearly nine-tenths of the town had been destroyed, including its train station. Of Saarbrucken's 135,000 inhabitants, only about 1,000 remained in the city.

On our second day in Germany, Ted and I went to an area of rolling hills and forests on the south bank of the Saar River. Between these wooded hills and the river lay the villages of Schaffhausen, Geislautern, Wehrden, and Hostenbach, small forgotten places where the 101st fought its first battles.

For weeks, as the cavalrymen waited for the signal to attack, they watched these villages from the high ground; then, at night, they would creep in to assess the strength of the German Army. By the time I went to Germany, I had spent years tracing battles and troop movements on maps. I was eager to see the towns and villages whose names had become so familiar.

It was a cold, gray day when Ted and I left Saarbrucken by train for Bous. At least the weather was dry, and we wouldn't experience the below-freezing temperatures and snow that had plagued the 101st when it first arrived.

In Bous, we caught a bus, even though it wasn't far across the Saar to Hostenbach and Schaffhausen. As the bus crawled

down the street, stopping every few blocks, we stared out the windows, searching for any sign that we were in one of these two villages. We discovered individual villages no longer seemed to exist. Instead, the suburbs sprouted along a now busy highway: houses, cafes, and cookie-cutter storefronts in an unbroken line.

A square mustard-yellow sign finally told us we were entering Hostenbach. We pulled the cord. By the time we got off, we were in Schaffhausen, right across the street from the Shaffhausen Kebap Restaurant, a type of Turkish fast-food restaurant springing up all over Germany. We needed time to study the map, so we went in for lunch.

As we ate, we pinpointed nearby villages on our map and circled the area where Hill 283 should be. The name, Hill 283, was, of course, a U.S. Army designation, and we had no idea what its German name might be, or if it had ever had a name. All we knew was that it existed somewhere nearby, and men from the 101st had lost their lives taking it. Hill 283 had been the focus of a difficult and bloody assault, but a necessary one. As the highest hill in the area, it was strategically important.

We felt confident we knew where we were going, so we tucked our maps into our backpacks and started off. I was less confident now than when I left home that I would be able to touch history the way I wanted. As I stood on that modern thoroughfare with Hondas and Chevys buzzing by and hundreds of possible Hill 283s on the horizon, it was clear that history was going to play hard to get.

I had seen a film made on March 13, 1945, by the Army Signal Corps. It was shot in Schaffhausen as the cavalry began its move into Germany. Today, the Hostenbach-Schaffhausen road looks nothing like it did then. Granted, the trees, bare and lifeless, were the same, and the backdrop of hills hadn't changed much either. But in 1945, the narrow streets had been filled with women, children, and elderly men, many struggling to pull wooden carts filled with their belongings over rubble that had once been their homes. What Ted and I saw in 2006 was a four-lane thoroughfare lined with Turkish kebab houses, pastry shops, markets, beauty parlors, and suburban homes.

We searched the horizon for a wooded area, hopefully one on a hill. Judging by our map, the highest hill in the area was Hoheberg, possibly high enough to have been a strategic asset. It was located in the correct location: in the center of the slightly flattened circle created by the towns of Schaffhausen, Geislautern, and Wehrden.

A steep, sawdust-covered path led us to the top, where we could look out over the Saar River valley to the river below. The haze we looked through wasn't caused by dust kicked up by 1945 artillery and mortar fire; it was instead a grim layer of smog from cars and factories.

Standing where the German defenses may have been located, I tried to imagine the sounds from the American Army, downhill and to the south: the shuddering rumble of tanks, the

The path winding down the hill to Geislautern.

whine and moan of armored cars and trucks, and the shouts of men eager to take possession of this hill. Or perhaps only the hushed murmur of voices rolled to the top of the hill, like wind-blown mist, a whisper that occasionally froze in mid-sentence as a shell burst or a mine was tripped.

We stood there a few moments more, trying to put our-selves into the past, but the present was in our way. Two slender, gray-haired women got out of a faded red car — a compact — and, chatting, headed off down a walking trail that led past a tennis club. They quickly disappeared into the woods, although we continued to hear their laughter for several minutes. In a field slightly downhill from us, a man tossed a stick for a golden retriever, who would leap and spin gracefully in the air, grab the stick, and lope back toward the man, head high. Sixty years is a long time, and nothing we had seen so far confirmed that battles had ever been fought on this hill.

For a while Ted and I walked along the top of the hill, trying to imagine where the German machine guns might have been placed. When we were ready to return to Saarbrucken, we decided not to go back east the way we had come, but to follow a path south that wound through the trees; according to our map, it would take us to Geislautern. We both felt confident that, if this path did come out at Geislautern, we had found Hill 283.

We followed a small stream down the hill, and, as we approached town, we passed an enormous crater in the earth. Pausing, we studied the hole and wondered what could have made one that size. The Americans and Germans had pounded each other with mortar fire for weeks as the stalled Americans waited to take this hill and cross into Germany. Since neither of us had any idea how big the hole would be from a shell the size of those being lobbed back and forth, we could only imagine this one might have originated during the war. It could, I supposed, have been caused by the same explosion that killed Lt. Robert Schafer, 2nd Lt. Charles Pierce, 2nd Lt. Alfred Kupferschmidt, and S/Sgt. Walter Mennel in those first days at the front. We would never know.

"I didn't walk around all day thinking of death and war," is how Ted described the day in his journal, adding, "But I have to admit it was a fine walk we were having."

True, it was hard to picture war and death in the stillness of these woods or imagine they had once been filled with trenches, foxholes, mines and booby traps, and deafening crash of artillery fire.

"We spent days in cold, wet, underground dugouts," one veteran had told me. "The nights were very dark, with no moon, and sometimes it looked like even the bushes crawled around out there."

These woods had been the final resting place of soldiers, both German and American, and I'd been told that during those long February and March nights men would sneak out of their foxholes to bury their dead in an effort to protect them from the wild animals. As Ted and I walked in silence through the trees, I wondered how many men might still lie hidden in these woods beneath a carpet of dried leaves.

Map 1
February 11-March 15, 1945

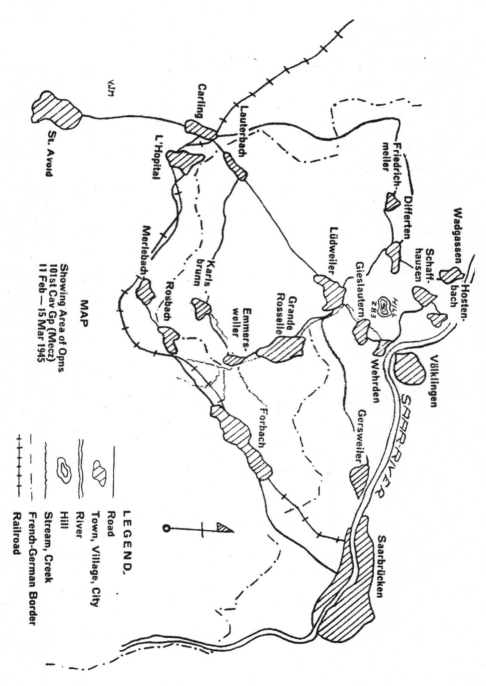

Vlm

St. Avold

Carling

Lauterbach

Friedrich-meiler

Differten

Wadgassen

Hosten-bach

L'Hopital

Schaff-hausen

Lüdweiler

Gieslautern

HILL 283

Völklingen

Merlebach

Karls-brunn

Emmers-weiler

Grande Rosselle

Wehrden

Rosbach

Forbach

Gersweiler

SAAR RIVER

MAP
Showing Area of Opns
101st Cav Gp (Mecz)
11 Feb — 15 Mar 1945

Saarbrücken

L E G E N D.
Road
Town, Village, City
River
Hill
Stream, Creek
French-German Border
Railroad

Front Lines: February 1945

Saarbrucken

On February 9, 1945, the men of the 101st Cavalry began a rather piecemeal relief of the 106th Cavalry along the Spurk-Schaffhausen line near the Saar River. Schaffhausen was a small village, and Spurk little more than a pub and an inn on Spurker Gasse Street near the village of Wadgassen, south and west of Schaffhausen.

A thousand men moving into the hills above the Saar River could have backed up traffic for miles, alerting the Germans, so the 101st slipped into the crowded chaos that was the front line, one platoon at a time. As one troop of the 101st moved in, one of the 106th Cavalry moved out. Troop B, 116th Squadron, my father's unit, settled in on one of the smaller hills between the towns of Differten and Schaffhausen. Squadron headquarters, administration, and maintenance remained in St. Avold, France, about five miles away.

"We stayed in houses in one little community," said David Gay, "and the enemy was about one mile away in another little community."

In a letter dated February 9, Lt. Col. Hubert Leonard, commander of the 116th Squadron, wrote to his wife, Mary, at home:

"I have been quite a busy little man, going places. Now I am settled again and, believe it or not, quite comfortable. All hands are well and they too are rather comfortable. Old Man Weather has not been too rough and our sick rate is almost nil. The not-too-tough Jerries are not too far away, and the Lord better help them if they don't pack up and move."

One thing I learned as I read the dozens of letters Lt. Col. Leonard sent home to his wife was that he tended to understate everything: weather, shelling, injuries, illness. Maybe he did it to protect her, but possibly from an officer's point of view things were sometimes a little more comfortable.

Lt. Col. Hubert Leonard, commander, 116th Squadron
Photo courtesy Jay Leonard.

While some houses and even whole villages had been abandoned by Germans fleeing the war, other villages were still populated. That made no difference to the cavalrymen. According to Lt. Col. Leonard, the troopers had little chance to meet the local people. He wrote that the men weren't allowed into the villages, nor were the civilian villagers allowed anywhere near the Army.

"We do not have any passes, leaves or furloughs, as we have more important things to do," he wrote.

In February 1945, the Germans, intent on defending their positions, stood between the cavalry and the Saar. Most of the activity between the two sides was limited to small scouting patrols, sniping, and occasional mortar and artillery fire.

Clinton Thompson, Troop B, 116th Squadron, remembers his first day on the front. It was his birthday.

"We pulled in," he said, "and — bingo! — just like that, we were in the middle of it."

Wilmer "Buck" Fluharty, who was stationed at headquarters, remembers the weather more than anything else.

"It was cold," he said, "and the cavalry hadn't been equipped for the cold quite as well as the infantry. All the overshoes went to the infantry, so my family sent me some. They didn't arrive until winter was over."

Earl Carmickle agrees with Fluharty, both about the weather and the supplies. "The worst part was we never got the stuff we needed," he said. "We wore the same clothes the whole time we were in and didn't have supplies for the cold. It was bitter cold, and sometimes we'd lay our heads down in the snow to sleep."

"If we had to sleep outside in the snow," said John Gorski, "we'd sometimes sleep under the fir trees that had branches hanging down to the ground. They hid us and kept the snow off us."

As shells burst in trees overhead, heavy chunks of ice and broken branches crashed on the ground, causing damage of their own, and none of the wood that fell could be used to build the fires they needed for warmth. That would have betrayed their positions to the Germans.

One night, Lou Gergley, B Troop, 116th Squadron, and two other men had to go to an observation post near a trench. It was cold and snowing, and the ditch was filled with water and had a crust of ice on the top. "I stepped onto the ice," Gergley said, "and my foot went through into the water, filling my boot. I took off the boot and wrapped the wool cap I'd been wearing on my head around my foot and set the boot and the sock on the ground. The next morning, my boot and sock were frozen solid. It was that cold."

Ironically, one of Gergley's duties was to make sure people changed their socks and kept their feet dry.

"Fortunately, we didn't spend every night sleeping out like that," he added. "We were usually pulled back to the main body and spent many nights in beds."

Clair Becker, Troop C, 101st Squadron, describes those first weeks as dismal:

"I joined as a replacement in early March," he said, "and from then until we reached Uffenheim in mid-April, the weather was very bad. We had snow squalls, cold wind, hard rain, and then the thaw, with foot-deep mud. Fields were an ocean of mud. We would be stuck for hours trying to get around roadblocks, running into other outfits with tanks or trucks swamped."

Fluharty took a photo of his tank, "Fightin' Bastard," resting at a precarious angle in an ocean of mud that nearly

Caption on the back of the photo: "Fightin' Bastard stuck."
Photo courtesy of Buck Fluharty.

swallows it. In the photo, two shovels lean against the tank; you have to pity the men who will be assigned to use them.

The 101st Cavalry spent most of February and early March waiting not just for supplies to come from the rear, but for the equipment needed to fight the war.

"We needed flamethrowers to break through the Siegfried Line. You couldn't crack through those pillboxes with anything else we had," Gergley said.

Within days of relieving the 106th Cavalry Group, the Army's XV Corps ordered the 101st to start planning an attack on the Saar River. No date was set for this attack; it depended entirely on the progress of other units in the Corps and the arrival of supplies.

Meanwhile, the Germans at the front line were strengthening their defense with both vehicular and foot patrols. Anti-personnel and anti-tank mines planted in November created a deadly defense line. None of these mines had yet been recorded, making movement through the area extremely dangerous.

During the long days spent waiting for the command to attack, both the Germans and Americans sent out aggressive patrols to monitor each other's activities. The cavalry's platoon-sized scouting patrols — around a dozen men — would go out to find and record the mines, locate the Germans, and count them. My father told me once that he crawled on his belly halfway across Germany. What he didn't say was that he was looking for mines, booby traps, and heavily armed Germans while he was down there on the ground.

John Almond remembers the day he and his lieutenant, Lt. Harvey Wood, were on patrol, detonating mines.

"His grenade fell," said Almond, and hit the trigger of a mine. "We froze. I expected to die. The mine didn't go off and neither did the grenade, but it was frightful."

Not everyone had the luck of Almond and his lieutenant. On the afternoon of February 11, Captain Francis X. "Bud"

Bages, from Brooklyn, N.Y., and an officer from each cavalry troop were checking for gaps in the mine fields that had been laid by the 106th and other Allied units. A few members of the 106th accompanied them to help locate the mines. As the group made its way through the area, someone accidentally tripped one of those anti-personnel mines.

The resulting explosion seriously injured 2nd Lt. John S. Halsey of the 116th Reconnaissance Squadron and S/Sgt. Doyle of the 106th. Lt. Halsey's was the first injury in the 101st since its entry into combat. It was noted briefly in the after-action accounts as "an event heavily felt by all."

David Gay's jeep was hit one night when they were on patrol. "We were headed back," he said, "coming down a hill, when a mortar shell hit about 20 feet away. All three of us were hit with shrapnel. One man had a piece of shrapnel tear through his leg between the bone and the muscle. He was out of it for good. A piece hit my helmet and a small piece hit the corner of my mouth. It was so small I barely felt it. The other boy was hit several times in the chest, but it didn't hurt him much, they were so small."

In spite of almost constant shelling and the danger of patrolling through mine-covered fields and woods, most of the men remember these days as relatively easy, at least compared to what would come later. Unless out on patrol, many of the men were billeted in houses and felt lucky to have some shelter from the cold. It was even better for officers.

"Up here the food is excellent, the cigarettes plentiful, and the morale is high," wrote Lt. Col. Leonard to his wife. In another letter the same week, he wrote:

> My Dear Mary,
>   All is well and everyone is fine and we eat pretty good. When one gets steak for lunch (and is even asked "How would you like it? Rare or

well done?") then you can understand that the mess arrangements could not be any better.

My present quarters are in a two-story house, our CP [Command Post] is on the ground floor and our living quarters (with beds) are on the second floor. We have a good roof, which is a rarity in this part of the country, and the same is true for windows. The house is well built and has a good cellar, just in case we need it. We have heat, too, so all in all we are quite comfortable.

At least for the time being. We are not going to be contented to stay put in one place — can't win sitting in one place — especially here in Jerry country. Otto Wichman is some help to me in reading German signs, streets, names, and the like. He is not too good, but usually gets some results as far as speaking the language is concerned. There is no one around here to talk to as the civilians are not allowed around here.

Father [Maurice] Powers is with us for a while and is quartered in the same building. He is quite a man to have around the men; regardless of creed, all the men like him. By the way, there is a mass today about a mile to our rear and another one later in the day. I will not be able to attend either (through no fault of mine). I am writing this at 0930 and will have a busy day – our working hours are (censored) our eating hours are fairly regular and as I have mentioned before, the food is good.

With loads of love, I am yours,
Hughie

Mostly because of the rumors that flew through the two squadrons, the 116th expected they would be sent to capture Spurk and Schaffhausen once the orders for attack came, while the 101st would capture Hill 283 and the town of Wehrden. Plans for a coordinated attack on the Saar River appeared to be taking shape. It was just another rumor, but still the men waited. They waited for battle, they waited for pay, they waited for supplies, and they waited for mail.

"It would be comforting," wrote Lt. Col. Leonard, "to receive a letter or two."

In addition to the lack of mail, three weeks had passed since the men had received pay, but with nowhere to spend it, that was a minor concern.

The men did have time for recreation of sorts. When Eugene Tharp got to the front, he found an abandoned motorcycle. Even though he had been injured on one before he left the States, he was ready to get on this one.

"Captain [Augustine "Gus"] Littleton asked me to take him for a ride one day," said Tharp. "He got on the back, and I took him for a ride all right. When we got back, he said, 'I'm sure never going on another motorcycle ride with you.'

'Still breathing, aren't you,' I said."

On Valentines Day, Troop B of the 116th Squadron was on reconnaissance when they saw five men around a house in one of the small villages in the area. They fired eight rounds of high explosives at the house, setting the surrounding woods on fire. Several more Germans ran out to fight the fire, and the cavalrymen fired four more rounds, killing those men. As more German soldiers came out to bury the dead, they too were fired on.

The next day, smoke could be seen rising from the direction of Wadgassen, where a fire that had begun with three houses was continuing to grow. Soon much of the town was burning.

During these early days at the front, the men listened with some fear to the popping of small arms fire from the villages and from Hill 283. Lt. G. L. Bricker was wounded by sniper fire, and Second Lt. John Muckstadt, who was in charge of

Troop C, led a patrol into an enemy outpost, where he, S/Sgt George Geissinger, and PFC Woodrow Ball were all captured.

After a few weeks, the novelty of their situation was wearing off and the reality of war had settled in.

Still, according to Lt. Col. Leonard, everyone was relatively comfortable "except the Jerries," who were, he wrote, "a bit weary. And we give no rest to the weary. Our artillery does a real bang up job, and they are capable of doing great things and are mighty comforting to have around. We have a standing order to all Troops: Be prepared to serve hot coffee to the Russians. Come on Joe [Stalin]!"

A priest, probably Father Powers, came to the camp one day in late February and told the men it was Easter Sunday.

"It wasn't," said Lou Gergley, "but he said that since he was there and might not be back for awhile, that we would celebrate Easter."

Perhaps the priest had a premonition that, come Easter Sunday, which would be April 1 that year, the 101st might not have time to stop and celebrate.

On the night of February 17, about 9 p.m., a patrol from the infantry regiment to which the 101st Cavalry was attached, left for Schaffhausen, reaching the outskirts of town at 10:50 p.m. They hid in empty buildings and watched the activities of the Germans all the next day. Enemy activity, they reported, was light, and few civilians ventured out into the streets.

At 7:30 the next evening, a patrol from Troop B, 116th Squadron, under the command of 1st Lt. Joseph Borkowski was preparing to relieve the infantry patrol when they received an urgent message from Schaffhausen. German soldiers were creeping up on the patrol, the message stated, and they were in danger of being surrounded.

First Lt. Borkowski and his patrol immediately set out to rescue the trapped infantry. Borkowski told his men to establish a protective screen along the road from Schaffhausen, which allowed the infantry patrol to escape, even though they were under heavy German fire.

Once the infantry passed through the screen, Lt. Borkowski's patrol began to withdraw, but as they were leaving, the Germans laid down a heavy barrage of mortar fire. The men dove for cover, causing confusion in the darkness. Eventually, the men in the patrol all gathered at the outpost, although it took some time. They quickly discovered two men were missing and three had been wounded. Lt. Borkowski immediately reorganized a second patrol and returned to the place where they had come under fire.

"I didn't want to go back," said Borkowski, "but, hell, men were missing."

The second patrol found one man sitting on the side of the road in a dazed condition, and they brought him safely to the outpost. They also discovered that Tec. 5 Thurman Swim, from Turley, Oklahoma, had been killed by mortar fragmentation. Lt. Borkowski earned a Bronze Star for his actions that day.

On another patrol, Borkowski and his men crossed the river into Saarbrucken:

> We moved slowly through this terrific thing — the Siegfried Line — with all these huge pillboxes, the concrete bunkers that made up the Siegfried Line. I remember [Grover Cleveland] Wilson, my radio operator, was with me and Sgt. Swanson. Your dad may have been there, too. We just kept going through those pillboxes, and we saw a guy, a German, waving a big white flag. It may have been a stupid thing to do, but we honored that white flag and went up to them. There was an officer and some men, and I said to the officer, "What's the problem?"
>
> And he said, "We're getting a lot of information that the Americans are disorganized, undisciplined, and have no equipment. We've been

watching you for half an hour. We think your men are very disciplined, and you have good equipment. I'd like to surrender to you."

I told him to call his men out, and he refused. He also refused to tell me how many men he had. He said that after all he had been through, he wanted to surrender to someone of higher rank; we were both lieutenants. Wilson called up to Captain Littleton, who came down and accepted the surrender of 22 to 32 German soldiers.

At 8:15 a.m. on February 21, the crew of an ammunition half-track assigned to Troop E was passing through the town of Werbeln, southwest of Hostenbach. The troopers on the half-track noticed a German soldier in a wooded area to the left of the road and shouted out a challenge to him. He immediately surrendered and told the crew that two other German soldiers who wanted to surrender were hiding in the woods, but they were afraid to come out. It took some persuasion, but eventually the German soldiers all surrendered, giving the Americans three German prisoners, who then provided interrogators with badly needed information on the German army's strength and location.

"Most of the German soldiers wanted to surrender at that point," said Earl Carmickle, "unless the SS were behind them. Then they had to fight us or the SS would shoot them."

The almost constant barrage of mortar and artillery fire began to unnerve the troops, and there was no sign they would be moving soon. Patrols continued as troopers collected all the information they could about the location and numbers of German soldiers in the area. They were especially interested in the number of Germans holding Hill 283. The cavalry dug a trench to help them move undetected between outposts and the base of the hill and get the information they needed.

"This escape trench ran to the tallest hill in the area," said Carmickle, "and that whole area was heavily mined. There were dead bodies all over the side of hill, German and American. Once we saw about 40 bodies up a little holler. We'd shovel dirt over the Americans at night to keep the animals away. I suppose someone came and got them after we pushed through. We kept their dog tags with them."

Sgt. Robert Klein, who enlisted when he was 21, had married his wife, Bea, in 1943. His daughter, Nancy, was three weeks old when he went overseas. It was only a stroke of luck that Bea didn't receive tragic news about her husband during his first days on the front.

"First platoon was the lead jeep on a mission right after we got to the Saar River," he said. "We weren't able to raise them on the radio, so we took off to look for them. Our jeep was blown off the road, and we lay there in a ditch for about four hours. When they found us, they told us that they had reported us dead. I thought, 'How awful for Bea to hear such news with a new baby and all.'"

Klein was happy to hear later that the message had been stopped before his wife heard of his close call.

Casualties in the 101st were light, but not unheard of, even among commanders. On February 22, as he returned to headquarters through the escape trench from Troop A's outpost overlooking Schaffhausen, Lt. Col. Leonard was wounded when a mortar shell burst in the trees overhead. The blast drove shrapnel into his forearm, hand, and leg. After receiving first aid, he was evacuated to the squadron aid station, and from there he was sent to the rear for hospitalization. Major Douglas Feagin, assumed Leonard's command until his return.

Mary Leonard received a telegram from the U.S. Army on March 6, 1945. It was short and to the point: "Regret to inform you your husband Lieutenant Colonel Hubert C. Leonard was slightly wounded in action twenty-two February in Germany. Mail address follows directly from hospitals with details."

That telegram was followed quickly by a more reassuring one from Leonard: "I am in hospital. Injury is not serious. Am getting along alright. H.C. Leonard."

Finally Mary Leonard received a longer letter, one that might ease her mind a little. In the letter, written on Red Cross stationery, Leonard made light of his injury.

My Dear Mary,

Yesterday I wrote a V-mail note, and I forgot to date it. You'll note that I am now in France, not Germany, and I must say I like it here, nice and quiet and no worries, but I feel a bit guilty about being here with only a slight bump on the arm, the right one at that, the one I am writing with, which should give you an idea how bad it is, yet it warrants a few weeks vacation and a Purple Heart thrown in.

Here, like all military hospitals, they will not let you out until they are assured that one is 100 percent and everything is okay. I am assured that I will be out in a few weeks even though I feel that I should be out now. Matter of fact, I don't know why I had to come here, but you know the Army. Anyway it's by no means serious. As I said before, your prayers have done loads of good.

I expect that Otto will get over here in a day or two and bring me some mail. They are pretty busy right now, so I must be patient. I suppose you will hear all sorts of stories, and they will all be different, so believe me when I say it's nothing to worry your pretty head about. I promise that I will take care of myself.

Hubert

ෂ෴

On February 24, while patrolling Hill 283, Tec 5 John Romano and PFC Bauldwin Moore stepped on a mine and were wounded, but one death that day was the result of friendly fire. While waiting for the command to cross the Saar, the men spent a lot of time training, drilling, and cleaning their weapons. On this particular day, a rifle accidentally discharged, killing S/Sgt. Bernard Lolos, B Troop. The name of the soldier who sat cleaning his weapon that day has been forgotten, but if he is alive today, he remembers. For him, it may have been the worst shot of the war.

Fluharty remembers a similar incident, when he almost killed his friend Ralph Nichols.

"He was working on a gun, and I was working in the turret," said Fluharty. "There were two triggers, one for the big gun and one for the machine gun. I bumped something and accidentally tickled the trigger. We had loaned the tank to the infantry, and they had returned it fully loaded and ready to shoot. When it went off, I popped up right away, since I knew

Clouds of black smoke pour from a German oil refinery in Wehrden after an attack by American P-47 on February 25, 1945.

Photo taken by Lt. John Moors, U.S. Army Signal Corps. Courtesy National Archives.

Nick had been working right in front of the guns. Bullets went through the brick wall in front of us. The captain stuck his head out the door and shouted, 'Who did that?' I'm just glad no one was hurt."

That evening, at a 7 p.m. meeting, Major Feagin and Major Edward French received the plans everyone had been waiting for. At 10:45 p.m., the long-awaited orders for the coming attack were relayed to everyone concerned.

∾ ∾

Since February 11, 1945, an Interrogation Prisoners of War (IPW) Team had been attached to the 101st Cavalry Group. One member of the team was attached to each intelligence section of a cavalry reconnaissance squadron. This made quick field interrogation of prisoners possible and allowed the 101st Group to get valuable enemy information before taking the prisoners to headquarters. The remainder of the IPW team was attached to the intelligence section at headquarters, where all prisoners of war were processed for more detailed interrogation.

Near the end of February, the situation began to change. Attack was imminent, and the tempo accelerated from being rather static to an almost breakneck pace. Two members of the IPW team instead of one were now attached to each squadron. Because prisoners of war could not always be evacuated to headquarters, detailed interrogation had to be conducted at the squadron level.

On the afternoon of February 25, 2nd Lt. Charles Pierce, Troop A, 116th Squadron, and 2nd Lt. Alfred Kupferschmit, of the IPW team, were at Troop A's outpost near Werbeln with a prisoner of war who had been captured earlier that day. The prisoner pointed out specific installations in Schaffhausen, and then he told Pierce and Kupferschmit that he and the second prisoner had thrown away their weapons about fifty yards inside the woods, near the spot where they exited to surrender.

Pierce and Kupferschmit asked the prisoner to show them the location, and, at about 5:30 that evening, the group headed down the hill. At the bottom, they met up with other members of the 116th: 1st Lt. Robert Schafer, S/Sgt. Walter Mennel, and Pvt. Earl Geiger, all of Troop C; and S/Sgt. John Schnalzer, Troop A. At the base of the hill, the men, with the prisoner in the lead, walked cautiously in the dark of early evening along the edge of a marked mine field that followed the line of the woods. They moved slowly, as one false step would mean disaster. Instead, disaster fell out of the sky when, without warning, a concentration of mortar fire fell all around them.

The blast killed 2nd Lt. Pierce instantly, and S/Sgt. Schnalzer jumped or was thrown into a nearby ditch. Lt. Schafer jumped into the same ditch, falling on top of Schnalzer. No sooner had they landed than a second mortar shell flew through the air and landed almost directly on top of them, killing Schafer instantly and hurling his body from the ditch to the edge of the mine field.

Wounded in the hands and legs, Sgt. Schnalzer managed to jump up and run back the way they had come to take cover in a small brick building. While running, he noticed the panicked prisoner run directly into the mine field. There was nothing Schnalzer could do but watch as the fleeing prisoner tripped a land mine and flew into the air. Also killed were 2nd Lt. Kupferschmidt, who died within an hour of being wounded, and S/Sgt. Mennel, who died later that day. Pvt. Geiger was seriously wounded.

As the shells began to fall, 1st Lt. Leslie Lewis and Sgt. John Noonan, Troop A, were nearby, standing close to a pump house. Seeing that several troopers had been wounded, they rushed under heavy fire to the ditch and surrounding mine field where Lt. Shafer lay. Not knowing he was dead, they tried pulling him to safety. Lt. Schafer's foot, or so it is thought, tripped the wire of a mine, and Lt. Leslie Lewis and Sgt. John Noonan were seriously wounded.

Several months later, in a letter written on May 4, 1945, Lt. Schafer's parents were still trying to find out what had happened to their son:

My dear Col. Leonard:

It is difficult to express to you how very much both Mrs. Schafer and I appreciated your letter of April 7. We were very close to Bob, not just as a son, but as a friend and companion who never did hesitate to reveal to us his dreams, hopes and ambitions. He spoke of you often with respect and genuine affection so your beautiful tribute to him had a particularly deep significance for us.

We understand that there must of necessity be restrictions on the information we may receive, but it is our sincere hope that when the war is over, we may have the opportunity of meeting you personally and learning anything you may be able to tell us of the time you spent with Bob and any circumstances surrounding his death. Even the slightest bit of information means a great deal to us.

It is almost unbearably hard to reconcile ourselves to the loss of our son, but we realize also that we are not alone in our sorrow and pray that He who gave His Son for the salvation of many may sustain us now and give us the strength and courage to face life as valiantly as Bob faced death for a cause he held so dear.

When peace comes again, it would give us a great deal of pleasure to meet you personally and thank you again for your kindness to us and to our son, Robert.

Sincerely,
Harry J. Schafer

The Schafers waited until August before writing again. The war had been over for three months, and they must have felt that it wouldn't be considered rude to try once more to get the story of how their son died.

> August 24, 1945
> My dear Col. Leonard:
>   I hope I am not presumptuous in writing you at this time, because I realize that since receiving your fine letter about Bob you have been far and wide and extremely busy and no doubt annoyed by other parents who are equally as anxious to know some of the circumstances surrounding the death of their boys.
>   Tomorrow, the twenty-fifth, will be six months since this happened, and we have heard about it only in a vague sort of way, but nothing of authority and only enough to keep us hoping that some day this information may come through. We realize that before the end of this war there were certain necessary restrictions and regulations concerning information of this kind, but now that World War II has finally come to an end — for which we have given thanks and sincerely hope that peace will now remain for ever — we do believe that detailed information if such is possible concerning Bob's going out and the mission he was on might be forthcoming to us.
>   It is still unbearably hard to reconcile ourselves to the loss of our son and naturally we live in hopes and anxiety that we may hear something about him and from someone, perhaps you yourself, who has authority to give this information.
>   Now that peace has come it would give us a great deal of pleasure to meet you personally

and thank you for your kindness to us and to our son, but I assure you that any information you or anyone else can give us concerning that which I have written in this letter will be appreciated from the bottom of our hearts and more than words can express.

Sincerely,
Harry J. Schafer

Finally, in October, Lt. Col. Leonard responded, explaining that their letter from August had only just reached him.

Headquarters
116th Cavalry Rcn Squadron Mecz
Camp Campbell Kentucky
26 October 1945
Dear Mr. Schafer:

Your letter of 24 August 1945 has just reached me at Camp Campbell, Kentucky. I am distressed that you have had to wait so long for an answer, but none of the mail was forwarded to home addresses while we were on leave.

Your son, Bob, was a fine young man. He had endeared himself to everyone in the organization and his excellent work and happy disposition had made him a favorite among officers and men. I am proud to have had him serve in my Squadron.

At the time Bob was killed I was myself in the hospital from wounds I had received a few days earlier. Upon my return I personally investigated the circumstances surrounding the tragedy and I can now give you what information is available.

I should like to give you a little background of the mission the Squadron was engaged in at the time. The Squadron landed at LeHavre, France, on 1 February 1945. After a few days at nearby Camp Twenty Grand we moved in organic transportation across France on the route Rouen to St. Avold, passing through Beauvais, Soissons, Laon, Meziers, Sedan, Charliville, Stenay, Verdun, and Thiacourt.

The 101st Cavalry Group received the mission of relieving the 106th Cavalry Group at Lauterbach, Germany, which is just over the border in the vicinity of St. Avold, France. The mission at the time was active defense of the front. The Squadron sector was about two miles long. Bob's troop was located in a small town named Werbeln and the enemy occupied strongly fortified positions at Schaffhausen about three-quarters of a mile away. Considerable mortar and artillery fire was exchanged daily.

On the morning of 25 February the Squadron captured two prisoners. During the day they were interrogated by the interrogation Prisoner of War Team and much valuable information was obtained. That afternoon one of the prisoners was taken up on a hill between Werbeln and Schaffhausen for the purpose of pointing out certain installations in Schaffhausen to Lt. Kupferschmidt our IPW officer, and Lt. Pierce of Troop A.

As they came down the hill about five o'clock in the afternoon they met Bob, S. Sgt. Walter J. Mennel, S. Sgt. John J. Schnalzer and Pvt. Earl Geiger, who were on routine patrol at the foot of the hill on the edge of Werbeln. They decided to have the prisoner direct them to the point of the woods nearby where the prisoner said they had thrown away their weapons that morning as they came out to surrender.

There was a marked mine field along the edge of the woods and just as the group moved along the edge of this, a concentration of enemy mortar fire fell in the vicinity. Lt. Pierce was killed instantly. Bob and Sgt. Schnalzer ran to take cover in a nearby shallow ditch. Sgt. Schnalzer reached the ditch first and Bob threw himself on top of him. At almost the same moment a shell landed very close to them and Bob was instantly killed. Sgt. Schnalzer was wounded in the arms and legs but managed to escape and run to the protection of a small brick building nearby. Sgt. Schnalzer undoubtedly owes his life to the fact that Bob threw himself on top of him just as the shell landed.

I sincerely hope that some day I may have the pleasure of meeting you and Mrs. Schafer. I feel almost that I do know you from the many conversations I had with Bob concerning his happy home life.

Sincerely,

Hubert C. Leonard, Lt. Col., Cavalry

❧❧

John Almond lost one of his best friends the same day that Schafer was killed. "We were up on a hill facing down into the town," he said. "We had a little machine gun nest there, and at night we'd pull back and stay in the little houses along both sides of the stream. We had mined the path with a trip wire, and one night I looked down and saw the tail of my overcoat dragging on that wire. I froze and lifted my coat."

Almond cleared the wire, but his friend, Grady Collins wasn't so lucky. "Grady, he was from Gainsville, Georgia," said Almond, "was coming in one night and forgot about the trip wire, I guess, and set off the mine." Almond's voice breaks, and he needs time to collect himself before he can continue.

"I rode with him to the aid station. He didn't make it."

❧❧

On March 1, Frederick Altizer and John Allen joined the 101st as replacements. Altizer had been drafted in April 1944 while attending Marshall College on a basketball scholarship. Because his father had a farm and help was in short supply, he received a draft deferment until fall, but by February he had been through basic training and was on his way to Germany.

The day they arrived, an artillery attack had just killed four men and wounded three, all but two of whom were medics.

"One of our best doctors was killed," said Gorski. "They were having some kind of conference and a shell came in and killed them all. We thought the world of those medics."

The attack killed S/Sgt. Edward Young, PFC Gilbert Hack, PFC Barzillai Lanning, and Capt. Louis Cowen. In addition to the medics, PFC Robert R. Harrington and Tec. 5 Eldridge Rodrigue, Troop A, and Tec. 5 Daniel J. Cuoco, Headquarters Group, were injured in the attack.

"Capt. Littleton was still pretty shaken by it when John and I reported to him," said Altizer. "He looked at our clean, pressed uniforms and frowned. 'What are you two doing here?' he barked at us. I snapped a salute and said, 'They sent us, sir.'"

Allen and Altizer became friends because of the Army's penchant for alphabetizing everything. "We spent most of the war together since both our names started with A. We were the first two men to pull K.P. or guard duty, any duty," said Altizer.

"I went right to the front line and helped to man an outpost on a hill overlooking a town full of Jerries," Altizer wrote. "We had field glasses, and every time we saw any of the enemy moving around, we would contact our big guns and send a few rounds over at them. One day, however, it was a pretty hot place for us to be, as they got a big gun zeroed in right on our position, and for every round we fired at them they fired

25 at us. It was there I received my first enemy fire. I got pretty scared, and dug a really deep foxhole."

If the men talk about having been afraid, their fear is usually expressed with humor, making light of an emotion that, at the time they experienced it, may not have been so funny.

"I had a sergeant who was a real old-timer," said John Gorski. "He had been around since World War I. He said to me, 'John, whatever you do, keep a tight ass.' I didn't know what he meant, but I found out. I told that to every new boy who joined the outfit, and they found out, too. When you get into the heavy action, everybody is crapping their pants."

Fluharty and his tank crew had their own way to deal with incoming fire. Fluharty was stationed at headquarters, doing maintenance on the tanks, heavier maintenance than what the troops could do in the field. Whenever the Germans began to shell camp, he and the rest of his crew — Ralph Nichols, Dominic Stolt, William Olsen — would dig a hole big enough for four men and back their tank over it.

The crew of "Fightin' Bastard" in St. Avold, France. Caption on back of photo: "Ready to fight." Bill Olsen, Buck Fluharty, Dominic Stolt, and Ralph Nichols.
Photo courtesy Buck Fluharty.

"It was pretty secure. The tank might blow up, but we'd probably be okay," he said. "The infantry didn't want us around; they would wave us away. A tank is a big target."

Allen described his first days at the front in a letter sent home at the end of the war.

"We made the trip by World War I French boxcars. These old cars were called '40 & 8,'" he wrote, "because they were meant to carry 40 men and eight horses during World War I. We were crowded into them for three days and nights. The train was slow, and it was really cold. The floor of the car was wet, because rain leaked through bullet holes in the ceiling."

"I was assigned as a scout to the Second Platoon," said Altizer, "replacing a man who had been killed. I rode in the back of one of the jeeps, and manned a 30-caliber, air-cooled machine gun."

The other two men in Altizer's jeep were Sgt. Giza, squad leader, and Grover Cleveland Wilson, the jeep's driver. Altizer described Wilson as a motorcycle nut and a bit of a hothead from somewhere around Danville, Virginia. Riding together in the same jeep for the rest of the war, Wilson and Altizer got to be pretty good friends, but Wilson apparently didn't get along too well with the Pennsylvania-born Giza.

In fact, there was often tension between men from different states or regions. The boys from Pennsylvania and the boys from New York didn't get along, I was told, and the boys from the south thought the New York boys got all the breaks. It seems they fought as many verbal battles with each other as armed battles with the enemy.

"We were the fighting unit," William Pierce, from Kentucky, told me. "We fought with each other."

And yet, the bond that was created in February 1945 has been unbreakable for more than 60 years.

First Steps

My father's room at the Veterans' Hospital was on the left, one-third of the way down a beige-gray hallway. When I arrived, it was empty. He should have been there, but the linens were taut across the single mattress on the bed. For more than a year, he had been in and out of the Veterans Administration Hospital in Portland, fighting lung cancer with nothing more than oxygen and morphine.

Theodore Roosevelt Welch was a man who starched his work shirts, ironed his t-shirts, and made knife-sharp creases in his pants. He owned boxes of cowboy boots, some never worn, and none with a scuff or a grease mark. He was not the kind of man to see his wavy blond hair end up in the bathroom sink or on a pillowcase. He would not have tubes running in and out of his body, or give up his voice box and endure the pitying stares of strangers. Long before the doctor made a diagnosis, my father had been telling people he had cancer. He had time to think about it, and his mind was made up: no radiation, no chemotherapy, no surgery.

For months he continued life as it had always been, only with more coughing, shorter breath, and increasing pain. He went from brief, infrequent stays in the hospital to brief, infrequent visits home. We spent Christmas of 1970 in the Veterans Hospital, using a large cardboard box, the kind used for shipping potted plants to my mother's floral shop, as a makeshift Christmas tree. It sat in the middle of the waiting room floor, overflowing with gifts. My dad sat in a standard-issue, metal waiting room chair covered with cracked gray vinyl. A plaid robe covered his narrow shoulders, and baggy pajama bottoms hid his unnaturally thin legs. His body folded in on itself, as if he were too tired to hold it erect.

Never one for small talk, he seemed even more silent than normal. Only a few gruff commands escaped through the cancer's pain. When my son Travis, nine months old, would drop to the floor to crawl, my father would struggle to fill his lungs with air and bark, "Don't let that baby crawl on the floor." We'd wait as he filled his fragile lungs once more with air so he could finish. "It's filthy."

In February, less than two months after that Christmas, I picked my father up at the hospital so he could spend a day at our house in Troutdale. It gave him a short respite from the doctors and nurses. At the end of the day, just as we left to go back, a light snow began to fall. We lived about 16 miles away through city traffic, and by the time we reached Portland's west hills, the roads were covered with snow and ice. The VA hospital was at the top of a steep winding street and, even though I made several attempts, my car couldn't get the necessary traction. I would move forward a bit, my father's harsh whisper hissing instructions, then slide back and start all over again. His face grew darker with frustration. He and I both knew that if he were behind the wheel — if he were well — he could drive up that hill. But he wasn't well. And he could no longer drive. After sliding sideways down the hill, I gave up, pulled into a gas station, and made a phone call. When the taxi arrived, I planted a hasty kiss goodbye on his cheek and turned my father over to a cab driver for the final few miles to the hospital. I had known intellectually for months that my father was dying, but it was in those moments in the snow that I knew it in my heart.

Ted Welch, in a photo he took of himself in Texas before the war. Note the string attached to his boot, which he used to snap the shutter.

He went home to Redmond for a visit in the spring that lasted only five days, which were spent in a hospital bed by the living room window. All I remember from that time is the sun streaming across his bed through the window and the moldy, decaying smell of cancer.

On June 1, 1971, he was rushed by ambulance back to Portland, on oxygen all the way. I wasn't able to arrange babysitting and transportation to visit him until June 4.

I drove my husband to work that morning, so I could keep the car. After feeding the boys breakfast, I dropped them off at my in-law's house and stopped to buy my dad a *Western Horseman* magazine. About an hour later, I was standing at the nurses' station on the fourth floor of the Veteran's Hospital, explaining that my father's room was empty and asking a nurse where Ted Welch had been moved.

She turned to a second nurse, who was standing with her back to us, filing medical records in a gray cabinet.

"Do you know where they moved Ted Welch?" she asked, giving the room number where he had been.

The second nurse kept filing and didn't turn around. She repeated the room number and thought a minute. "Oh," she said, "that's the man who passed away an hour ago."

At 22, I must have looked terribly young to those two nurses that day. I had no idea what I was expected to say or do at that moment. I was too much like my father to break down and cry, not here, not in this public place. But I felt something was expected of me. What does a person do when she hears her father has just died? What are the rules? I stood there, waiting for someone to tell me what to do, but no one did.

To break the silence, one nurse said, "We've notified your mother. Would you like to talk to the doctor?"

"No," I said. "Why would I?"

I wasn't trying to be sassy, as my dad would have said; I was truly confused. It seemed a silly question. My father was dead. Weren't doctors only for the living? And before the nurses could respond, I turned and walked to the elevator.

Now, when I watch that confused girl as she turns and leaves the nurses' station, I wish someone had took her hand and led her to her father so she could say goodbye. She might decline at first, and they might need to insist, but please, I want to tell her, please go. You can't imagine how important it will be someday.

In my car, I put my head against the steering wheel and cried. Later that day I learned how desperately my mother, husband, and in-laws had been trying to reach me. Had they been successful, that frantic relay of phone calls would have prevented what had just happened. But each call came in, first at my house, then at my in-laws, just moments too late.

Even though I couldn't imagine my father dying surrounded by relatives, the center of attention — he wouldn't have liked that — I still hated the thought that he had died alone, maybe wondering why I hadn't been to see him yet. Someone should have been there. I should have been there.

The truth is that I wasn't there nearly as often as he would have liked. When I did visit the hospital, I would sit in a straight-backed chair near his bed and watch the clock. What passed for conversation between us would begin with awkward questions about how he was, awkward because it was obvious how he was doing: he was dying. Then we'd talk about the weather and the children. For a long time I had brought Gary and Travis to the hospital to see him, but by spring 1971, he was too ill to meet us in the lobby, and children that young weren't allowed in his room. Soon I would run out of things to say, and it was hard for him to talk. I would start to mutter about needing to pick up the boys or that I had things to do at home, and I would wonder how soon I could leave without hurting his feelings. No matter how long I waited, as soon as I stood to go, he would whisper, "Do you have to leave already?" So I'd sit back down, and we'd go on as before for just a while longer, listening to the hospital hum around us and struggling to find something to say.

We hadn't always had that problem. Mother and Daddy had been married for 12 years when I was born; eleven of those years in Texas and one in Oregon. Growing up, I was closer to him than to Mother, at least from the time I was old enough to trot behind him as he irrigated our pasture or to help him drive in our few cows at milking time. When we had to walk through a flooded field, he'd lift me onto his shoulders and carry me piggyback. Since I had no brothers or sisters to play with, my parents by default became my playmates.

But my later teenage years had been difficult, and I wasn't long out of those when he became ill. For one thing, he hadn't approved of my decision to get married at 18. At my wedding, six months after my graduation from high school, a friend of my father's walked up to shake his hand and said, "Ted, why are you frowning? Your daughter's getting married today."

"It's not the happiest goddamn day of my life," my father replied, still not smiling.

So we entered into his illness without the closeness we had once enjoyed, at a loss for words. I lacked both the interest and the maturity to force my way past through our silence and talk about things that mattered. It would be many years more before I realized how much that silence had cost me.

That realization began with a desire to know more about what he did in World War II. Movies like *Band of Brothers* and *Saving Private Ryan* had brought the war to mind in a way it never had been before. I had never been able to see my father as a soldier, not in any real way. I had seen him in uniform in a formal portrait, and I had examined a few of the things he brought back from Germany, but it wasn't a topic he brought up, so neither did I. Watching the stream of new movies and documentaries, I kept thinking, "My father did that. He was there. That's what he was going through."

I wanted to know more. Unfortunately, I had waited until my mother was gone, all my father's brothers and sisters were gone; anyone in the family who might be able to help me had died. I wasn't sure where to begin.

My father's military records couldn't help me; they were destroyed on July 12, 1973. A fire at the National Personnel Records Center in St. Louis destroyed about 80 percent of the records for Army personnel who were discharged between November 1, 1912, and January 1, 1960. All I had were his separation papers: two pages of only the most basic information.

Theodore Roosevelt Welch was a private first class in Troop B, 116th Cavalry Reconnaissance Squadron Mechanized. His permanent address was listed as Canadian, Texas, although he had been inducted in Oregon. Even his description was there: blue eyes, blonde hair, 5'10" tall, 156 lbs.

His Army papers tell me that he had worked 10 years for Dr. F. D. Teas in Canadian, Texas, as a farmer on a 2,400-acre stock farm, handling up to 2,000 head of cattle. (He probably would have preferred the word "rancher.") His duties were listed as breeding and caring for stock, riding and tending herds, planting, cultivating, and harvesting wheat and cane, and driving a tractor and pick-up. He personally owned six head of cattle.

The date of his induction was December 22, 1942, in Portland, Oregon. He was living at the time in Redmond. His military occupational specialty was Mortar Gunner 607, and he was qualified for Carbine M-1 SS Rifle M-1 Expert (81 MM Mortar 2d C Gnr SMG 45 Cal Expert 60n MM Mortar Expert ASR Score (2 Sept. 45) 49. A lapel button was issued.

His war record was summed up in a few lines at the bottom of the page:

> Battles and Campaigns: Rhineland Central Europe

> Decorations and Citations: European African Middle Eastern Campaign Ribbon with 2 Bronze Stars

> Wounds: None

> Immunized against small pox, typhoid, tetanus and typhus.

> Left for Europe October 30, 1944, arrived November 12.

> Returned to the U.S. July 23, 1945, after leaving Europe on July 22.

> His mustering out pay was $300.

Ted Welch and his nephew, James Paschal King, who was lost at sea December 18, 1945, in a typhoon.

These two sheets of papers tell me that he spent eight months and 24 days in Europe, two years, 10 months and four days in the service. They tell me that his military occupation was reconnaissance car crewman in the European Theater of Operations. In combat, he performed scouting missions on foot or in a jeep to gather information about the enemy. He could read maps and a compass, and he drove a jeep on which a 30-caliber machine gun was mounted. He could fire that gun in accordance with fire orders from the reconnaissance car commander, and, when radio silence was not prescribed, he maintained radio communications where necessary.

His papers tell me he left Europe a month ahead of his troop, and he flew home while they took a ship. What those papers didn't tell me is why.

They aren't much, these two faded sheets of paper, but they are all I have. Unfortunately, for many years, I didn't see it as a place to start; I saw it as the end. I couldn't think of any way to learn more.

Then, one evening while watching *Band of Brothers*, I noticed actual veterans talking about their experience. It occurred to me that if Stephen Ambrose could interview veterans, then maybe I could, too.

Ted Welch, 1944.

What if I could find some of the men who served in the 101st Cavalry? A door creaked open; it was a place to start again. From there, I went to the Internet. I began searching for the 101st Cavalry and for the one man I knew had served in the war with my father. This man had visited my father when I was in junior high or high school.

I couldn't remember his name, but I had a vague memory of how the sound of it played against my ear. I believed that I would recognize it if I found it somewhere.

This man had called our house several times, wanting to visit when he came to Oregon. Mother had nagged at my father to return the call, but he wouldn't. Then one night the man caught my dad at home, and he had no choice but to take the call. They began to talk, and soon my dad was laughing. My father was repeating the man's name over and over, alternating it with a rhyming nickname. I had never seen this silly side of my father before, and this surprise helped the bouncing, rhythmic nickname remain as a shadow in my mind. All I needed was to hear it again or see it, and I'd know it.

I hoped a roster with names of the men who served in the 101st might exist somewhere. I got lucky. Almost immediately I found a website created by John Altizer, whose father had served in the same troop as my father. As I read down a short roster of names, I saw the name Charlie Kashuba. Kashuba, Kashuba. That was it. Further searching turned up a phone number for him in Tennessee.

Even more exciting, Altizer's website announced a reunion of the 101st Cavalry in just two weeks in Goldsboro, N.C. I didn't know a thing about the 101st Cavalry, but I was ready to get on an airplane and fly three thousand miles in order to learn about it.

The 101st Cavalry: A History

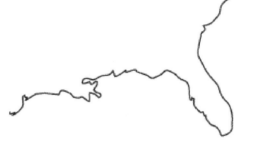

My father told me he signed up for the cavalry because he thought he'd be riding horses. Then he'd laugh, either at his own naiveté or at the joke he was having on me.

It's true that the 101st was a horse cavalry regiment – right up until the time my dad was drafted. He may have been disappointed that horses were a thing of the past. As a Texan suspicious of Yankees, he may have been equally unhappy to learn the 101st was a New York outfit.

In 1940, the 101st Cavalry was made up of three squadrons: Squadron A, located in Manhattan; Squadron C, Brooklyn; and Geneseo Troop in upstate New York. Headquarters for all three was on Bedford Street in Brooklyn.

The 101st had grown out of several other organizations, all starting in the 1800s. The two main groups were the 10th Regiment, which was created from companies of the New

York State Militia and became the New York National Guard in 1862, and Troop C of Brooklyn, which was mustered into the service of the National Guard of the State of New York on December 16, 1895. At that time, the Arsenal for the 101st was located on Portland Avenue, just north of Fort Greene Park in the heart of Brooklyn.

The drill floor of the old arsenal was converted into a riding ring, but the Troop soon outgrew these inadequate quarters. In 1904 they moved to more spacious quarters on Bedford Avenue in Brooklyn.

The 101st Cavalry saw its first action at Coamo in Puerto Rico in 1898 during the Spanish American War. They were under the command of Captain Bertram T. Clayton, a graduate of West Point, who was later killed in France during World War I. In 1916 the regiment was ordered to the Mexican border, where it spent about nine months, returning to Brooklyn in the spring of 1917. Shortly thereafter, the entire regiment was assembled at Spartanburg as machine gun units and a wagon train, before heading to France, where the regiment spent about 18 months during World War I.

On May 20, 1925, the Coat of Arms of the 101st Cavalry was approved. Designed in strict compliance with the rules of heraldry, it included three gold, interlaced chevrons on the azure body of a shield. The three chevrons represented the three times the regiment had been in federal service up to that point: the Spanish-American War (Puerto Rico), 1898; the Mexican Border, 1916-17; and World War I, 1917-19. The interlacing is for decorative purposes. In heraldry, the use of gold or yellow signifies "elevation of the mind" and "nobility of purpose," and it is the distinctive color of the U.S. Cavalry. Blue (azure) signifies "loyalty." On

the gold upper third of the blue shield, a falcon, which is portrayed in natural colors, stands with wings folded and bells on its legs. The falcon signifies readiness for action, although it is normally at rest. The falcon is associated with courage, speed, mobility and impetuosity of attack, like the cavalry.

Some time later, another design was created for the 116th Squadron. The motto of this squadron is "Advance without delay."

Called to active duty

PROCEDE SINE MORA
Advance without delay

In 1940, the regiment was called up for active duty and re-organized as a combination horse-mechanized regiment. Some of the horses were replaced with motorcycles.

"They added tractor-trailers to transport the horses," said Sgt. Bill Hurley, who had joined the 101st Cavalry in 1939, "and they gave me a motorcycle. My job was to stop traffic so the trailers with the horses could go through town. Then I'd work my way back to the head of the line to do that all over again. I was a trainer and had to teach men to drive trucks, men who had never even had a driver's license. And we had to train the horses. They weren't used to riding in trucks, and they would fall over. By the time we finished training, the horses were veterans like the rest of us."

Many of the men who were "unhorsed" and sent to the mechanized units were not happy about it. They continued to wear boots and breeches and were authorized to wear spurs when in uniform off duty. These were men who, before the war, had joined the 101st because of the horses. Many of them were from society – polo players and recreational riders – and the horses meant everything to them.

The men began intensive training at Fort Devens, Mass., and on September 29, 1941, the regiment transferred to North Carolina to participate in maneuvers with the First Army. For the first time as a horse-mechanized outfit, the 101st moved over the road in a single column. With its circus of scout cars, motorcycles, tractor-trailers, and trucks of various sizes, the column extended several miles down the highway, as daring young motorcycle troopers like Hurley dashed up and down the column riding traffic control.

The horse troopers experienced a special kind of thrill, riding in the tractor-trailers as they barreled down the main highways on their first long trip. Each trailer held an entire eight-man squad with its horses, feed and equipment. The men rode in a small compartment in front, separated from the horses only by removable bay boards. Their main fear was that if the tractor-trailers had to slow down suddenly, they would surely end up with several tons of horseflesh in their laps.

Once they arrived in North Carolina, a tent camp was established in a field near the small town of Candor. This camp would be used as a base camp for the next nine weeks. The only amenities in Candor were a small restaurant and a barbershop with two bathtubs, where a customer could get a haircut and hot bath for two dollars.

As the maneuvers progressed, it became clear to many that the inclusion of horse and mechanized units in one regiment was a mistake. Their capabilities were entirely different. They did not complement each other as the field manuals said they would, nor was it

Lt. Col. Hubert Leonard before the war.
Photo courtesy Jay Leonard

easy to move men and horses from one battle area to another by tractor-trailer. They were cumbersome and virtually impossible to camouflage. In one instance, the column commander was embarrassed to find himself on a narrow dead-end road. It took half a day to turn the column around. In another situation the tractor-trailers became bogged down for almost an entire day in a field after an all-night rainstorm.

After maneuvers December 3, 1941, the regiment began its 800-mile march back to Fort Devens, arriving on Saturday, December 6. They believed that their year of active duty would be over in a few short weeks. This hope collapsed the next day.

"Three friends and I had been to a Sunday matinee," wrote Clinton Gosnell. "When we came out of the movies, we heard the newsboy yelling, 'Sneak attack by Japan means war.' I called home to speak to my mother and asked if it were true. She said yes."

John Gorski had enlisted in 1939, expecting this day or one like it would come eventually. "I was sick and tired of hearing about the Germans invading all these countries," he said. "I figured something was going to happen, and I wanted to be ready."

Lt. Col. Leonard wrote to his sister about how much morale changed in just that one day.

> December 13, 1941
> Fort Devens
> Dear Catherine,
>   Back again after being one of the 300,000 men fighting gnats, flies and dust in the Carolinas, and I am glad to be here. The past maneuvers in the South have put the finishing touches on us and has ironed out many rough spots. All of us feel that we are ready, willing and able to do our share and more, if necessary, to bring the present situation to a successful end or die doing it. Before Sunday, December 7, the esprit de

corps and morale of our regiment was high, but since that day it has multiplied a hundred fold. I believe this is true throughout all the arms and services.

I expect to be in New York on Tuesday, if everything works out …

Hubert

After Pearl Harbor, things changed dramatically for the 101st. The Army's VI Corp, including the 101st Cavalry, had been earmarked for the Philippines in event of war with Japan, but when those islands were overrun, that plan was canceled. In January, the regiment was ordered to provide security to Dow Air Base at Bangor, Maine, which was being used by the U.S. Army Air Force to ferry P-38 fighters to England. They would also be responsible for securing the Maine coast in the vicinity of the base. The mechanized troops were dispatched to Bangor on a rotation basis and, according to several written accounts, patrolling this windy, snow-blown airfield on foot and in open scout cars and motorcycles was not a choice assignment.

Bangor was an old lumber town that had suffered through generations of young loggers letting off steam. In spite of its history of tolerance, the town sometimes had to be patient with the rowdy troopers. One Saturday night, Col. Charles Graydon, at the time Troop Commander for F Troop, was summoned to the city jail where three of his troopers had been incarcerated. Apparently two of them had tried to clean out Kerrigan's, a local bar, while defending the honor of a young lady customer who had been insulted.

Another time, a young homesick private spotted a telephone through the window of a Chinese laundry around 1 a.m. He decided he just had to get in to make a phone call to his girl friend in spite of the hour. The frightened proprietor, who thought that he was being robbed, called the police.

According a front page story in the local newspaper, one patrolman was injured by the soldier's spurs while attempting to put him in the patrol wagon.

Because of the social and political connections that many of the men enjoyed in the early days of the 101st, they believed they would spend the war stateside. Walter Winchell, a noted columnist at the time, was promising as much.

"He wrote in his column that if mothers wanted to keep their boys at home," said Gergley, "they should have their sons join the 101st Cavalry."

However, Lt. Col. Leonard, however, was preparing his family for a different future.

Dear Mary,

Just a line or two to let you know we are here on the east coast and expect an overseas movement in near future

I hope that you will be able to collect all the furniture, boxes, crates and trunks and that you get them in our house without further delay and it will be a big job for you so take it easy and do a little at a time. ... Perhaps Mr. Rabb and Matt can give you a hand with the heavy crates and boxes as you will need a hammer and crowbars to open most of it. ... winterize the car before freezing weather sets in. If there are any repairs to the house better get them fixed and off your mind soon as possible. Don't wait too long. Now, how did Junior make out with the x-rays and examination? Did he get the gum? Great little guy, he is your big job as Patricia seems the type that should give little trouble as far as health goes. And did you get your candy?

So much of that. Even if we have had some disappointments, anyway everything we do is the work of God and usually for the best.

Hubert

Farewell to the Horses

In the late spring and summer of 1942, as hundreds of draftees were being added to the 101st, the horses were leaving. In April the regiment became fully mechanized and was designated 101st Cavalry (Mecz). Jeeps began arriving to replace the motorcycles, a relief to many of those who had risked their lives riding them in the snow of New England and mud of the Carolinas.

Emotions were mixed the day the last horses left the regiment. As they paraded down the street past Regimental Headquarters, men, many with tears in their eyes, lined the route to say good-bye. One sergeant, quoted by Col. Charles K. Graydon in his unpublished history, *With the 101st in World War II*, expressed his feelings this way:

"We were proud of continuing in the old tradition, but we soon became envious of the mechanized boys who at the end of the day simply parked their vehicles and took off on pass, while we had to unsaddle, groom, water and feed our horses and stow our gear. Our romance with horses was soon over. Anyway, who wants to go to war on such a noble animal?"

On September 4, 1942, the regiment left Fort Devens. They were scheduled for eight weeks of field training at Pine Camp near Watertown, New York. Pine Camp was familiar to the older troopers who had participated in summer training there for many years, but they noticed a few changes. For one thing, parking lots had taken the place of picket lines for the horses.

Clinton Gosnell was inducted into the U.S. Army on December 26, 1942, and reported to Fort Devens on December 30 for basic training. Gosnell's father had been gassed in World War I, and he thought his mother was probably more concerned than the average mom about his going into war.

"She had watched my father struggle with the after effects of the chemicals on his health for years," he wrote. "She knew better than many what the horrors of such an attack could be."

At about that same time, my father and mother moved to Oregon to be near my mother's family. They planned to find work, see if they liked the Pacific Northwest, and, if they didn't, to return to Texas in a year or two. My father, who was 33 years old, believed he was safe from the draft.

Unfortunately, he was wrong. Around the same time as Gosnell, my father was ordered to report to Ft. Lewis, Wash., for basic training. He arrived on December 22, 1942, a date less than one week before his 34th birthday and three days before Christmas. Age was not the barrier he had hoped.

Even though the 101st had originally been a place for New York boys wanting some time on a horse, the war made the regiment a truly diverse outfit with farmers, hillbillies, cowboys, watermen from Maryland's eastern shore, mill workers, steel workers, and a few underage students who lied to get in.

I envy those who have boxes of letters and diaries left them by parents and grandparents. All I have from my father are four wrinkled, beige sheets of paper: two letters sent to my mother while he was at Fort Lewis, and one letter mailed to my mother's parents from Fort George Meade in Maryland. Everything I know about my father on the eve of his going to war comes from a few emotionless words written in faded pencil.

> January 1, 1943
> My dear wife and all.
> How are you? I am fine, tired and sleepy. Got here yesterday at three. Got asinged (sic) to barracks. Been in here every since. Wish I was there. Have you got a job yet? Do you stay home? When you leave the pickup out, cover it with the tarp. Reins (sic) here all the time. I guess can't tell you any dirt, don't know it. Have got to line up for mess.

Members of the 101st Cavalry at Pine Camp, New York, 1933
Photo courtesy Jay Leonard.

And on a second sheet in the same envelope:

> Try and write you a few more lines. Gee I just don't write. I have gone through that building where the sign on the door says, 'Through these portals the finest soldiers pass.' Have got all my clothes. Everything is too short ecept (sic) the necktie. I guess I look pretty (good). What are you doing? I went to a show this afternoon. Had to. 'Article of War' was the name. No glamour or western to it.
> There are lots of soldiers here. The feed is fine and plenty of it. Will send my Lincoln clothes home soon as I can. Have got to go.
> Teddy

After basic training at Fort Lewis, my father joined the 101st at Fort Meade. Since March 10, 1943, the regiment had been serving as mobile reserve for the Eastern Defense Command. Its job was to defend the coastline against saboteurs who might enter the country by submarine or parachute drop.

From where they were stationed, the men could stand at night watching the flash of explosions as torpedoes struck tankers only a few miles out at sea. Oil slicks from those sinking ships splashed up on the coastline from Maine to Florida. War was heating up in Europe now, and some of the men were eager to go into combat. This seaside duty was seen as a secondary, though important mission. Plus, they were tired of the endless training.

At Fort Meade another First Army team showed up to conduct a training test. Using the main highway between Washington, D.C., and New York as an axis of advance, the regiment was required to "reconnoiter in zone" up through the center of Baltimore and other towns along the way, all jam-packed with civilian traffic. The training concluded with an attack on fixed positions in the Fort Dix Military Reservation.

I had to wonder if my dad had participated in this exercise. I can imagine him, the small town Texas cowboy, fighting highways and traffic to attempt reconnaissance up through a city like Baltimore. It would have been a long way from the Teas Ranch in the Texas Panhandle, and I can't imagine it helped the ulcer that was already giving him trouble.

He spent a few weeks in June of 1943 in the hospital at Ft. Meade. From there he wrote a letter to my Grandpa and Grandma Chamberlain, my mother's parents. The letter, mailed on Saturday, June 7, 1943, was more personal than either of the letters to my mother.

> My Dear Folks,
> Two o'clock Saturday afternoon in the United States. I'm in a hospital and I bet it is 110 degrees in the shade. Hottest country I ever seen. Have been in here since Tuesday just eating and sleeping. Don't know how long I will be in here. Not long I hope. My stomack has been bothern (sic) me. Wish when I got out of here I was com-

ing home. I was too old when they got me in the Army.

How is every one out there? I dreamed the other night I was home and had a tank full of gas. Wish I could drive that green pickup. Are the wheels off the ground? If not could you put blocks under axles?

Got a letter from my mother here the other day. I guess she is mighty fickle. I haven't seen her in so long. Bill [his twin brother] said she took it mighty hard when dad died.

Looks like Tutts [nickname for his wife] would be happier out there but I don't know. I want her to be where she wants to be and is the best satisfied while I'm in here. Maybe some day I can make her happy. I'm living for that day. Anyway I haven't seen a pleasant day since that nite I left your home, a home indeed it was to me, except the few I spent with Tutts in Kansas. Is very pretty and green out there. Would love to see that country this time of year.

Junior [brother-in-law serving in the Pacific] should have a furlough before long, maybe he can come home. Well I can't think of anything to write. Hope you are all well and happy. Write me a long letter. My address is the same.

Love to all, your son, Teddy.

Shortly after he wrote the letter, he was sent to South Carolina to patrol the eastern seaboard; my mother joined him there. All I had heard about those months from either of them was that Mother hated the humidity of South Carolina, and that all her clothes molded in the suitcase under the bed.

August 20, 1943-June 30, 1944:
Eastern Defense Command

On August 20, 1943, Colonel Charles B. McClelland, a young, aggressive officer, assumed command of the 101st. "Mac" made his mark early by emphasizing physical fitness for all officers and enlisted men.

"Wherever we went thereafter," wrote Col. Graydon, "obstacle courses were built that would challenge the ability of an orangutan. Soon we were swinging on ropes with the greatest of ease across gullies twenty feet deep and climbing walls like monkeys. In one location, all officers had to negotiate an obstacle course to get to their mess hall."

In October 1943 the regiment was guarding the Chesapeake Bay Sector of the Eastern Defense Command, which extended from the eastern shore of Maryland to South Carolina. Regimental headquarters was established at Camp Ashby, Virginia, which became known as "Camp Swampy," a former prisoner of war camp near Virginia Beach, where Lou Gergley remembers living in tar paper shacks.

First squadron headquarters was at Camp Branch, North Carolina, and second squadron had its headquarters at Somerset, Maryland. Scattered look-out posts were established along the beaches, and troopers patrolled constantly between them. In one interesting twist, a stretch of coastline south of Virginia Beach previously patrolled by the Coast Guard mounted on horses was now covered by ex-horse soldiers on foot and on motorcycle.

Trained as a radio repairman, Clinton Gosnell was now riding a motorcycle, searching the coast for German submarines, which sometimes brought saboteurs in close to the shore. "We had several alerts," he wrote, "but never actually witnessed any landings."

As soon as the regiment became well established in its new locations, it went through its third major reorganization:

from an all-horse regiment to a horse-mechanized regiment, then to a completely mechanized regiment, and this time to a mechanized cavalry group, organized as follows:

> Hq and Hq Troop 101st Cavalry Group, Mecz.
> Hq 101 Cavalry Recon Sq. Mecz.
> Hq Service Troop
> Troops A, B, and C (recon troops)
> Troop E (75 mm assault gun)
> Company F (light tank)
> Hq 116 Calvary Recon Sq. Mecz.
> Hq Service Troop
> Troops A, B, and C (recon troops)
> Troop E (75 mm assault gun)
> Company F (light tank)

In this configuration, the two squadrons were attached, not organic, to the group. By adding a headquarters and service troop, they became administratively and logistically independent. The addition of an assault gun troop and a tank company made the squadrons even more capable of independent action.

In the new organization, Col. McClelland commanded the regiment with Lt. Col. Leo Mortenson as executive officer. Lt. Col. Milton Kendall commanded the 101st Recon Squadron with Major Henry Brock as executive officer, and Lt. Col. Hubert Leonard commanded the 116th Recon Squadron, with Major Feagin as his executive officer.

Soon after this reorganization was completed, the Squadrons began drawing the new M8 armored cars to replace the old and battered scout cars. Scattered as they were, the units had little opportunity to train with these new vehicles or with the tanks and assault guns they were receiving.

Each recon troop had three platoons, consisting of an M8 armored car section with two armored cars and a scout section with six jeeps. The platoon leader rode in the third armored car. The M8s carried one turret-mounted 37mm cannon and a 30-caliber, coaxial machine gun. Later a 50-caliber, anti-aircraft machine gun was mounted on a ring-mount in the turret. The M8 was rated to withstand a 50-caliber machine gun on the front and on the turret. The scout jeeps had pedestal-mounted 30- or 50-caliber machine guns.

The assault gun troop consisted of three assault gun platoons, each containing two 75mm Howitzers mounted on armored-track vehicles.

I found myself learning a new vocabulary that used words like half-track — a kind of truck — and caliber. I learned the difference between tanks and armored cars. I learned the tank company of the 101st had three platoons of five light M5 series tanks each and what an M5 tank was. I learned it was powered by two Cadillac v/8 engines with automatic transmissions and carried a 37mm turret gun and one .30-caliber, coaxial machine gun next to the turret gun. Both of these were sighted through a telescopic sight and controlled by the gunner. They were stabilized by a gyro-tank that moved up and down, even though the sight stayed firmly on the target. One bow gun, also .30-caliber, was operated by the assistant driver, and one .30-caliber was mounted atop the turret for anti-aircraft fire. This tank was rated to withstand 20mm cannon fire. At the beginning, this was like learning a foreign language.

The men's explanations of armaments and artillery floated over my head and around me, but never lodged inside. I read books and studied photos on the web, and I have begun to slowly acquire the most basic kind of understanding.

Even with all this artillery, cavalry squadrons, with their lightly armored vehicles and jeeps, were never designed for combat with the heavy German tanks and infantry, but they were fast, maybe the fastest units in the Army. They also had great flexibility and excellent radio communications. Their best hope in a battle was to outrun the enemy.

July 1-November 12, 1944:
Camp Campbell and a Sea Voyage

On July 1, 1944, the scattered units of the 101st were brought together and transported by train to Camp Campbell, Kentucky. It was their final training before heading to Europe. Camp Campbell had the training facilities they had been lacking: adequate firing ranges for the tank and assault gun weapons, as well as for the small arms.

Clinton Thompson, who was drafted in 1941, recalls the training at Camp Campbell, especially one incident involving a plain-spoken enlisted man and a captain, who he described as "quite a character."

"When we were at Camp Campbell, taking our tests for going overseas, we had to hike so many miles in so many minutes," he said. "We were having trouble doing that. We never could meet our time objective. B Troop's commander, Augustine "Gus" Littleton, was losing patience fast. John Gorski, this guy from Pennsylvania, stepped out of the ranks and told the captain that it was a problem of leadership. Gorski said that if he could be allowed to lead the Group, they'd be able to make their time. The next time we went out, Littleton ordered Gorski to the front and made him set the pace. I'm sure that captain thought he'd fail, but sure enough, we made the time."

Gorski remembers the story, but in his version he didn't take the lead. He just set the pace.

"Littleton really liked to do all that hiking and marching," said Gorski, "but for crissakes he was a little guy and we were for crissakes practically stepping on him all the time. He was too proud to let me get out in front him, like Thompson said, but I kept stepping on his heels, so he had to walk a little faster. But, I don't know, maybe Thompson was right."

On October 23, the Group left Camp Campbell for Camp Kilmer, New Jersey, a staging area for overseas movement, but Sgt. Bill Hurley, who had been with them throughout their training, didn't leave with them.

"I had a problem with my left eye," he said, "so I went to see the medics. I was immediately hospitalized. As time passed, I wanted to sign a waiver so I could return to active duty, but to no avail. I spent five months at Camp Campbell station hospital, eventually losing the sight in the eye. I was then sent to the Veteran's Administration hospital at Kingsbridge Road in the Bronx to be discharged. It was a dark and dreary place. My father picked me up the day before Thanksgiving. It was a sad day at Black Rock for me, not to have gone with the outfit."

Hurley may not have gone to Germany with his men, but his loyalty to the cavalry never waivered. When I'd call or write to the veterans, asking questions about the history of the unit, many of them would respond by saying I needed to talk to Bill Hurley, that he was the man who knew all about the 101st Cavalry.

In New Jersey, the men received additional equipment, medical shots, and physical examinations. Their next stop was the Port of Embarkation, Staten Island, New York.

Eugene Tharp was just 18 years old when he was drafted in 1942. "I was excited at the time," he said. "We were just kids, and we thought we were fixing to get into something great.When we got our shots in New Jersey, our arms were so sore that we couldn't salute our lieutenant. He couldn't salute us either."

Tharp, like Hurley, almost got left behind. During training he was riding a motorcycle when a half-track ran over him, badly injuring his knee. He was in the hospital right up until the Group was ready to leave, but he was discharged in time to board his ship, the USS Uruguay.

The men of the 101st boarded their ship, an old South American cruise ship converted to a troop transport, in the late evening of October 31, but they did not leave that night.

They anchored off-shore until the next morning, when they left in a large convoy of merchant ships, oil tankers, and other troop ships, all guarded by a destroyer escort and all bound for England. Some of the men remember being told that it was the largest convoy ever to set sail during the war.

Although converted cruise ships like the Uruguay were once elegant, they now had men stacked like cordwood in the hold, sleeping three to four deep in bunks.

"We called it the 'banana boat,'" Gosnell wrote of the Uruguay. "It was 2 a.m. when we went aboard and a band was playing 'East Side, West Side.' I remember wondering at the time, 'How in the world did I ever get myself into such a mess?' Since there didn't seem to be any practical way of getting out of it, I just gritted my teeth and continued on."

Gosnell got a bunk on the bottom, or "D" deck. "The hammocks were hung in layers clear up to the ceilings," he wrote. "I was in a top hammock; somebody told me it was better to be up on top, in case somebody got sick."

Members of the 101st Cavalry cross the Atlantic.
Photo courtesy of Bill Hart

David Gay was 22 years old when he was drafted in April 1942. He had been farming with his dad, raising tobacco, corn, beans, and other crops. He was lucky. He didn't get sick on the way over, although a lot of soldiers did. "I remember one boy," he said, "who was so sick that he stayed in his bunk the whole 13 days."

They ate twice a day, said Buck Fluharty, "because there were 6,000 men on the ship and that's all we could do."

Fluharty grew up on the water, so he didn't get seasick like a lot of the guys.

"Another guy and I scrubbed the passageways at night," he said, "which gave us access to the mess hall. We survived on cold cuts for the 16 to 17 days we were at sea."

Fluharty said the weather going over was good, and the men walked the decks in shifts in order to avoid crowding. Gosnell remembers that he spent a lot of time watching the other ships.

"In a way it was like looking at old movies," Gosnell said. "Destroyers would dart in and out and all around, listening and looking for enemy subs."

William Pierce remembers zig-zagging to avoid the U-boats and sleeping in hammocks on the lower deck, and he laughs when he tells about the thing he remembers most clearly.

"The thing that bothered me were the latrines on the ship," he said. "They were up high, and my feet didn't touch the floor. I had to get a box to put my feet on. I don't know why, but that really bothered me, not touching the floor."

Lt. Col. Leonard saved one of the menus from the trip, the one for November 11, and it was signed by Leo Mortenson, E. Davis, Milton Kendall, Irving Odell, George Hull, all lieutenant colonels, and by a colonel whose signature was illegible. They dined that night on olives, fruit cocktail, spring onions, celery, dill pickles, cream of asparagus soup, fried filet of cod in sauce portugaise, fried breaded veal cutlet in tomato sauce, roast prime ribs of beef au jus, mixed green vegetables, carrots vichy, steamed rice, potatoes, cold cuts, salad, cream cheese and crackers, angel cake, ice cream tea, coffee, and cocoa. I doubt that my father or any of the other enlisted men had the same for dinner that night.

While at sea, Leonard wrote home, describing his experience on the trip to England:

> November 5, 1944
> Dear Mary
> Life Aboard Ship. Not too bad as far as I am concerned. Although the men do not find the luxuries on board, I have everything one would want on a peace time cruise aboard a fairly good ship. We have two meals a day, excellent dining room for officers, food and plenty of it and with a wide choice at that, especially at dinner. I am seated at the Transport Commanders table with Col. Mc., Leo, Milt and three other Lt. Colonels. Dinner is rather formal, blouses are worn, dinner music, supplied by three enlisted men. As quarters are assigned by rank, I share a large stateroom with Milt, two single beds, separate reading lamps, comfortable chairs, separate toilet with shower and what not. No sign of the hardships of war yet.
> The other officers are not so well off. They are quartered six or more to a room and sleep in three-tier bunks and a bit crowded. The enlisted men are a little uncomfortable in various parts of the ship, and they have the chow line and stand at high tables, Bickford style. It is an interesting trip for all concerned and an experience that will never be forgotten in the years to come.
> An important factor in making the trip a pleasant one to date is the weather. It has been good to us, not a bit rough, little or no rolling

with the exception of one afternoon which was not enough to cause seasickness. However, a few of the men were not quite normal. I think it was caused by a combination of homesickness, cramped quarters and possibly the uncertainties of the voyage. To date we have had no cause for any excitement.

I get up around 0800 and prepare for breakfast, which is served at 0830, then on deck for some fresh air and a little exercise, and I mean a little as there is not much deck space available. At 1100 an inspection is made of the quarters occupied by military personnel while they are on deck. I am one of the inspecting officers; the inspection only takes one half hour. At 1330 I go to mass, usually said by Father Powers; we have one other Catholic chaplain aboard and several of other faiths. After mass, back in the room for a nap or maybe a little reading or writing until about 1630, then wash and dress for dinner which is at 1730. After dinner, a movie or a game of cards. I play for small stakes, but there are some pretty big games way out of my class. I have seen several movies, including *White Cargo* and *Major and Minor.*

November 8, 1944
My Dear Mary,

As long as I have the headquarters portable in my room I might as well take advantage of it and do a little thinking. You understand of course, no mail is received by us while we are aboard ship and I assume it will be a few more days after we land before we can accept any. Regardless you all are close to me, mail or no mail.

This afternoon I was a busy little man. I got out my laundry, a few pieces of underwear, socks and handkerchiefs and did a little washing, using the wash basin in the bathroom, some Palmolive (the complexion soap) and the rinse and squeeze method. I managed to get fairly good results, at least my laundry smells nice.

We have heard via radio that Dewey has conceded and forwarded his congratulations to his nibs. Such is life.

Excellent weather has kept all hands fine and in good spirits, anxious to get on the move and do something as we approach our destination, wherever that is.

Well, my fair one, from now on you must call on nothing short of your all out best to be your best. You must, and you can keep your head high, your spirit high and pleasant thoughts, remembering of course that I not only love you, but I salute you.

November 10, 1944
Dear Mary,

Another day and everything is fine. As we near our destination, rumors are plentiful as to when it will be. Anyway, it makes good conversation. It's an old saying, "Everything comes in bundles," so look for several letters arriving all about the same time.

That fruitcake sounds good. I hope it gets to me in good shape and not highjacked. Today I purchased five cartons of Camels at 50 cents a carton. They should last me awhile.

Hubert

Barrow-in-Furness

England

"I **remember looking down on the dock** and seeing this English fella who was playing spoons," wrote Clinton Gosnell. "He held multiple spoons in both hands and tapped them on his knees and thighs and arms to make different sounds. I had never seen anybody play spoons before."

In Liverpool, more than 10,000 men disembarked and caught buses to the train station, where children begged them for gum.

"'Any gum chum?' they would ask," said Gosnell. "We had some fruit from our mess on the boat, and we shared it with the children, some of whom hadn't seen oranges and apples before. It was late evening before all of us were on the train, and we set off. Nobody told us where we were going, and we had to keep all the blinds on the train completely closed in case of German air attacks."

The 101st was on its way to the northwest of England, to Lancashire, Barrow-in-Furness, described by Major Mercer W. Sweeney in the Group history, *Wingfoot* as a "rugged Old World peninsula" that "sparkles like a lovely jewel when the stubborn north-country sun brushes aside the eternal rains that come sweeping in on high winds from the Irish Sea."

The troopers saw little of this beauty when they first arrived in the middle of the night, marching up a country lane with high stone walls on either side.

"Nobody knew exactly where we were," wrote Gosnell, "or where we were going." Where they were was about 100 miles north of Liverpool. They would be staying in Quonset huts, which had been originally built for refugees coming from the south of London to escape the air raids, and sleeping on wooden beds with small mattresses.

"[Those beds] were short," wrote Gosnell.

Stationed at Camp Anty-Cross, the men of the 101st settled in to wait for the orders that would take them to France. They were the first Americans to be billeted in that particular place, used most recently by a Scottish Highland brigade that had just left for the continent. After several days of quarantine, which were required of all troops coming into England, they were given passes to go out on the town. The chaplain arranged some dances, and the locals invited them to their homes for tea.

"I met a young lady who worked in a shipyard," wrote Gosnell. "I made plans to meet her one evening at a dance. During the course of the evening, I decided to ask another girl to dance. There were about 25 girls to every man, so I went through quite a crowd before I came to this young lady who really interested me. I asked her to dance and discovered she was the one for me. We danced several times, and I asked her for a date. She accepted."

Gosnell was late for his first date with Eileen Windle, and she thought he had stood her up. He saved himself by arriving just in time and taking her to the movies. After the movies, he walked her home, and she invited him to dinner and to meet her parents.

"When her five-and-a-half-foot-tall father met me at the door that evening, he said, 'Come in lad,' and asked me to sit down. Then he called out, 'Eileen, looks like you caught a big one.' Over the next few months he and I became very close and remained so for all of his life. Tobacco was virtually impossible for him to obtain, so I made a point of getting cigars in my rations for him, along with other small items he had trouble getting, which he really appreciated."

This home in England was the first place Gosnell wanted to go when the war was over several months later.

∽⌇∾

The ships with the heavy equipment the cavalry needed had been diverted to higher priority units, lengthening the cavalry's wait. When the equipment finally arrived, the supply and maintenance men put it into service and made several modifications. For example, the M8 armored cars and other vehicles needed to be fitted with 50-caliber, anti-aircraft machine guns on ring mounts before they would be ready for the battle ahead.

In a letter home, Leonard wrote:

> ... here I am, somewhere in northern England
> and quite comfortable, at least for the time being.
> We are quartered out in the country just outside
> of a small, quaint old town, most every building
> and fence made of stone. Our camp is considered
> one of the best of its type, and we are fortunate to
> have warm, dry buildings this time of year. The
> weather compares with that of New England in

the early spring when it's cold, damp and dreary. Although we have been here only a short time, we are quickly getting acclimatized. We have no idea how long we will be here. American money cannot be used in England so it was necessary for us to exchange it for British money. The pounds, shillings and pence sort of threw me for awhile, but now I can handle it fairly well as I have so little of it.

～～

Earl Carmickle described those months in England as "the worst winter ever. It rained a lot and it was too foggy to go anywhere sometimes. One night we couldn't even find our barracks in the fog."

He's not alone in his assessment of the weather. Most of the men remember England had friendly people and dreary weather.

They spent most of their time training, but sometimes Father Powers took them on tours to London. Lt. Col. Hubert Leonard wrote home often, and his letters tell a lot about life in England – as least for the officers.

> November 17, 1944
> Dear Mary,
>   I too miss the cocktails before dinner, but do have a bottle of ale, which is better than nothing. This noon, the Colonel and the Lt. Colonels Mortenson, Kendall and myself kept a luncheon engagement in a nearby city. We were the guests of a British colonel and in the company of a British admiral, major and a city official. It was quite a social visit. We met our host in the lounge room of a fairly nice hotel where he and the other Britishers were waiting for us, all standing in front

of a fireplace – sort of picture one might see on a painting in a good tavern, or on liquor advertisements. All had a drink either in their hand or on a nearby table. We were introduced around and joined in a drink, called gin and vermouth, sweet vermouth, no ice (not near as good as one of our mixed drinks). After a few minutes of general conversations, no business – all talk being weather, cigarettes, cost of living, etc., we moved to the dining room for lunch. Soup, rolls, boiled beef, potatoes and carrots, pudding (rice), celery and a small cup of coffee which was not too good. Several typical English stories were told, the kind that makes them laugh, and we laugh because they do, not at the story. The colonel was very polite to us and so were his friends, and as they had other business to accomplish, they bid us "Cherrio" about 1430. All in all it was a pleasant experience.

Last Sunday aboard ship I went to Mass. Father Powers is a busy man during the week taking troops on sightseeing tours of the various old churches, abbeys, etc. He has asked several times about you all.

I hope you are able to get the storm windows up and you got back the knack of baking. Receiving mail is a treat, but it's a real thrill when it comes from you.

Much of what Leonard wrote home related to the dismal weather and the lack of mail. Mail delivery was often held up, and letters arrived in batches. In one letter he wrote, "Seems that the mail has yet to straighten itself out. Today I received your v-mail letter dated November 11 and your airmail letter dated November 4, and according to your letters, you have not heard from me. Seems strange, but I know that by now you have several letters."

In Germany events were leading up to the Battle of the Bulge, which would begin in mid-December.

November 19, 1944
Dear Mary,

According to the news, another push is on over on the continent and apparently the beginning of a winter drive. As for me, I am quite comfortable and there is no evidence of activity around here. I would not mind putting up here for the winter, but who can tell?

I have not mentioned it before, but our food has been excellent, just about the same as we received in the States. Today, roast chicken, etc., so as far as that department is concerned, we are doing well.

November 21, 1944
Dear Mary,

.... we are just starting to "cook" and are beginning to have things to do.

Today the weather was perfect, comfortably warm. This morning the staff took a short hike, three or more miles. We expect to do this every day, doing a little more each day until we can do ten or twenty miles without exertion.

Our nights have been rather quiet, matter of fact too quiet, so several of us scraped together twelve pounds and bought a radio. It sure brightens the evening. We can sell it on a short notice if and when we move – let's see, my share is thirty shillings, more or less.

Today I took a look in our cook house (mess hall) and was surprised at the amount of food we received for Thanksgiving: turkeys, nuts, candy, and all the trimmings. We have everything, including the day off. The only thing missing will be the folks at home – and everyone misses that.

The men spent Thanksgiving Day in 1944 far from home, celebrating with a half-day holiday and a traditional meal. The afternoon was spent like many Thanksgiving afternoons at home.

> Thanksgiving Day, 1944
> Dear Mary,
>   Thanksgiving Day, half a day holiday. Noon meal was typical American, everything but nuts, plenty other food for all. It should not be hard for you to guess what most of us did this afternoon – right – I took a little two and one half hour nap. As it drizzled most of the day, sleeping was in order, and I really knocked it off, until four thirty. I have just finished supper, turkey soup, cold turkey and cheese, bread, jam and coffee, and now as I struggle with this typewriter I am nibbling on hard candy. Two Sunkist oranges are sitting on my desk, staring right at me. I'll get to those a little later.
>   Leo Mortenson has been laid up for a few days with a slight cold, but was up and around today, feeling no worse for the wear.
>   My room is next to our sitting room and I can hear the radio, an American band just finished playing a new song which caused a bit of laughing: "Got Any gum Chum?" Whoever wrote it must have been over here, as that is just what the local inhabitants call for when one or a hundred soldiers pass them..., listen to it if you get a chance. The radio program that comes from the U.S. is usually a special broadcast and has all the headliners without any commercials.
>   Hubert

My father had written to my mother from Ft. Meade, telling her how to care for his car, and Lt. Col. Leonard was no different. Letters to his wife, Mary, were often filled with instructions for her and complaints about the boredom of every day life.

November 24, 1944
My Dear Mary,

About the car, I believe it may be well to lay it up for the winter and suggest you have a good garage man prepare it, that is, remove the battery, drain the radiator, engine block, etc., and put the car up on blocks. The winter months are pretty hard on a car and it requires much more care to keep it in operation during the cold weather.

No cigarettes available at the time being, which is causing a lot of griping and conversation throughout the UK – an unsolved mystery. It's an unhealthy situation, but I am sure it will be back to normal before long. The shortage does not affect me as I have five cartons which I purchased on the boat for a nickel a pack.

November 27, 1944
Dear Mary,

Today, or rather this morning, we had our first frost and it has been cold all day. Tonight it is raining and hailing, nasty and cold, but inside it is quite comfortable. For several hours after supper we sat around our coal burning fireplace and listened to the radio, drank a few bottles of beer and discussed things in general. I had planned to take a hot bath, but French and Weinheimer beat me to it and used all the hot water. Besides, the bathroom is cold, so I'll take one tomorrow.

November 28, 1944
My Dear Mary,

It seems that this is brussels sprout season here in England as we are getting them three and four times a week. At first they tasted pretty good, but now it takes a little effort to eat them. All in all, our meals have been excellent, at noon today we had steak and I had a good one, and I was tempted to have another, but I thought of my figure and I passed it up.

I am feeling fine, which is quite true with all of us, little or no sickness, even if the weather is not of the best. The sun can be out (which is not often) and without a moment's notice it will be pouring rain. Generally it is just dull, dreary and damp.

November 29, 1944
Dear Mary,

Milk? What's that? We get evaporated and powdered milk, also powdered eggs, once in awhile cold storage eggs show up, however, the rest of the food, including butter, is plentiful. ...

I am looking for that fruitcake, but I must restrain my anxiety as parcels are not handled as promptly as other mail and too the lid might have blown off and sunk a boat or wrecked a train. Anyhow, when it gets here, I will do it justice. ...

When Leonard wrote about special events the officers attended, I could never be sure if these were also opportunities for the enlisted men to get out and have fun.

December 2, 1944
My Dear Mary,

Last night I had the pleasure to attend an amateur show done by a dramatic society of a Royal Air Force station not far from us, the play *Hay Fever*, a comedy in three acts by Noel Coward. I went over with Leo Mortenson and we were the guests of the commanding officer of the station. We sat in the first row centre. The party consisted of the CO, his wife, Leo and I. They were very pleasant and cordial. They play was done fairly well and I enjoyed it after a fashion. After the performance, we retired to their club and, believe it or not, the Scotch began to flow, of which Leo and I had just enough to keep us from getting cold on the way home. Not too bad, what? We were in bed by twelve.

The fruitcake etc. has not arrived yet. Maybe it blew up, anyway it will be a long time before I give up looking for it as they say packages may be late but they finally get to their destinations. All mail with the old APO is sent right to us without delay so we will not worry on that score.

I would like to send you and the children something for Christmas, but to date I have not seen a thing worthwhile, not even a card, so in the interim, think of all the year has brought you, look at all the blessings still in view, friendships, comfort, home joys, health and my love.

Sunday, December 3, 1944
Dear Mary,

Today we had a few good laughs. But first I must say that I did my duty and went to mass. Our building facilities are rather limited and the chaplain holds the services in a small chapel located in a cold English cemetery about two or three hundred yards outside of our camp. It is the kind of a chapel and cemetery one would find in a ghost story. Now for a few of the events of the day which caused the laughs, first we got paid, in English money, the highest denomination being in one pound notes. Well, Ed French made some change on his pay form regarding the allotment and some how it did not go through and all his pay came direct to him, so he has a bundle of money about two inches thick and no place to carry it.

Of course tomorrow he will arrange to purchase a money order and send some home.

Still looking for that fruitcake.

December 4, 1944
My Dear Mary,

No mail today – but we have other news. The cigarette situation is cleared up. We now can get five packs a week, which is enough when it is supplemented by the packs from those who do not smoke, such as French. By the way, Ed tells me he received your letter. It is now eight twenty and Fred Waring and his Pennsylvanians are giving forth over our radio. It is a rebroadcast of one of their shows – that radio of ours helps to make things right pleasant especially in the evening.

Tomorrow, if I get time and the weather is a bit clear, I will go down to the town and see if I can pick up a little something in the line of gifts for you all. If I am successful, I will send them along, however, don't expect much as I understand things are pretty grim.

As Christmas drew closer, Leonard contacted his sister to arrange for presents for his family. And in letters to his wife, it is clear the fruitcake is still on its way.

Monday, December 11, 1944
Dear Catherine,

A day or two ago I sent to you the following telegram:

"Unable to purchase appropriate Christmas gifts for Mary and Children. Please shop, pay, sign Daddy, and deliver. Will send you money order."

I have no way of knowing whether you received it or not. In any event, your help will be appreciated as I think it will be a little surprise, even if it is after Christmas, you being Mr. Santa Claus on my behalf. You can let me know all the costs and I can send you a money order from here. Mary does not know of this plan, it's just between you and I so that we can effect surprise.

As for me, I would appreciate the overseas edition of the *New Yorker*. Can you arrange it? A little package of fancy eatables would also be appreciated.

Tuesday, December 12, 1944
Dear Mary,

I see by the *Daily Mail*, an English newspaper, the chances for the people over here in getting turkey for Christmas is one for every ten families and they are selling from 45 cents a pound to 85 cents a pound. Fresh eggs or even storage eggs are a treat to them. They use powdered eggs and they are called 'reconstituted eggs.' Butter they get little or none, use margarine instead, so after all you are quite lucky.

As for the fruitcake, other officers have heard that packages have been mailed to them as far back as November 5 and still they have not received them. Matter of fact, very few packages have been received considering the number of men here. My officers are planning to have a little party on Christmas. Each one to donate some eatables (if he has any). As far as spirits, that's the real problem. It is still possible that someone will produce it. If not, we will be contented with beer.

December 14, 1944

Dear Mary,

The weather continues to be ugly, rain every day, sometimes for an hour or so. Other times all day and longer. For instance, it started raining early this morning and it is now 9:00 o'clock and it is still coming down. Most of my work is such that it keeps me indoors when it is raining.

We have found a place, or rather an 'inn' about five miles from here where we can go after hours, which is open until 10:00 o'clock (no beer or spirits are sold in the UK after ten) where we can relax, drink beer and if one is lucky, two and sometimes three shots of spirits. I don't think they are over an ounce (rationed, you know). The place is known as Fisherman's Inn, built about eight years ago and it is quite modern for this part of England. It has three different rooms, adjoining one another: a tavern with a bar, table and chairs, a dart game and a ping pong table; a cocktail lounge, a smaller room with a glass top bar and red leather chairs; and another room more on the typical pub style, the latter used mostly by local folks – not a jute (sic) box in the place and no singing allowed – it's a change from the camp, once or twice a week – now don't worry I go out as a very much married man with my devoted affection for one and only.

Saturday, December 16, 1944

Dear Mary,

Still no sign of the fruitcake.

I had some Britishers here yesterday as my guests: two navy officers, two home guard officers, and two army officers. We entertained in our little room, bitter ale and stout were the liquids, sandwiches and coffee were served.

Leo Mortenson and I are going to Fisherman's Inn tonight to pour a few if we can get it. At dinner tonight he said he felt a little blue, I replied that I felt the same way – so, to Fisherman's Inn to chase the blues away. Doug Feagin went to London (with Sweeney and Brock) on business, Ed French left a few minutes ago to go to Liverpool to meet his brother at the Red Cross.

Plans were already being made by December 17 for a Christmas celebration. The men were building an altar in one of the mess halls for midnight mass and making arrangements for flowers, an organ, and a choir. After church services, the Red Cross would serve coffee and doughnuts.

And finally, on December 19 after weeks of waiting, Leonard wrote that the fruitcake arrived.

It's here! And what a pleasant surprise. The package was in perfect condition. The fruitcake looks right good and it tastes as good as it looks. I had to sample it as soon as I opened it. The aftershave lotion and the hair tonic were really a surprise, every bottle in perfect order. I had to try some immediately. It is 100 percent better than the stuff over here. I intend to save it for my personal use and for special occasions only.

That night, Leonard wrote, Chaplain Eastman had arranged for a choir of young boys from a local church to sing Christmas carols in the mess hall.

Happy Holidays

Some men of the 101st celebrated Christmas by going to midnight services on Christmas Eve, then to the mess hall for hot coffee and thousands of Red Cross doughnuts. They listened to Christmas carols sung by local singers, and, over the radio, they heard Bing Crosby sing "White Christmas" for the first time. Some of the entertainment was provided by the men themselves.

Buck Fluharty bought an old guitar in an English pawn shop for $12. It was not playable, but since he had experience with low-budget guitars at home, he knew what to do.

"I sawed a piece of bolt rod out of the ceiling of a bombed-out railroad station," he said, "drilled through the guitar body where the neck joins and out through the rear, extended the rod through the holes, drilled and tapped the rod under the fingerboard and with a screw pulled the fingerboard into alignment, strings laid flat, easy to fret. No Gibson, but playable."

A couple of guys would sing along as he played, and the locals were taken with their music. The company office had a steady stream of phone calls for Fluharty and his friends to come to dinner each evening and bring the guitar.

A family Fluharty knew invited him and two other men to go with them to visit relatives on Christmas Eve.

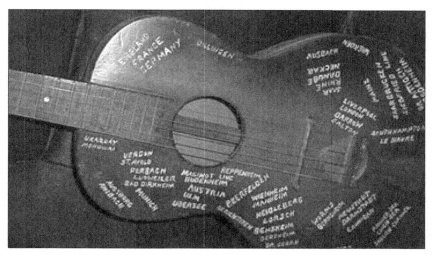

Fluharty still has the guitar hanging in his hobby room, and across the front of the guitar are painted the names of towns he passed through, from Barrow and Dalton to LeHavre, Verdun, Saarbrucken, Worms, Heidelberg, Lorsch, and a dozen places in between.

Photo courtesy Buck Fluharty.

"We had dinner with the family," Fluharty said, "and on the midnight train ride back, we had to switch trains. During the lull in the station, they had me play and the boys sing over the telephone to some of their friends who could not be with them. They seemed to enjoy it as much as we did."

December 25, 1944
Dear Mary,

Another holiday and come and gone. Most everyone went to one of the two services. The Catholic services were well planned. It was known as a Military Mass with a guard of honor. Only one thing was missing and that was the choir. Some place along the line that did not work out, which was too bad as choir singing at midnight mass gives it additional beauty. After the mass I went to Brock's quarters to join him in a drink of brandy (he received a package, too, with little bottles) and a bite of cake. Then we went to my quarters and repeated the performance. Believe it or not, we felt a little high and did not get to bed until three thirty. I managed to stay in bed until eleven, and then cleaned up for Christmas dinner, turkey with all the trimmings. Somehow the whole day was dull and empty.

Tonight the gang – Feagin, French, [Capt. William] Weinheimer, Perkins, (Bages has a date) and I are going to the Fisherman's Inn and try to wrangle some gin from the barkeep. Weinheimer has promised us a little party on our return: cold shrimp, Kraft cheese, and Ritz crackers. I will add a little fruitcake.

Hubert

December 26, 1944

Dear Mary,

The day after Christmas is called Boxing Day over here, just why I don't know.

Last night at the inn, the spirits were scarce, the place crowded, but we did wrangle a round each, that is five drinks each (wee ones) of gin, and it was decided that we should go someplace where we could sing, so we left about nine and went to a not-so-fancy inn (another pub) and joined in song with the local patrons. An Englishman, complete with cap, cigarette and a mug of beer played the piano, then we had a few beers and then came ten o'clock closing time, so back to home to Willie's shrimp and cheese and a few more of our bottled beer, more song.

A small package would be appreciated, say some hors d'oeuvres, sweet pickles, olives, shrimp, cocktail franks, anchovies and the cake.

For the past few days it has not rained hard, just a damp mist. The sun has been seen once or twice and only for a few moments. Most everyone has a slight cold or a cough.

Hubert

On December 28, the mayor and "mayoress" of the town invited about 150 enlisted men and 20 officers to a dance in honor of the U.S. forces. Leo Mortenson and Mercer Sweeney represented the 101st Group, while Robert Feagin and Leonard represented the 116th Squadron. According to Leonard's letter to his wife about this event, the group representing the 101st Squadron "failed to appear."

The dance was held in the town hall, which Leonard described as "almost as big as the armory in Brooklyn," although broken up into municipal offices and a large reception hall. In his letter, Leonard describes the event:

Now, we were met by an old gent in tails who showed us around the building, and shortly we met another younger man, also in tails, who introduced himself as the town clerk (apparently an important position) who suggested we go to the mayor's office and meet the mayor and the mayoress and also join in a spot. Well, we followed along and met the mayor and mayoress – the mayor – a fine little old lady and right pleasant, the mayoress a daughter-in-law of the mayor (about 38).

We also met the mayor's husband, a little old gent and the mayoress' husband and the town clerk's wife. After we were introduced around, we each had a spot. The mayor then requested us to go out to the dance floor as she had to welcome the soldiers. To do this properly, it was necessary for her to wear her badge of office, a big gold chain with a locket that weighed about fifteen pounds. So, complete with locket, out we went. The mayor and Leo mounted the bandstand, the town clerk adjusted the mike and the mayor made her welcome speech. It was short and she received quite a hand. The town clerk asked Leo to say a few words, but Leo was taken by surprise and declined (with a red face). Shortly after they returned to the floor, Leo mentioned to me that he felt like a big chump as he at least should have acknowledged the mayor's hospitality. Anyway, as the major did not dance, we returned to the office and talked about everything.

The mayoress' job is to handle all the details for social functions, and she saw to it that we received our share of spirits and a bite to eat. She also introduced us to the councilmen and their wives who came in a little later. I had a grand time with the exception of three occasions, and they were three duty dances which I got roped into: one with the mayoress, one with the clerk's wife and one with a councilman's wife. The enlisted men and officers who attended all had an enjoyable time (most of the ladies were in evening dress, which added a little something).

Hubert

Plans were made for a New Year's Eve party to help the men celebrate the beginning of 1945, the year everyone hoped would be the last year of the war.

A committee rented the hall and arranged for music, drinks, and food. The cost of the evening would be two pounds each (about $8.10).

"Sounds like a lot of money," wrote Leonard, "but as we have to have it out of the camp, everything adds up and we do need to blow off a little steam. All work and no play makes Jack a dull boy."

In just a few weeks, the 101st would move on, but, as Sweeney wrote in *Wingfoot*, "Camp Anty Cross and its people will always hold a special place in the hearts of the men."

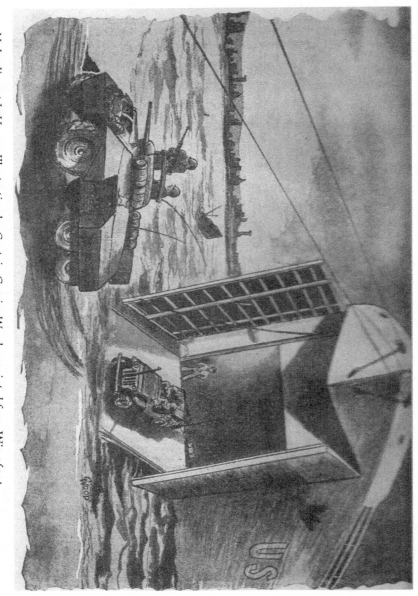

Unloading at LeHavre. Illustration by Captain Crozier Wood, reprinted from Wingfoot.

Road Trip

Southampton

On January 4, the men finally received orders to move across the English Channel and join the war. They moved out by rail and motor convoy to Camp C, Barton Stacey, Hampshire, in southern England. There they would prepare for the crossing. They spent three weeks, from January 5 to 28, servicing and modifying approximately 250 vehicles, readying them for the front line. A few men attended a mine and booby trap school, which proved to be useful once they got to Germany. Others participated in an overnight training exercise near Stockbridge.

Lt. Col. Leonard's letters continue, keeping his wife informed of their journey.

January 5, 1945
Dear Mary,

Surprise! We are now in our new home; at least we will call it our home while we are here. As for comfort and convenience, we still have them. The buildings are warm and comfortable and the facilities adequate and our stay here should be pleasant regardless how long it is. It is not quite as damp down here as it was up north.

I have plenty of cigarettes at the moment and probably for several weeks to come I shall be very comfortable. Let me briefly describe the staff officers quarters, where I live, a building with eight small single rooms (I have a double room) with two bathrooms complete with bathtubs, plenty of hot water, they are located on one end, on the other end, a room about the size of your living room – which we use as an office in the day and sort of a sitting or a club room in the evening. This room has a fireplace going all the time; it is smaller than the one in Morehead. We burn coal in it and we have four Morris chairs always occupied in the evening, sitting around the fireplace pouring a bit of ale and telling stories. Quite comfortable. My rooms, one I use for an office and the other a bedroom, a little smaller than a hall room, complete with clothes closet, a dresser, a spring bed, mattress sheets, pillows and blankets. Wichman is always puttering around fixing and cleaning things.

We do not have too much to do as yet, but we manage to keep busy and comfortable.

Back to the little things I could use, I just thought of one or two: G. Washington coffee (separate servings), and perhaps bullion cubes or the like.

Hubert

The new barracks didn't allow room for an officers' club, so Leonard had his radio put in his room, which he wrote was fairly large and furnished with a "large wardrobe, a dresser, a table, a rug, and a comfortable single bed."

A little snow fell, but the weather was described as mostly fair and cold. Perhaps to keep warm, Bages and Nawn began to grow mustaches.

> Southern England
> January 11, 1945
> Dear Mary,
> Today we had snow flurries, but not enough to cause any more than a thin covering on the ground. Tonight we had another school, radio this time. It helps to pass the evening. It is now nine-thirty and by the time I finish this letter it should be around ten-thirty as it takes me a good hour to write.
> I believe I mentioned before that the cake lasted about a week and the other contents about the same time. I still have a little of this and that in the wardrobe to nibble on; however, it soon will be gone, so I will make a request. Please be so kind to send me some snacks to nibble on and also see the druggist and get him to fill the prescription; it has given me relief on several occasions.
> We get plenty of fruit and fruit juice, canned and fresh, so don't worry about that. Candy and cigarettes, although they are on a ration basis, we get enough. The liquid refreshment department is really grim here in this part of England. There is a liquor ration which amounts to about one-third of a bottle per officer per month. We work it by drawing lots so that the lucky ones get a full bottle: twenty bottles of Scotch, ten of gin and six bottles of wine. In other words, thirty some odd officers out of ninety get something, the rest, nil.

Our staff did not fare well. Weinheimer drew one scotch and Feagin one gin, which will not go very far among our bunch.

Sunday, January 14, 1945
Dear Mary,

Just got back from London. Yesterday arrangements were completed to have about 350 men and a dozen officers go to the big town. A special train left here yesterday at 9:00 o'clock and by noon the population of London was increased by 350 some odd men. The enlisted men were put up for the night by the Red Cross who also had a program for those who desired it, such as sightseeing, dances, etc. The officers from our squadron, Feagin, [Capt. Louis] Bossert, [Capt. Albert F. Jr.] Burgess, [1st Lt. Ezra B.] Mann, [2nd. Lt. Frederick] Mack, and [1st Lt. George] Harden used the facilities that the Red Cross provided and were able to get rooms at several different hotels.

Shortly after our arrival and after we checked in our hotel (Feagin and me) the Park Lane, we went to another hotel for lunch. Here the Army has taken over and operates a mess for officers, which holds around 1,200 at one time, so you can imagine what size it is. The service is cafeteria style. After lunch we stopped at the officers' bar and had a couple of pours of scotch and went to the officers' clothing store, another crowd, like Macy's basement, here I bought heavy socks, heavy wool underwear, a hat and handkerchiefs. Feagin bought just about the same. So with our purchases which we could not get wrapped up, we got a cab and had the driver take us around the town. We saw the Tower, Buckingham Palace, House of Parliament, Hyde Park, etc., getting back to the hotel at dark, and I mean dark. The only lights are those of the vehicles.

Well, we cleaned up and went to another place for dinner, the Senior Officers' Club. There we had two scotches, that's all one is allowed, and it is not sold after dinner. We had a good dinner, although it was crowded. I thought that I might run across one of the Leonards while we were there, as it is the gathering place for field officers. However, I did not see them, but did meet an officer that was in Riley with me and also one from Ft. Devens. Nope I did not go anywhere from there, went back to our hotel. It was about a mile and we walked it in the dark. Took a bath and so to bed about eleven thirty.

Sunday morning was foggy and when it is that way one might as well stay in bed, because if you don't know the way around, you get lost, believe it or not. So I stayed in bed. After lunch, it cleared up and I took a walk to see the sights. Everything closed and a bit battered up. I did not know where I was most of the time, but managed not to get lost. We had supper and left London on the special at eight o'clock.

Southern England
January 15, 1945
Dear Mary,

Here we go again. Another week and all is well. According to the news reports, the Jerries have been dropping a few V bombs on southern England, so far I have not been anywhere near any place either to see or hear them, and I am assured that we have little to worry about in this part of the country. To realize that there is a war on it is necessary for us to listen to news reports and to read the newspapers. So far we do not know just what part we will play, but we do know that in the not-too-distant future, we will be on the continent.

Bages, [1st Lt. Raymond] Paquette and [2nd Lt. Robert] Schafer (the great lovers) are away in London on a three-day leave. This is their second day there and they must be raising whoopee as Bages phoned Ed French this afternoon, long distance, and asked for money as they are dead broke. Neither Ed nor any of us are going to finance them, if they need money bad they can go to the finance officer there and get a partial payment on this month's pay. At the time he phoned, we did not think of this, so I guess they are sweating it out washing dishes. Wichman just came in my room to fix the fire. I asked him how he enjoyed his trip to London. He says he would like to go back there next weekend and it was better than Barrow. I asked how come. He came back with that big laugh and said nothing. I said, how are the girls. He said words to the effect that they did not bother with any, just looked around, but maybe next time.

Hubert

For a few hours in the afternoon on January 18, it rained, hailed, and blew up a storm. The officers stayed dry inside, taking classes led by Capt. Irwin Olenik on how to take care of themselves in cold weather.

A brush with the law

While in Southern England, some of the men had a special adventure with law enforcement that almost kept them in England.

"We were on our way to Cardiff to get some vehicles," said Almond. "A fellow from Scotland Yard showed up at our camp about midnight that night and made us take off our clothes."

Almond said they didn't have any idea what was going on, but, used to taking orders, they dropped their trousers.

It turned out that a local girl in the village had been raped that night, and the investigators suspected the men from the 101st. It caused a few tense moments, as the men stood there in their underwear, waiting for a decision from Scotland Yard. They were finally cleared and able to go on their way.

FRANCE

On January 29, the group departed Camp C and marched to Southampton in the middle of a snowstorm, which later turned to rain. After waiting for hours in the miserable downpour, a party of 553 officers and enlisted men embarked on a troop transport, and the rest of the Group left on four LSTs and two Liberty ships.

An overcast sky and a moderate sea made for an uneventful crossing of the English Channel, but when the LSTs and troop transports arrived in LeHavre on January 31, they found the city was a sprawling heap of rubble, and the people of Le-Havre greeted them with angry glances.

"It was our first real look at the war damage," wrote John Allen in a letter to his family at the end of the war. "The town had been a target on D-Day, and it was blasted to rubble. No buildings were standing, and the harbor was filled with sunken ships; only their masts stuck out above water."

"I just couldn't believe the destruction," said Bennie Hawkins, who was single, 20 years old, and working in a shoe factory in Lynchburg, Va., when he was drafted. "A lot of towns were just shot to pieces."

From LeHavre, the units from the LSTs marched 44 miles to Camp Twenty Grand near Duclair, France. Cavalrymen who had been on the Liberty Ships were routed up the Seine River to Rouen, where they disembarked February 1, 1945.

David Gay remembers that when the sun came up that first morning in France, they could see both sides of the river as they sailed in from the channel. "We had vehicles on the small ship," he said, "and when we landed, we unloaded them, got right in, and drove off."

The Group remained at Camp Twenty Grand, mired in mud, from February 1 through 4, waiting for their assignment. Finally the word came that they were to report to the Sixth Army Group's Seventh Army and the XV Corps, under the command of General Jacob Devers.

> February 2, 1945
> My Dear Mary,
> This is our third day in camp. We have some of the comforts and few conveniences as it is a tent camp. No electricity, but plenty of candles and each tent has a stove. All in all it is not too bad, generally it reminds one of Pine Camp, but instead of sand we have mud, as long as we have mud it is not cold. The weather is still with us and we see the sun every once in a while. Everyone feels fine and a'rarin' to go. When and where we do not know.
> Sightseeing and the receipt of mail will be postponed for a few more days, but we can take it. We have many odds and ends to clean up before we can be on our way.
> Hubert

The Group left Camp Twenty Grand at 9:30 a.m., February 5, headed toward Soissons, France. They arrived, 120 miles later, at 6 p.m. and prepared for overnight bivouac. It was a short stay, as they left Soissons at precisely 7:10 a.m. the next morning, and arrived in Verdun at 5 p.m. While there, the Group learned that their destination would be Faulquemont, behind the battle line south of the Saar River in the 7th Army sector. The front was now just one day away.

The 101st departed Verdun early on the morning of February 8, with squadron and unit commanders going on ahead to see what points were held by the 106th Cavalry Reconnaissance Squadron. Over the next few days, the 101st would be taking their place on the front. As they departed Verdun, they reflected on the WWI battles fought there, and they began to think about how they would react in battle for the first time.

"I remember passing by the cemetery at Verdun," said Lou Gergley. "No one said a word as we passed. We were all wondering if we were going to be one of those. It was very disheartening, wondering if we would end up there."

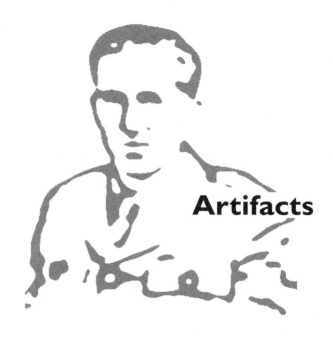

Artifacts

My father had grown up as Theo in Texas, but the people in Oregon called him Ted, and Mother sometimes called him Teddy. He was a collector of things, a man who could take a load of trash to the dump and come home with more than he had when he left. Every bit of available space he could find was filled with mysterious antique tools, battered and rusty license plates, Japanese fishing floats, and cooking utensils. For his outdoor cooking, which was often done for hundreds of people, he had giant cast iron pots, Dutch ovens, frying pans, and pie tins. He had a covered wagon and a surrey he had picked up from an old homestead somewhere in Eastern Oregon. He hoarded his treasure in the barn, the garage, the house, the chicken house, and a stone lean-to.

When he died, my mother held a garage sale and sold everything she could. She didn't sell a Nazi bayonet, dagger, and knife that my father brought back from the war. These were meant to go to my three sons.

The few items I salvaged from my father's stash include an antique hand iron; a silk map of France and Germany, the one he carried tucked under his collar during the war; a gray, tattered plaid dress that he wore as a baby; the book *Wingfoot*; three letters he wrote home from the service; and his separation papers. Enough to bring rough outlines to my father's shadowy portrait, but not enough for any detail.

The pots and pans used by the author's father in his outdoor cooking.

Most of what I knew about my father came from the artifacts he left. I knew that he once wore a baby dress of gray; I knew he loved to collect antiques; and I knew that somewhere in Germany he had acquired a dagger, a bayonet and a knife.

As a child, I loved looking at those weapons, and would often take them from their place on a shelf inside an oak cupboard, unsheathe them, and run my fingers along the blade. The hilt of the dagger was ivory, carved and polished into gentle coils bound with braided brass wire and decorated with a swastika and an eagle. The bayonet, too, was adorned with the swastika. I liked them for their ornate beauty. I never imagined – or even tried to – how he might have acquired them. In fact, I didn't associate them with the idea of war at all. They were art.

I learned later that a lot of men brought back weapons and other souvenirs of war. Some took special pride in the rifles and pistols they took from German soldiers, although they often hesitated to share how they had acquired their loot. Others told how they sometimes risked their lives to hold on to their treasure.

"We had been told that we would be killed if we were captured by the Germans and had those weapons on us," said William Pierce. "One day I was in a tough spot, so I threw the German pistol and rifle I was carrying into the woods. We all did. I didn't know if that story was true – that they would kill us – but I didn't want to take any chances. Once we knew we were safe, we ran into the woods to retrieve our weapons."

Lt. Borkowski came home with a rifle he took from a boy near the end of the war.

"This boy came up out of a foxhole with his rifle," said Borkowski, "and I yelled at him in German, 'Don't shoot.' That confused him. The boy looked about 14 years old, and he dropped his weapon and began to cry. I took his rifle and the guys gave him candy and gum. He ran off and I told my men to hold fire and let the youth go. Maybe we shouldn't have, but we're the ones that would have to live with it after the war if we shot him. To this day, my conscience is clear. I'd sure like to know what happened to that boy."

Altizer told of running into a bunch of Hitler youth, 14-, 15-, 16-year-old kids, who were enthusiastically shooting at them.

"What to do about them was a problem," he said. "Nobody wanted to shoot kids, but their rifles could kill us just as dead as those manned by a 30-year old man. The kids refused to surrender. That wasn't a good day."

My father's small knife was exactly like those carried by Hitler Youth, and my father once told my cousin that having to fight children was one of the things he hated the most about the war. So where, I wonder, did he get his knife?

Orders to Move Out

Saarbrucken

Oン March 9, the 116th Squadron was defending its positions around Hill 283 and Wadgassen and conducting raids to gather information and take prisoners. Along the Group's right flank, the 70th Infantry Division was embroiled in battle, and until it was over the cavalry couldn't advance. They had been in position for a month, and the men had been fairly patient. They had plenty to do besides watch the infantry's displays of mortar fire. They made about one raid per week, mopping up scattered bands of German soldiers trying to escape over the mountain trails in the daytime. And at night, they slipped through woods littered with schu mines and booby traps, trying to learn all they could about German strength.

Bennie Hawkins was on night patrol with a platoon that had orders to capture one of the small towns in the area.

"They got us up at 3 a.m.," he said. "There was a mine field going in, and I was scared. Six of us were bringing up the tale end, and when the engineers who had marked off the mine field said they needed someone to guide the others through, I volunteered. I got down on my knees and told each man going through where to step to avoid the mines."

In woods filled with mines, booby traps, and hostile German soldiers, some days the men needed all the help they could get. Even a little spring of water played a role in helping them capture a few prisoners.

"We found this spring," said Clair Becker, "and we used it to fill our canteens. The next day we returned, thinking the Germans would probably appreciate some fresh spring water, too. Soon several German soldiers did come to fill their canteens. We captured them, and we all had a little joke about the good spring water."

On March 12 the 116th Squadron finally got the chance to live their motto: "Advance without Delay." On the day that Lt. Col. Leonard returned from the hospital, the order came to cross the Saar. Troopers on foot were to lead the attack the next morning, supported by close air support and artillery. Training had ended.

"I knowed it was coming," said Carmickle. "I was glad when it did. I didn't like the waiting. I enjoyed being on the move. It's harder to hit a moving target."

Sixty years after the war, William Pierce remembers feeling differently. "When you are in a safe place," he said, "you aren't in a hurry to leave." Then he laughs.

By March 13, the 101st and elements of the XXI Corps were moving away from their long-held positions south and southwest of the Saar River as the 63rd and 70th Infantry Divisions began their attack. The 70th, on the Group's right flank, had cleared the town of Forbach and was entering the towns of Stiring, Wendel, and Petite Rosselle.

My dad's squadron, the 116th, was to take Schaffhausen and Hostenbach. Hostenbach was dominated by elaborate defensive works on the high ground north of the Saar River, and, on the southeast, Hill 283 remained in German hands. To get into Hostenbach and Schaffhausen, the men had to get past entrenchments, foxholes, strong points located in houses on the southern fringe of the town, and several broad belts of anti-tank and anti-personnel mines.

To get close enough to take out these defenses, the Cavalry had two options: walking single file down a narrow road or spreading out to cross a gently sloping terrain. Either way, they would be without cover or concealment for more than 1,000 yards, in clear view of any German soldiers who might be watching.

The taking of Hill 283 and the towns of Geislautern and Wehrden was assigned to the 101st Squadron, with Lt. Col. Milton Kendall in command. It turned out to be one of the most difficult objectives faced by the Group. Hill 283 was the tallest hill in the area, and because of its clear view of the entire valley, it was surrounded by mine fields and fiercely defended by German soldiers. Taking possession of Wehrden would be nearly impossible while Hill 283 remained in enemy hands.

Germans guarding the high ground above a city.

Photo taken from a prisoner by Lt. Joseph Borkowski.

Approaches to Geislautern could be easily defended by the Germans from inside the houses that lined both sides of the single street leading into town. Ted and I saw those houses, or ones like them, when we walked along the curving street that led downhill into Geislautern. Delicate lace curtains covered the windows of tidy homes, and gardens of evergreens and flowers lined the sidewalks. When the 101st was asked to take the town in March of 1945, German soldiers had been stationed behind the lace curtains of those houses, and mines were buried along the street.

When I was there, only an old American Army jeep parked in the driveway of a white house with green trim reminded me of that other March.

Reliable sources had told the cavalry that Geislautern and Wehrden were garrisoned by the 2nd Battalion, 861 Volksgrenadier Regiment, which also occupied the towns of Schaffhausen and Hostenbach. Prisoners of war confirmed this information, adding that the total number of German soldiers in the zone was estimated at 800 men, supported by the defensive works on the north bank of the river. Not an insignificant obstacle to overcome.

At 6 p.m. on March 13, Lt. Col. Leonard ordered Capt. "Gus" Littleton, commanding officer of the 116th's Troop B, to form a combat patrol and reconnoiter the approaches to Schaffhausen by way of the Werbeln-Schaffhausen road. They were to determine whether or not the road was strong enough to withstand the Cavalry's vehicles and see if they could discover where the Germans were located and what their strength was in Schaffhausen. This patrol was placed under the command of 1st Lt. Joseph Borkowski.

Charlie Kashuba

Lt. Borkowski said he often chose my dad and Charlie Kashuba to go with him on such patrols, and they were most likely with him on this patrol to Schaffhausen. "They made quite a team," he said.

Altizer wrote a story about the time Charlie Kashuba saved his life. He called it "Charlie and the Panzerfaust":

One afternoon we had fought our way into a small town (can't remember which one), where the Germans had put up some stiff resistance. When we established a foothold in the edge of town, Charlie Kashuba and I had dismounted from our jeeps and were scouting carefully and quietly along the main thoroughfare of the town. We returned to the jeep, parked at a corner where several streets intersected, and were looking at a map on the hood of the jeep, talking in low voices, trying to decide what to do next.

Suddenly, Charlie swore and spun around toward one of the side streets, firing his rifle. Startled, I turned, crouched and began to fire my weapon, too. About half a block away was a German soldier squatting in wood-covered dugout with a panzerfaust pointed directly at us. Whatever his intent, we startled him. It seems he was waiting for a vehicle to pass by so he could destroy not only a vehicle, but block the streets, too. He hesitated a fraction of a second too long, and I am here to tell this story and he's 60 years dead. That day Charlie Kashuba saved us both by his quick thinking. Later, for an entirely different action, Charlie received a Silver Star for bravery. He was a fine soldier and a good friend.

Charlie Kashuba was one man I really wanted to meet. I knew he would remember my father. But he had died quietly at his home in Knoxville, Tenn., not long before I called. It was the first time I got this message, but it wasn't going to be the last. It became a litany, heard over and over again: "I'm sorry, my father or my husband or my brother passed away a year ago, a month ago, a few weeks ago."

Bill Hart

At 7:30 a.m. on March 13, the 101st Recon Squadron had begun its attack against Hill 283 and along the Ludweiler-Geislautern road. Troops A and F were commanded by Capt. Ralph Ritchie.

One man wounded during that first advance was Bill Hart, who always wondered how he ended up in the cavalry.

"Can you believe it, I'm an aircraft mechanic," he said, "and I end up in the damn cavalry. They gave me a horse-riding outfit: boots and spurs. How the hell do you dig a fox hole for a horse? Then they gave me a Harley motorcycle."

Hart remembers the day he was wounded in great detail.

> I was one of the lucky ones. I was hit on the first push going into Wehrden. Frank [Smith] and I stopped the SS in no-man's land near Wehrden at 1:30 a.m. The moon was out bright. The street was sandbagged, and I think about three dozen of them with submachine guns were shooting at us. I had a crank telephone, so I called and yelled into the phone, "They have us surrounded. The sons a'bitches are everywhere."
>
> Our side started firing – you could have walked across the street on the .50-caliber shells.
>
> I was laying down on top of the tank when I was hit. That's how I got my arm blowed off. Smitty was squatting down by the side of the tank and he was hit too. Dale [Weirick] and Glenn [Eanes] were on the tank with me when I got hit. Eanes helped lift me off the tank.

"There was Captain Ralph Ritchie, myself, and one other trooper," remembers Eanes. "A sniper hit Hart. Glen Blackwell was there, too. Blackwell and I had to hold Hart on the side of the tank. The captain jumped up on top of the tank with a machine gun when he saw where the bullet came from. I never heard such a sound as when he started firing that machine gun."

As he was being evacuated, Hart's arm, which was hanging by a radial nerve, was dragging in the tank tracks. He still remembers Blackwell and Eanes — or someone — there beside him. "A buddy held my arm up out of the mud. I guess it was a buddy. Everyone looks alike with dirt all over their face."

Hart remembers a curve in the road as it climbed a hill. "I was losing blood like crazy. I was about to run out of gas."

It took Hart nine months to recover, first in France, then England, South Carolina, and, finally, Georgia. For four days in the French hospital, he walked around with a bullet in him.

"I picked up a chart and said, 'Some bastard has a bullet in him.' Found out it was me," he said. "I was soaking my hand in hot water when a doctor came in. He asked me if I had a knife."

Hart said he must have reacted strangely to the request, because the doctor then said, "Hell, I'm not going to cut your arm off, I'm want to cut off that shirt."

"I was wearing an SS blouse," said Hart. "We had come across a basket of freshly laundered clothing in a building, and it was jersey wool and warm, so I took it."

"You know you have a bullet in your chest?" the doctor asked. "We'll have to get that cast off."

"It took two doctors to cut off that cast," said Hart.

He went back to the U.S. on the British ship Atlantis. "I was in a body cast that would float like a damn anvil," he said. "That worried the heck out of me."

Eanes, who had helped hold Hart's dangling arm out of the mud, was wounded soon after.

"It was one evening just as it was getting dark," he said. "We were in a building setting up booby traps. We noticed five or six German soldiers coming across the street. We noticed them because the steel heels on their boots made sparks on the street where they were walking. We had a radio, so I called some of our other guys to drop a couple of flares. That would help us see the Germans well enough to get a shot at them with our machine gun. The other guys set off the flare, but the Germans had a bazooka. Luckily we were behind a brick wall, but still, I got hit in the head with shrapnel."

Eanes was sent to a hospital in England to recover. "It was horrible," he said. "The hospital beds were everywhere, even in the middle of the floor, wounded were everywhere. I was there about 30 days."

Taking Hill 283

By 8:45 p.m. on March 13, first platoon, Troop A, and one squad from Company C of the 290th Engineer Battalion, with 1st Lt. Robert Ulmschneider in command, had gotten through the enemy minefields and booby traps and reached Hill 283. The Germans did not allow the balance of the troop to pass so easily. Most of the leadership of first platoon was part of the mission and at risk of being wiped out. In the ensuing battle, Captain Ritchie was wounded, but he refused evacuation.

Richard Bischoff took this photo of a pillbox on the Saar River.
Photo courtesy Frances Lerner.

During that long night, Lt. Robert Ulmschneider ordered artillery fire on the Germans, and Capt. Ritchie was wounded a second time. Again he refused to be evacuated.

"We were doing night patrol in a heavily forested area," said Sgt. Robert Klein. "It was dark, dark, dark. We took a small spool of telephone wire and a telephone, since we couldn't use radios in the woods."

As they patrolled B Troop's lines, the telephone wire ran out. Klein telephoned back to headquarters to tell them that he was coming back for more wire.

"The guy answering the phone asked me for the password, and I couldn't remember what it was," said Klein. "Fortunately, I recognized his voice. I just called him by name and he let me through."

Klein headed back through the woods alone, with flares going up all around him.

"Heavy fire was coming in," he said, "and in the light of the flares I saw our fellows rushing by me carrying Capt. Ritchie. It was the third time he had been wounded, and this time he was shot in the head. I never saw him again, but he did survive the war."

Ulmschneider then assumed command of the unit, and the 101st Squadron's Troop B and Troop E's first platoon began attacking early that morning toward the northeast along the heavily wooded south and southeasterly slopes of Hill 283. With Capt. Abraham Friedman in command, they were moving through the woods when they found themselves in the middle of a well concealed and closely sown *schu* minefield. Within just a few minutes, they suffered seven serious injuries and were forced to withdraw and change the direction of their attack. In spite of the density of the mine field, all the wounded were successfully evacuated under the personal direction of 1st Lt. John M. Sullivan.

The *schu* mines that were causing so much damage to the men were made of wood and undetectable by normal mine

A platoon from B Troop, under the command of Lt. Joseph Borkowski, was given the mission of taking an oil refinery near Schaffhausen.

Photo couresty of Joseph Borkowski.

sweeping. They took a terrible toll on the American troops, and the injuries were nearly always the same: a man's foot would be blown off and the remainder of the bone split upwards like a stick of rhubarb.

"I remember that several of our men stepped on mines that day," said David Gay. "It usually tore up their legs, and one boy had his hip broken."

With Capt. August Bielss in command, Troop C; first platoon, Company F; and first platoon, Troop E, all of the 101st Squadron, staged an attack along the Ludweiler-Geislautern Road. The nature of the terrain forced them to move through the area in narrow columns, and a determined rear-guard action by the Germans slowed their advance even more.

Lt. Harold Meyer was in command of first platoon, Troop C, 101st Squadron as they advanced down the road between Ludweiler and Geislautern. Road craters made travel difficult, as did anti-tank and anti-personnel mines all along the way. The men moved forward, successfully navigating the obstacles

in their path, only to be stopped later by strong enemy machine gun and mortar fire at the southern edge of Geislautern,
forcing them to withdraw to Ludweiler, where they had to wait
for reinforcements before continuing.

Troop A of the 116th Squadron was north of Werbeln at the
junction of the roads to Schaffhausen and Wadgassen. Captain
Bages had the job of controlling and coordinating this patrol.
A roadblock of timber and sandbags, which had been constructed by the 106th Cavalry, was approximately 300 yards
north of this outpost, on the Werbeln-Schaffhausen Road. The
roadblock was heavily mined and filled with unmapped booby
traps. Knowing these had to be removed before the patrol
could proceed over the road, 1st Lt. Harvey Wood of Troop
A crept in under blackout conditions and removed the booby
traps from the roadblock.

At 9:00 o'clock that same night, Lt. Borkowski's patrol,
which included Troop B and the engineers, was moving slowly
down the heavily mined Werbeln-Schaffhausen road with
orders to take Schaffhausen. At 10:15 p.m., they received word
that a prisoner of war was giving Headquarters important
information about their mission, so Captain Bages ordered
Borkowski's patrol to stay put until this new information could
be analyzed and evaluated.

The prisoner told them that the German Army in Schaffhausen had received orders to withdraw and then assemble
north and east across the Saar River at 10:30 p.m. The prisoner
also pointed out on maps the mine fields in the town of Schaffhausen. Split-second timing and strange plays of coincidence
and luck, as much as anything else, often saved men's lives
and, just as often, got men killed. How many men's lives were
spared because of the information given at the last minute by
this prisoner of war?

Armed with this new information, the patrol moved out
accompanied by ten engineers. Progress was still slow because

of the mine fields and other obstacles, and the work of clearing the road had to be done in the dark. Additional engineers were rushed to the patrol's assistance to move it forward more quickly and to deal with the mine fields in Schaffhausen.

As the patrol reached the southwestern edge of town, heavy enemy artillery and mortar fire interrupted their progress. Their advance was slowed again when they found 41 Germans partially buried in foxholes along the road. They dug them out and took the entire group as prisoners.

March 14, 1945

On March 14, the 116th attacked on foot against the towns of Schaffhausen and Hostenbach. Troop A, with Capt. Alfred Burgess, commanding, and Troop B, with Capt. Littleton in command, were the primary units staging the attack.

A dense fog settled over the 101st Cavalry Group and didn't lift until almost noon. It covered the initial stages of their attack, hiding much of their movement from the Germans. Even with this protective curtain, sniper fire from church steeples and houses along the road accounted for more than fifty percent of all casualties that day and made it necessary to clear each and every house.

Attacking on foot was necessary because a carpet of anti-personnel and anti-tank minefields protected all approaches to the town, making the use of vehicles impossible. At around 12:15 a.m., Lt. Borkowski and his platoon, which included my father, began creeping through the fog into Schaffhausen on hands and knees, feeling their way in the darkness, hoping to avoid the mines and booby traps.

The rest of the 116th Squadron quickly exploited the success of Lt. Borkowski's patrol. A second combat patrol from Troop B, led by 1st Lt. Ezra Mann, left its command post a little later and followed Borkowski's route. A third patrol, led by 1st Lt. George Harden, moved out at 1:50 a.m. At 4:30 a.m., the mission was extended to include Hostenbach, and by 1:00 o'clock the next afternoon, that town was occupied and mop-up had been completed.

Altizer describes that early morning patrol in his written account of the war:

> It was cold and foggy; you could barely see 15 to 20 feet ahead. About a dozen of us had spread out over a city block, walking quietly along a narrow cobblestone street. Four of us were up front: two combat engineers; Lt. Borkowski, who was the officer in charge, and me. After several minutes, the lieutenant stopped and told me to go back down the line and tell the men to close up a little. Visibility was so limited that he was afraid some of us would get lost. I had just turned and started down the line, when, from somewhere behind me, a voice with a German accent yelled, "Halt! Hands up!"
>
> Everybody, including me, hit the street face down. Somebody — we assumed it was the man who had yelled — began to fire a machine gun down the middle of the street, spraying lead from side to side, just where we had all been walking until he had called out his command for us to halt.
>
> The German kept firing, and I began to crawl over to the edge of the street, hoping I could find a wall to get behind, or a doorway to get in, but the street, typically European, with houses crowded very close together and with narrow sidewalks, left me no place to go. My first thought was to throw a hand grenade at the gunner, but when I reached to pull one off my harness, they were gone. Apparently, when I fell flat on my face, I had lost all my grenades, and in my present position, didn't feel like it was too wise to

go hunting for them. I was turned wrong way around anyway, since I had been heading down the street with my back to the gunner when he opened up on us.

The lieutenant and engineers were closest to the enemy, and we figured they were either dead or wounded. The rest of us lay pretty still, or took off for cover if there was any, except for 'Pop' Bretz (called Pop because, at 40, he was older than most of the other soldiers). He began firing his 'grease gun,' an automatic that fired .45 clips, in the direction of the gunfire. This naturally attracted the attention of the German gunner, so he turned his gun and began to fire directly at us. I could see the red tracers through the fog over my head. Pop called out and asked why we hadn't all fired our rifles at the same time he did. Considering the amount of attention it called to our position, most of us didn't think too much of that idea.

We were lucky. Nobody got hit. Meanwhile, Borkowski and the combat engineers began

Members of the 101st Cavalry milk a cow in Geislautern. This photo was reprinted in the National Geographic *in 1945.*

Photo taken by Lt. John Moors, U.S. Army Signal Corps. Courtesy National Archives.

firing at the Germans. Suddenly, the shooting stopped. We got ourselves together, reorganized the patrol, and started, very cautiously, back up the street. The lieutenant and engineers were coming back toward us. Borkowski said they had wounded one of the two machine gunners, who had been dug in at the corner of a building, and they had seen one of the soldiers carrying his wounded comrade into the basement of a nearby building. We tossed a grenade into the basement, and one German came out with his hands up. We found the other soldier, badly wounded, but could not stay to see what happened to him. We turned our prisoner over to somebody else, and proceeded to the house that had been our original destination with no further trouble.

We set up an outpost overlooking the Saar and stayed there for the rest of the day and that night. Having no food or sleep for about 24 hours, we were very glad to see the Infantry when they relieved us next morning.

By nightfall on March 14, Troops A and B, 101st Squadron, held all of Hill 283, and Troop C, 101st Squadron, had completed mopping up Geislautern. The cavalry had advanced about 2,700 yards during that operation and captured the towns of Geislautern, Wehrden, Schaffhausen and Hostenbach. Fifty-four prisoners of war were taken, and two men from the 101st Cavalry Group were killed and 31 were wounded.

"I don't remember seeing many civilians," said Almond of their entry into Schaffhausen. "We were the second platoon into town. Troop B was first. I remember seeing one German rolled out of a house in a wheelbarrow."

In the Signal Corps film of the 101st, which is dated March 13, a man is seen in a wheelbarrow in a sequence shot in Schaffhausen. I've watched the short, silent film over and over again, trying to see a face that I recognize from the nearly 100 photos that I have received from veterans, but I don't. And none of the veterans who have seen the film recognize the events pictured there. Filmed in Werbeln, Ludweiler, and Schaffhausen, the film shows the 101st Cavalry loading wounded soldiers into a jeep-turned-ambulance, called an ambo-jeep in the archive's description of the film. It also shows troopers interrogating German soldiers and the Americans helping evacuate the few civilians left in one of the towns. Women and children and a few old men struggle with hand-carts and wagons down the rubble-filled street and load their possessions into Army trucks. I don't know which troop of the 101st is helping them, nor do I know where these people are going, but the film shows one day in the life of my father. Even though he's not in the film, it casts a spell over me, and I watch it again and again.

The film captures only a few moments in each of three separate locations, and the chance is small that out of the 1,200 men or more who were in the 101st Cavalry Group, one of the few I know might be there, but I keep hoping. More than once, when I asked a man what he remembered from the war, he told me that a soldier only sees what is directly in front of him and maybe a foot or two to either side. The same can be said of a camera's eye.

Their victory in those first few days was more than combat success for the 101st. The men knew the Germans were willing to fight, but now they also knew they could fight back – and they could win. It was an emotional victory as well.

March 15, 1945

Units of the 101st were tested one more time in battle before reaching the Siegfried Line. In *Wingfoot*, Major Sweeney writes, "Some of the Group's best young leaders and troopers paid for the ground gained at this point. The dueling of artillery was awful and awesome, but ultimately the troopers had the upper hand."

One of those wounded on March 15 was Tec 5 Andrew Matanin, Troop A, 101st Squadron. Matanin had been working in a Pennsylvania coal mine when he was ordered to report for induction at Fireman's Hall, New Salem, Penn. His order to report is not only dated, but time-stamped at 6 a.m., December 16, 1942.

Matanin responded to my first letter with a short note and a newspaper clipping that ran in his local newspaper right after he was wounded. Later he sent me a file that included his order to report for induction, photos from a Motor Course he took, and certificates from the Cavalry School at Ft. Riley, Kansas.

Matanin, like Hart, received his injuries outside of Werden and ended up in a hospital in France. Eight days later, on March 23, his parents received a Western Union Telegram: "The secretary of war desires me to express his deep regret that your son, Matanin, Andrew, was slightly wounded in Germany on March 15, 1945. Continue to address mail to him as formerly or until new address is received from him. Signed, Dunlop acting the adjutant general."

They heard no more until March 31, when they learned of his continued improvement. This letter also referred to a shell fragment in his right thigh. Like Hart, Matanin never received a Purple Heart for his injuries, although he tried for years after the war to get his.

The same day Hart and Matanin were wounded, Tec 5 Alvin J. Romero, Troop A, ended up under heavy small arms and machine gun fire. Five of his comrades lay wounded around him, and safety was more than 500 yards away, across an open field and in view of the Germans.

Romero was a man who some remembered as a big guy and described as "primitive," the kind of guy who "didn't have shoes until he went in the Army."

Romero's father had died in 1928, when he was eight years old, and his mother died a few months later. An aunt took his baby sister, and an older brother had already left home. Romero stayed in the house alone, feeding himself by hunting and raising vegetables.

That day during the war, when he rushed to the aid of his comrades, he may have thought about the families they had at home and the fact that he didn't have one, or maybe he wasn't thinking at all, but relying on instinct. Whatever his reason, Romero crept through heavy fire for three hours, killing enemy snipers along the way and getting the wounded troopers into the woods. From there, they were successfully evacuated. Romero, who was from Elton, Louisiana, received the Silver Star for his actions that day.

When I called to talk to Romero, it was too late. His wife, Mary, said he had died just months earlier. She told me what she could about his life, adding that he always wondered why the five guys he brought back, whose lives he had saved, never tried to contact him after the war.

"He talked about that a lot, but never had too much else to say," she said.

Photos on facing page

Top: 7th Army Engineers cleaning debris and sweeping for mines in Geislautern after the town was taken by 101st Cavalry on March 16, 1945.

Bottom: German civilians of Schaffhausen prepare for evacuation to a safe area behind the lines.

Photos taken by John Moors, US Army Signal Corps, Photos courtesy of the National Archives.

Map 2
March 16-20, 1945

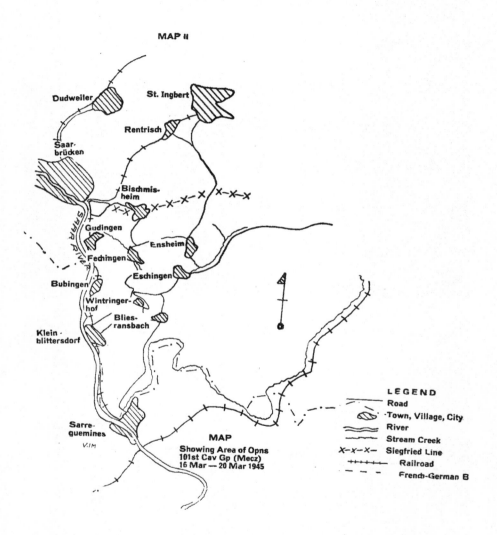

MAP ii

Dudweiler   St. Ingbert

Rentrisch

Saar-
brücken

Bischmis-
heim

Gudingen

Ensheim

Fechingen

Eschingen

Bubingen

Wintringer-
hof

Blies-
ransbach

Klein-
blittersdorf

Sarre-
guemines

V.IM

MAP
Showing Area of Opns
101st Cav Gp (Mecz)
16 Mar — 20 Mar 1945

LEGEND
———— Road
〜〜 Town, Village, City
———— River
———— Stream Creek
x–x–x– Siegfried Line
+++++ Railroad
– – – French-German B

SAAR RIVER

Reunions

McCall's Bar-B-Que and Seafood Restaurant is a solid, country-style restaurant on Millers Chapel Road just off of Highway 70 East in Goldsboro, N.C. Its all-you-can-eat buffet holds the barbecued chicken, shrimp, fried chicken, pork, deviled crab, string beans, slaw, potato salad, butterbeans, corn, cornbread, field peas, baked beans, sweet tea, peach cobbler, and banana pudding with vanilla wafers – the food my southern-raised parents always cooked, the food I grew up eating. In addition to all of that, McCall's waitresses kept our table supplied with red plastic baskets filled to overflowing with hush puppies.

It was 2006 and my second time at a reunion of the 101st Cavalry. About six veterans, their wives and children, and I ate dinner at McCall's on Friday night. I felt a lot more at home now, chatting with the men and their wives, not nearly as uncomfortable as I had felt at the first reunion I had attended two years earlier.

In October 2004, just weeks after reading about the reunion on John Altizer's website, I was on an airplane, flying across the country to meet some of the 101st Cavalry's World War II veterans. I hoped I would find someone who knew my father.

I didn't know any of these men, and they had never even heard of me, so it was with a great deal of trepidation that I walked out of my motel room in Goldsboro, N.C., and approached the group of men and women seated on folding chairs in front of the motel.

I didn't need to worry; I was welcomed with a warmth and an intensity that I hadn't expected. Jane Fields, widow of Ivy Fields, was my contact, and she had paved the way.

"What was your father's name, sweetheart," one woman asked. "Which troop was he in?"

Then the women divided my photos and carried them from one man to the next. "Welch," they would shout in ears that had trouble hearing. "His name was Welch. Troop B, Squadron 116." And I watched as the men's head shook. No, they didn't recognize the face or the name.

Around 1,200 men served in the 101st Cavalry, split between two

William Pierce, Troop C, 116th Squadron
Photo taken by the author at the 2006 reunion.

squadrons. There were close to 100 men in my dad's troop, and men rarely knew anyone other than those in their own platoon. With odds like that, only a few men might have been in a position to know my dad. At that reunion, I met only two men who had been in my dad's troop. They didn't remember him.

Seeing that I was discouraged, Jane Fields offered an explanation. "I've heard," she told me, "that a soldier only knows what he sees here." She brought her hands in close to her face. "They only see what's right in front of them and a little to the right or left." This idea would be repeated to me over and over again, as men told me it's unlikely they would remember my father, since they only knew the men on either side of them, the men they were defending and in whose hands they had placed their own lives, the men in their own jeep, tank, or armored car.

Frederick Altizer, one of the men at the reunion who had been in my father's troop, said he didn't remember my father, but the name was familiar. He went into his motel room and called Lou Gergley, who had also served in B Troop. He thought Gergley might have known my father.

"Gergley remembers your dad," said Altizer, returning from his phone call. "He said he was a real Texas hick."

"Yes," I said, "that would be my dad."

When I got home, I called Gergley.

"I remember Welch," he said, dropping the "hick" reference. "He was a real Texas cowboy. "Welch, Vandenburg, and Shaker were in a jeep together. I was in the armored car behind them. Welch was friends with Shaker, but he hated Vandenberg, who was a Yankee from Massachusetts. One day he said if they were ever in combat, he was going to kill the son of a bitch, meaning Vandenberg. On the night of February 18 they were on patrol, when they came under fire and Vandenberg took some shrapnel in the back. Welch ran over to help him and said, 'Oh, God, I'll be court-martialed in the morning. Everyone knows I wanted the son-of-a-bitch dead. They'll blame me.' He was like that, a typical cowboy. He walked like one, talked like one."

I had another question for Gergley. One of my cousins had worked with my dad for awhile, and my dad had told him a few stories about the war. One had to do with teacups hanging outside a store. The soldiers with him made a bet that he couldn't draw his gun and hit a target – in this case the teacups – when one of them dropped a cigarette to the ground. When the cigarette hit the dirt, my dad drew and fired, breaking every one of the cups. Hearing the shots from inside the store, two Germans came out with their hands in the air.

Gergley said yes, he remembered that incident, but his story was a little different.

> We went into a small village, not a village really, just three tall buildings. Between two of the buildings, a wire was strung as an antenna with a tea cup used as an insulator. I fired at it eight times, but missed every time. I was just putting in another clip when a bunch of Germans came out waving a white flag. One of the Germans went back in for some reason and caught his coat in a wire with a potato masher (a stick grenade) hanging on it. He started jerking on his coat, trying to free himself, and that potato masher was flipping up and down, up and down. We hit the dirt, but it didn't go off.

There's no way to know which of these stories reflects the truth, or maybe there were two separate shoot-outs with china cups, and they are both true. I like to think of my father as the hero of the story, but Lou Gergley tells the story with conviction, and I've only heard my father's version second hand.

Gergley also told me that he remembered my dad wearing a big silver and green onyx ring, square-shaped. I had never seen my dad wear a ring, and so I was sure he must be mistaken. Still, I was checking every fact I could, so I went through all my pictures, studying his hands under a magnifying glass. Sure enough, in pictures with my dad when I was just a baby, a large ring was clearly visible on his hand. Between the war and 1955, he quit wearing it; maybe he lost it or gave it away, but it was gone. Gergley had been right.

I learned at these reunions that my dad hadn't been the only veteran who had kept his thoughts to himself. Most of the men told me that they came back home and just wanted to get on with the business of living. Many didn't talk about it at all until they began coming to these reunions in 1982.

"There were things we grew up knowing not to ask about," said Chris Singleton, whose father had been in the 101st, "things that maybe we didn't want to know about."

But, after the reunions began, the men started sharing their stories. Jane Fields told me, "There is a fellowship they still share today; these men have fought together and cared for each other in ways we can't imagine."

Bill Hart, Troop A, 101st Squadron.
Photo taken by the author at the 2006 reunion.

Edith Holloman loaned me two photos from her scrapbook. I took them home and scanned them into my computer, beginning a collection of photos that, through generosity like hers, continues to grow.

Within weeks of returning home from the 2004 reunion, I receive a large envelope filled with photos from Frederick Altizer. Not willing to wait until I got home, I sat in my car and opened it. One by one I went through those small black-and-white photos, looking at the faces of the young men.

One photo in particular caught my eye. It was a picture of four men in an armored car. One man peers out from inside the car, and another man sits with his back to the camera, looking over his right shoulder so his face is only partially visible. Two other men stand outside the armored car, leaning into it, resting their elbows on the top. One of those men stands slightly in front of the other, his face in the shadow of his helmet. It is my father.

Sitting there in the parking lot of the post office, I stared at that photo for a long time, wondering what my dad was thinking as the shutter clicked. He looked a little cocky, with his hand on his hip, one knee bent, gazing unsmiling at the camera. Then, just as I had done almost 30 years earlier, on the day

Members of B Troop, 116th Squadron. Standing to the right of the tank and wearing a helmet is Ted Welch, the author's father. Next to him is a man identified only as Cline.

Photo courtesy Frederick Altizer.

my father died, I pressed my head against the steering wheel of my car, and I cried.

❧❧

On that Friday night in 2006 at McCall's Bar-B-Que and Seafood Restaurant, only a handful of men showed up. On Saturday a few more trickled in; there were more children and wives than veterans. On Saturday night, I presented a slide show that combined photos from my trip to Germany with dozens of photos they had sent me, photos taken in German in 1945 with quotes from *Wingfoot* as captions. I had done the presentation before, but it felt strange to present it to the men who had lived it. Here I was, this whippersnapper, telling them, "And here is the Tauber River, where you crossed in April 1945."

They often asked me questions about particular battles or events, as if I had been there and and they hadn't. It reminded me again that each man was fighting his own war, often unaware of what happening two miles away.

2004 reunion of the 101st Cavalry in Goldsboro, N.C.

2006 reunion of the 101st Cavalry in Goldsboro, N.C.

Beyond the Siegfried Line

Gudingen

On March 16, the 101st was assigned to XXI Corps and attached to the 63rd Infantry Division, which would make the main thrust of the 7th Army through the Siegfried Line. Made up of two wide barriers about a mile apart, the Siegfried Line's defenses included "dragon's teeth," concrete pyramids a few feet high; anti-tank ditches, each about eight feet deep and 12 feet wide; pill boxes staggered all through the woods; and mine fields.

Just east of the Saar and south of Saarbrucken, the 63rd was preparing a final assault, and the 101st Group was put into the front facing the line between Gudingen and Ensheim. They were ordered to patrol aggressively, seeking weak spots in the German defenses.

A command post for the 101st Cavalry Group was established in Wintringhof, and the 101st Squadron was headquartered at Eschringen and the 116th in Bubingen.

Any daytime movement of the troops was immediately met with small arms, mortar, and artillery fire. The Germans were not going to give up this line easily.

Altizer remembers a time when this artillery fire was a little too close for comfort. "One day we were working with tanks," he wrote, "and an artillery shell landed within about 10 yards of where I was standing. Thank goodness it was an armor piercing type, so it penetrated deep into the ground before it exploded. It made a hole big enough to bury a cow, and my ears rang for days."

The noise of the battle did more than make Joseph Coccia's ears ring. "Howitzers were going off over our heads," he said. "My ear starting running so bad; the medic said there was nothing he could do. I was sent to the 63rd evacuation hospital." Sixty years later, Coccia still has trouble hearing.

On the night of March 16, the 253rd Infantry Regiment, to the immediate right of the 101st, began its initial assault on the Siegfried Line, methodically working its way through the German line section by section, blasting dragon's teeth, demolishing pill boxes, and filling anti-tank ditches.

The troopers watched in awe as the regiment's high explosive artillery shells raised a curtain of fire. The flames, sparks, and smoke danced between the night sky and the black outlines of engineers, tanks, and tank-dozers that inched along behind it toward the line.

"We were sent on reconnaissance through the line," Eanes said, "then we had to back off and let the infantry go through. They used tank-dozers to push dirt up to the line, and we were all behind that dirt."

Major Sweeney described this night in *Wingfoot*: "The relentless attack continued through the night, illuminated by eerie artificial moonlight created by bouncing searchlight beams off the low flying clouds. The cavalrymen thanked God that they had not been chosen for this task, and their admiration for the infantry and engineers increased one-hundred fold."

At 8:05 a.m. on March 17, the 116th Squadron relieved the 253rd Infantry Regiment, and by 2:30 p.m. the 101st Cavalry Group relieved the 63rd Infantry Division, still in the area around Ensheim and Gudingen.

"We spent several days in cold, wet, underground dugouts that had been constructed by the Infantry troops we relieved," wrote Altizer. "There were three men in our group, and we took turns standing guard duty at night, theoretically two hours on and four hours off. The only problem was that none of us had a watch and no way to tell how much time had really passed. Sometimes you got kicked out in what seemed like 30 minutes, instead of the four hours you were supposed to have for sleep. I remember that the nights were very dark, with no moon, and sometimes it looked like even the bushes crawled around out there. Spooky."

Three combat engineers stand on the dragon's teeth of the Siegfried Line,
U.S. Army Signal Corps photo. Courtesy of the National Archives.

Exploiting a narrow breech that had been made through the line, the 101st discovered that German troops were withdrawing on both sides of the break-through to avoid encirclement. Troop A, 116th Squadron, was selected to make the initial passage through the line and seize the town of St. Ingbert, about four miles away, and to block all roads into the area. The remainder of the Group had orders to protect the 63rd Division's flanks as it completed breaking through.

"We were held up briefly at the Siegfried Line," said Clinton Thompson from Oklahoma, "while they cleared things out ahead of us. We had the opportunity of seeing the Germans leave; they loaded up their vehicles and took off."

As the combat engineers cut and blew their way through barbed wire entanglements and rows of concrete dragon's teeth, the cavalry made its first deep run into enemy-held territory. Passing through the hole punched in the outer crust of the line, elements of the Group struck out through miles of narrow valley roads dominated by great frowning pillboxes, which were now unmanned. The Siegfried Line had been penetrated throughout its entire depth.

"You can't imagine the number of pill boxes and dragon's teeth tank traps," wrote Allen about his first impression of the Siegfried Line.

This initial penetration of the Siegfried Line on the Seventh Army front gave rise to an interesting anecdote. A Brooklyn war correspondent overdid the glorification of his home town unit by writing a press release for *Stars and Stripes* headed: "101st Cavalry First to Break Siegfried Line in 7th Army." Reading this, or so the story goes, the commanding general of the 63rd Infantry Division, who had been promised that his division could be the first, dashed off a letter to Col. McClelland, thinking the correspondent got his information from the 101st.

"It was understandable that the 63rd wanted credit for being first," writes Sweeney in *Wingfoot*, "since they had lost

Map 3
March 21-23, 1945

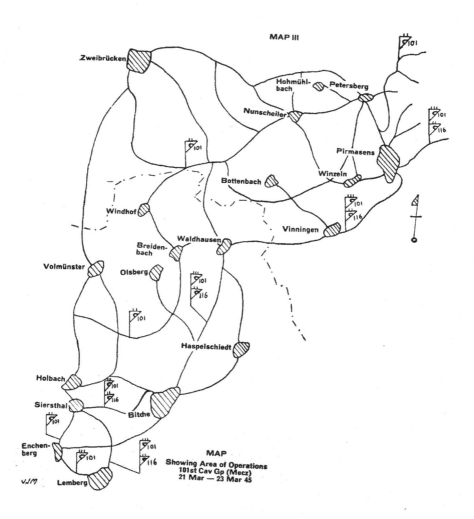

MAP III

Zweibrücken

Hohmühl-bach

Petersberg

Nunscheiler

Pirmasens

Bottenbach

Winzeln

Windhof

Vinningen

Breiden-bach

Waldhausen

Volmünster

Olsberg

Haspelschiedt

Holbach

Siersthal

Bitche

Enchen-berg

Lemberg

MAP
Showing Area of Operations
101st Cav Gp (Mecz)
21 Mar — 23 Mar 45

many good men fighting through the line, and the Cavalry had passed through after most of the heavy fighting was over."

In spite of the retraction, Lou Gergley and many others maintain that the cavalrymen were, in fact, the first to go through, at least unofficially.

> About 10 of us were out on patrol one night, and we were supposed to go only as far as the Saar River. At that spot, it was just about three feet wide, so we just walked in and waded across. We kept going, walking through abandoned pill boxes — all the Germans had pulled out of that section — and went into Saarbrucken. No one was in the town either. It felt deserted. We could see an infantry division back behind us, so we radioed our position, letting them

On March 20, 1945, U.S. cavalry troops penetrate several hundred yards through a wooded mountain area to survey terrain surrounding a village in the 7th Army Sector, 12 miles west of Kaiserlautern.
U.S. Army Signal Corps, *courtesy of the National Archives.*

know where we were. The next day, Lt. Borkowski had to write a letter of apology to the general
of the 63rd infantry, since they had been promised they could be the first through. But they
weren't. We were.

Lt. Borkowski doesn't remember any letter of apology he
had to write, although perhaps Gergley was thinking of Mc-
Clelland's letter. Borkowski does remember several patrols that
took his men across the Saar, including one where they went
straight through with no roadblocks as far as Volklingen. "We
were to take a steel mill on the north side of the Saar River," he
said. "And we did pass through the Siegfried Line."

Frederick Altizer, somewhere in Germany 1945.
Photo courtesy Frederick Altizer.

Most of the men I interviewed will state absolutely that the
101st went through ahead of any other unit.

"We were the first men in the 7th Army to break through
the line," wrote Allen. "After cleaning up a few pockets of resistance there in the woods, we left for the Rhine."

"I remember us being the first ones through the Siegfried Line," said Tharp. "Most of the bunkers were empty, but the Germans were still inside one. They wouldn't come out, so we poured gasoline in it. When they fired their big gun, it caught on fire. Then they came running out."

"We were the first," said Eanes. "Bill Evans and I were the first through the line."

March 20, 1945

On March 20, the commanding officer of the Group ordered the 116th to conduct reconnaissance to the north and to be prepared to move forward and "gain contact with the enemy." It's an interesting expression: to gain contact with the enemy. As the 116th was a reconnaissance group, it wasn't clear to me if they were being ordered into combat, or just to get close enough to snoop around. "Gaining contact" seemed to mean both.

"We weren't supposed to fight," said William Pierce. "Our armored cars were light and fast, meant to slip in and out; that was the point. Not combat. But we did what we had to do. Sometimes we got into situations we had to fight to get out of."

The 63rd Infantry reported that the 17th SS Panzer Division appeared to be withdrawing and requested prompt information as to whether or not there were other withdrawals in the area. Patrols from the 101st were sent forward, and they reported the details of what they discovered: a German motorcycle messenger going from pillbox to pillbox; five German soldiers picking up telephone wire; a heavy dust cloud, indicating a vehicular column moving west, although the number of vehicles was not visible; a second column following the route of the first column; two German soldiers leaving a pillbox and entering a house; 15 to 20 men observed entering houses in the vicinity and leaving in overcoats; the sound of track-laying vehicles moving northwest; and the sound of vehicular traffic on a trail leading over the ridge just north of the Group's location.

These were the things my father was looking for every day. His job, in many ways, was to be the eyes and ears of the infantry. I don't know if the scouts wrote these things down or just had to remember what they saw, but it seemed clear that they were the flies on the wall that helped defeat the German Army.

In the middle of March, combat patrols were organized in Troops B and C, and Troop B went on foot by road and cross-country to Neufechingen, then to Ander-Schafbruck, Stahl-hammer, and Scheidt, which was its objective.

Troop C moved by road from Gudingen to Brebach and then to high ground near Sankt Johann, a borough of Saar-brucken located near the train station. Both patrols encountered roadblocks, road craters, and mined areas, which made vehicular movement impossible. As these impediments were eliminated, the soldiers brought their vehicles forward slowly,

German refugees leaving Saarbrucken on March 20, 1945.
U.S. Army Signal Corps photo. Courtesy National Archives.

blowing up dragon's teeth and improvising stream crossings. They encountered little enemy resistance, even at many of the principal defensive sites.

Units of the 101st were ordered to drive to St. Ingbert by any available route, and at 3:35 p.m., first platoon, Troop E, and 1st platoon, Company F, entered St. Ingbert against light resistance. By 5:45 p.m., they had cleared the town of the enemy.

After moving through the main fortifications of the Siegfried Line, Troop C and Company F, 101st Squadron, occupied the town of Bischmischeim. Sometime during that day 1st Lt. Lewis A.R. Innerarity's foot landed on a mine, killing him instantly.

The 116th's Troops B and C had gained their objectives, so the squadron was then ordered to sweep the area from Brebach to Rentrisch, Ensheim, and on to St. Ingbert, checking the roads and trails and protecting the left flank of the 63rd Infantry Division. At 10:50 p.m., word was received that the units were to assemble in Bubingen by 8 a.m. on the morning of March 21.

March 21, 1945

On March 21, the 101st Squadron had completely breached the Siegfried Line and was relieved of its attachment to the 63rd Infantry Division, although it was still under direct control of XXI Corps. Units of the 116th, which had assembled in Bubingen, received orders at 4:10 p.m. that they were to head for Lemberg, France. They arrived by 7:30 p.m.

Lt. Robert Ulmschneider, in command of Troop A, 101st Squadron, since Captain Ritchie had been wounded, was on a special mission for the Sixth Army Group, and the remainder of the 101st Group entered a war of movement, for which the lightly equipped but highly mobile, cavalry had been designed. The squadron commanders organized troops and platoon-sized task forces made up of reconnaissance, tank and assault gun elements. The task forces normally operated too far from the main infantry to have support provided, but their excellent radio contact helped coordinate movement, except when they ended up at night behind German forward elements and had to exercise radio silence.

The duty of the 101st was now to mop up all resistance in the 20-mile-wide zone behind the XXI Corps. The German forces did all they could to block the narrow roads in the mountains, but the cavalry kept moving.

"We were going through the mountains," said Erwin Perkins, "and I was in the lead car. Abe [Friedman] was behind me. Out of the corner of my eye, I saw about 20 Nazi soldiers. My weapon was a carbine – I hated that weapon. The clip was always breaking out. Some of the Germans put their hands up, but a couple didn't, so I raised my gun to fire. Sure enough, the clip fell out. Abe had his machine gun, and when he pointed that at them, they surrendered."

Along the way, the cavalrymen found abandoned supply dumps, ammunition stores, weapons, and hospitals. The relative comfort of a house to sleep in and good food was now a thing of the past.

"From that point on," wrote Clinton Gosnell, "we never really stopped. It seemed like we drove all night and fought all day, with never enough sleep. We went straight across Germany, sometimes doing 40 miles an hour. If the village church steeples didn't have white flags prominently displayed on them, we'd blow off the steeple to keep it from being used as an observation tower, and move on to the next town. One time we even got as far as 40 miles in front of our own troops. We waited in one position four nights and three days, until the 4th Infantry Division came up and relieved us."

On their push through Germany, the men carried almost everything they needed on their backs.

"We carried a thin sleeping bag and two blankets in our bedroll," said Fluharty, "which was made up by rolling up the bag, blankets and sleeping bag in the half-shelter, a canvas piece that, when joined with another, made a pup tent large enough for two."

Marching, they wore a harness, webbing that held the bedroll bent around the musette bag like a horseshoe. In the bag were toilet articles, a few clothing items, a canteen, trench knife, first aid pack, gas mask, all on a web belt, including spare ammo clips.

"We sometimes slept in an old barn or whatever we could find," Fluharty said, "with rats as big as cats jumping on our chests. Mostly though, we slept on the ground under our half-shelter."

"The hardest thing was trying to sleep," said Hawkins. "I was too scared to sleep. I didn't know if I was going to get through the next day."

"War is mostly just being tired, or scared to death, or bored out of your mind," Altizer wrote, "but most of all, it is never, I

There will be deer for dinner. Lt. Joseph Borkowski (right) skins a deer shot by one of the men.

Photo courtesy Joseph Borkowski.

repeat NEVER, getting enough sleep. The food was never very good; it was just portable, and it kept you from starving. Occasionally we would 'liberate' a few eggs or a chicken or two, but not very often. We were a mobile group, and there was never enough time to stop and cook anything, even if you had anything that needed cooking."

"Our cook was Roskowski," said Almond. "Before Germany he did a good job. The men would complain, but I bet a lot of them ate better than at home. Once we started, we ate out of cans, but sometimes we'd get potatoes out of cellars. One fellow got some and cooked them up for us."

Sometimes the men would shoot a deer for dinner, which was a big boost to the normal C rations. Once they shot a small deer in an open field, and Becker carried it slung over his shoulders back to the town where they were bivouacked.

"I had deer blood all over me," he said, "and the German women in the village thought I had been hit by fire and were fussing all over me. This was our little humor for the rest of the day."

Fluharty remembers passing through towns where women had put fresh-baked bread on towels in their front yards to cool. "In a few cases, the women would throw warm bread to us," he said. "I never had better bread in my life."

Fluharty describes one member of his tank crew, Dominic Stolt, as a scrounger. "If we stopped in some black hole of a field or village for the night, where you couldn't see your hand in front of your face, Stolt'd disappear and come back with a helmet full of eggs. I don't know how he did it."

An anonymous writer posted a story about his father on John Altizer's website about the 101st Cavalry. In it, he tells how his father's unit had bivouacked in a field next to a farm one night and, for the first time in weeks, they received mail. The soldier's mother had sent him some sausage, which he thought would go real well with eggs. He knew the farmer's wife had gathered eggs that morning, so he walked to the house and knocked on the door – it was one of those split type doors where just the top half could be opened.

The woman of the house opened the top half, and the soldier tried to communicate that he wanted to buy some eggs. She became very agitated and kept trying to close the door and send him away. He kept pointing to the basket full of eggs on her table, trying to make her understand what he wanted.

After a minute or two of her trying to say no and push him out the door, he just opened the bottom half of the door and walked in, grabbed a couple eggs and left a dollar on the table. She then started to try and push him out the back door, but his intent was to walk out the front. In spite of her attempts to stop him, he walked towards the front of the house protecting his precious eggs in his helmet. His rifle was slung over his shoulder, of no use in a pinch. As the soldier reached the front room, he realized why she had been so agitated. Sitting in her front parlor were four German soldiers having coffee. He almost dropped his eggs.

One of many destroyed German towns the cavalry passed through.
Photo courtesy Joseph Borkowski.

They had him cold, and he wouldn't have had a chance. Fortunately, they wanted to surrender, and he never had to touch his rifle. They had seen enough war and just wanted to go home, so he got his eggs and sausage and four German prisoners on the side.

∝∝

At some point in those first few days after the 101st started their push into Germany, Eugene Tharp, Patty Walsh, and John Dembowski added a Polish boy to their jeep crew.

"All his family had been killed, and he had been forced into the German Army," said Tharp. "He rode with us for the rest of the war. We called him 'Pedro.' He hated the Germans, so he would shoot anyone if he had the chance – soldier or civilian; we had to break him from that habit."

As the cavalry approached villages, many of which were in ruin, they continued looking for that white flag flying in a church steeple. They had now learned through sad experience that the steeples weren't just used as observation towers. Snipers also hid in those steeples, and many of their friends had been lost to their bullets.

In 2006, Ted and I passed through similar villages, but we were seated comfortably on a regional train. I would look for the church steeple in each hamlet and question its age. Was it an old steeple, saved because in March of 1945 someone had flown a white flag from the top? Had a sniper in that steeple killed one of the men from the 101st who didn't get to go home? Rolling from village to village on a regional train, it was a small curiosity for us; for the men of the 101st it had been information that could mean the difference between life and death.

During the third week of March, the 101st Cavalry learned that the German Army planned to make a determined stand on the east side of the Rhine River, sixty miles away. It wasn't good news.

March 22, 1945

As they traveled along the mountain roads toward the Rhine, the troopers witnessed the results of allied air power, and the victims in a few instances deeply affected the cavalrymen, with their historic ties to horses. On one particular road, for more than a mile, they saw at least two hundred dead horses, still harnessed to their wrecked wagons, killed when a German supply column was strafed by American aircraft.

On another day, David Gay was on patrol, headed with several other men toward some cabins in the hills where German soldiers were known to be. "We went through a village where a horse was badly burned," he said. "Some of the men wanted to put it out of its misery, but they couldn't shoot it. The Germans would hear the shot."

The men continued into the hills and eventually captured the Germans who had been hiding there. Some of the men headed back with the prisoners. "We told those who were headed back through the village that they could kill that horse now," he said. "No one wanted it to suffer."

Some of the dead horses ended up as food for the German people. "They were so hungry they would cut quarters off the horses," said Borkowski. "It was an awful sight. Blood was everywhere."

For long-time cavalrymen like Col. Graydon, who had entered the 101st when it was still a horse regiment, is was a sorrowful sight.

"I for one," Graydon wrote, "was not ashamed to feel for those horses almost the same anguish that I felt on seeing dead GIs or, for that matter, even the teenage German soldiers who had died."

March 23, 1945

The 101st was entering every village and town they encountered, reporting their location every four hours, and giving the condition of bridges and roads, the location of enemy minefields, roadblocks and other pertinent information. The Corps zone at that time was bounded by Walschbrand-Hinter-Weidenthal to the south, Waldfichback-Elmstein-Lambrecht-Neustadt to the north. By March 23, it seemed that German resistance west of the Rhine River in the XXI Corps zone had collapsed.

As the 101st moved by night into the eastern outskirts of Pirmasens, they were reminded once again of the devastating power of aerial bombing. Col. Graydon described how the town of perhaps fifty thousand was practically leveled.

> German families were huddled together wherever they could find shelter. Others wandered in a daze through smoking rubble. Broken water mains spouted water and the smell of death was everywhere. That night the Group found a place to bivouac near a mausoleum and cemetery at the edge of town. In back of the buildings were row upon row of coffins of the unburied dead and within the mausoleum was a large room completely filled with corpses. We were glad to soon move on.

Earl Carmickle remembers a night in a cemetery near the Rhine; perhaps it was the same night and the same cemetery.

"Our lieutenant wanted to set up in a cemetery," he said. "He said it would be safe there – the Germans wouldn't fire on a cemetery. We were in the middle of setting up when an artillery barrage started – right there in the cemetery. That lieutenant was wounded in both legs."

March 24, 1945

Early on March 24, all units moved forward against scattered resistance from German soldiers the infantry had bypassed earlier. Two problems made speed impossible: the rugged character of the terrain and the detailed reconnaissance required by their mission. The forward units reached the Landau-Edenkoben line at 6 p.m., and the entire 101st Squadron assembled near Elmstein. The 116th Squadron assembled at Sarnstall, arriving there at 9:18 p.m. They had traveled almost 60 miles since leaving Bubingen on March 21.

Saarbrucken, March 1945
Photo courtesy National Archives.

During this mission, the Cavalry took 135 prisoners and found and reported a number of supply dumps, ammunition stores, weapons, hospitals, and transport. They reported on the condition of the roads and bridges, and the roads were cleared of displaced persons. One soldier was killed in action.

Map 4
March 24-28, 1945

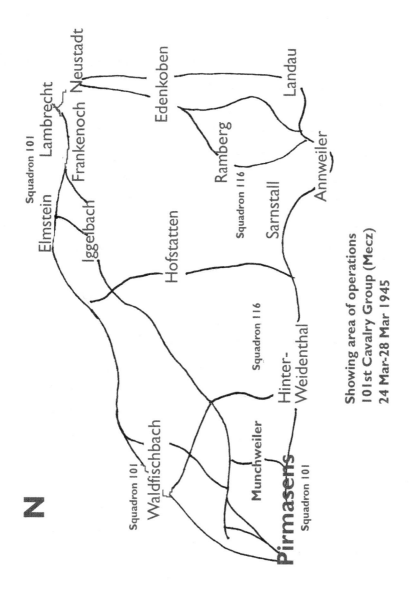

Neustadt

Landau

Lambrecht

Frankenoch

Edenkoben

Squadron 101

Ramberg

Elmstein

Annweiler

Iggelbach

Squadron 116

Hofstatten

Sarnstall

Showing area of operations
101st Cavalry Group (Mecz)
24 Mar-28 Mar 1945

Squadron 116

Hinter-
Weidenthal

N

Munchweiler

Waldfischbach

Squadron 101

Squadron 101

Pirmasens

On March 24, Lt. Col. Leonard wrote to his family, telling them that he had just returned from "another trip in Germany."

> We have a few days to clean up a bit, and we will be on the way to the Rhine again. We have been through the Siegfried Line in various places, so often that it is monotonous and the novelty of it has worn off. Our squadron has done fine work, down to the lowest private. We had a few casualties, very few, almost nil. The morale is excellent and I hope we continue to do things as we have in the past.
>
> In a very few minutes (this being Saturday night), I am going to take a bath in a wash boiler filled with hot water with two candles providing the necessary light. The house we are in is in pretty bad shape, no windows and plenty of rubble, but we manage to make it livable for our purpose.

The Children

When I first began looking for information about my father, I posted a request on a couple of websites: "I'm looking for anyone from the 101st Cavalry Division, 116th Squadron, B Company, who might remember my father, Ted Welch." I learned very quickly that I wasn't alone. The web is filled similar requests, not just for the 101st, but from every unit of the Army, Navy, Coast Guard, and Air Force:

> Did anyone know my father? He was with the 189th heavy artillery.
>
> I miss my dad very much. He was a member of the 45th infantry. Does anyone remember him?
>
> My father fought at El-Alamein in June 1942. Does anyone remember him or that battle?

Did you know my dad? He was a physician with the 101st Cavalry.

My father was James Melvin Kellie. Killed in action, Luxembourg, Thanksgiving forty-four. No luck locating records.

My father was Paul Schneider, a medic, wounded in a minefield, November forty-four. Earned a Bronze Star. Please, if you have information ...

Sergeant Romich. A tree, weakened by bursts from a German 88, fell and crushed his spine. He was partially paralyzed the rest of his life.

Lieutenant Charles D. Lemons. Injured November forty-four, Hurtgen Forest. We were writing his war stories when he passed away.

Private Sol Geffner. Killed in action seven December forty-four, Bergistein, Germany. Born in New York City. Buried in Henri Chapelle, Belgium. I want to locate someone who knew my dad. Please, if you did, send me an e-mail.

Wilbert Phillips. On his military gravestone: 'PFC ENGINEERS,' the sum total of my knowledge of my father's war experience.

Charles O'Neil. Killed in action, March forty-five, near Senden, Germany. I would like to know about my father. Please get in touch with me. I want so much to know something, anything, about him.

❧

So many missing fathers, and so many of our generation out there desperate to hear our father's stories. Maybe our interest has been sparked by the phenomenon of "The Greatest Generation" together with the romance of World War II in the movies we grew up watching, but whatever the reason, it has certainly been aided by the open door to research that the Internet has provided.

As I began to receive photos and stories from the men I interviewed and their children, I created a website so I could share them. Soon I was getting e-mail from other children and grandchildren of World War II veterans, asking if I had heard anything about their father or grandfather. Sometimes proud family members ask me to post their fathers' names and stories on the website.

Janet Willemain of New York was one of the first to contact me through the website. She hoped I had talked to someone who remembered her father, Bernard Willemain, a lieutenant with Troop B, 101st Squadron.

Bruce Peele was searching online when he found his father's name listed on the website. He wrote: "My father Louis Peele was in the 116th, Troop E. He was a tank gunner who served with Sgt. Pollack. My father was awarded a Silver Star and Purple Heart. He was from Chicago and currently lives in Raleigh, N.C."

He wanted to make sure his father's Silver Star was listed, and I wanted interview his father. Before that could be

Bernard Willemain
Photo courtesy Janet Willemain.

arranged, I received another e-mail from Bruce.

"My father was never sick a day in his life that I remember, and never complained about anything. He died on Friday. He opted not to do chemotherapy and died relatively quickly from lung cancer."

Lou Kiessler, whose father David Gay served in the 101st Squadron, B Troop, became interested in her father's war record when she was around seven years old.

"It was when *Rat Patrol* and other World War II television shows were popular," she wrote. "I would see these fictional heroes and wonder what my father had done. I ask him one time if he had ever killed anyone during the war. My dad is a gentle man and never loses his temper, but that did it. He became very upset and even grabbed me, yelling, 'Don't ever ask me that again.' It was so unlike him that it even frightened my mother. She was afraid he might hurt me. I never asked him personal questions about his time in the war after that. I would just ask about generalities, like where he was when the war ended or the people he remembered."

Before Kiessler's cousin shipped off to Vietnam, he came to visit her father. She walked into the living room where they were talking. Both men were both crying, so she left immedi-

David Gay, with his daughter Wanda at the 2006 reunion of the 101st Cavalry in Goldsboro, N.C.

ately and never asked what they had been talking about. War was something they could share, and she could not.

"All the time we were growing up, Dad instilled in us the deepest respect for this country, its military, and the flag that represents it," she said. "He had nothing good to say about the protesters and flag burners of the Vietnam era, especially the media that insisted on showing things from the war, which he felt women and children should not have to see."

Kiessler wrote that her dad really opened up when he and her mom read Tom Brokaw's *The Greatest Generation* and saw Ken Burns' *The War*.

"Dad started talking about the war and telling stories we had never heard before. He told us about his Purple Heart, the men in his outfit who were killed, patrolling the beach in Virginia, battles, encounters with civilians in the war-torn countries, and about coming home. He got on a transport for home on the day before his birthday, and when he woke up on his birthday, he was at sea headed for the U.S."

When he was discharged, he hadn't received his medals. After seeing a story on the news about a veteran getting his medals after all these years, Kiessler said that her father decided he wanted his.

> He told Mom that he thought he'd like to get them. Mom wrote to the appropriate places, and with a little help from Senator Jesse Helms, he got his medals in 1988. The medals hung in their house in Wilson until Mom died. After her death, Dad was going through a drawer and pulled out his silk map [of Germany], still in its oilcloth envelope. He told me that since I had always been interested in it, that he wanted me to have it. I took it back to Asheboro and had it framed with glass on both sides, so that we could take it down and look at it.

"It has been in a drawer for 60 years and look how good it looks," he told me.

He was so touched that I decided to establish a wall of honor and do a little more framing. In addition to the map, the wall now includes U.S. coins from the war years and money from France, England, Germany, Italy, and Austria. His summer and winter "Go to Hell" hats are there, as well as a flag that few over the U.S. Capitol to honor the 101st Cavalry. My sister won it at one of the reunions. His medals, a B Troop banner, his dog tags (one is on his key ring) also are part of the wall of honor.

This year I matted and framed his discharge papers. For someone who never talked about the war or his service, it is almost like we can't shut him up now — of course, I don't want to, even though I have heard some of the stories until I can almost repeat them verbatim.

Kiessler and I could barely imagine the young men our fathers were, and all the others like them: farm boys from North Carolina and Texas and Louisiana, who had never left their home states, much less their country. Almost overnight they were plucked from the lives they knew, taught to march and shoot, and then put on a ship and sent halfway around the world. Once there, the new rule was kill or be killed.

Abe Friedman served in the 101st from 1940 or 1941 until 1946 and was the recipient of the Bronze Star. His son, Lev Friedman, has a video of their dad telling some of his stories. "Certainly his experiences affected us profoundly," he said.

Sheila Ramuar Abshire's father, Roy W. Ramuar, was in Troop B, 116th Squadron, the same troop as my father. He served from December 21, 1942, to November 21, 1945, as a truck driver.

"I was in the dark about his service," she said. "Dad didn't want to talk about all of that with us. He was not a conventional man and not highly talkative."

Her father died on November 9, 1989, "the day the Berlin wall came down," she notes. "We buried him on Veterans Day. It was fitting."

Abshire became interested in her father's war service as a child watching old WWII movies.

Roy Ramuar

Photo courtesy his daughter, Sheila Ramuar Abshire.

John Wayne, Audie Murphy and the like. I love old war movies. Mom gave us tidbits about how it was for her and Dad during that time, so I wanted to know more. I tried very unsuccessfully to get something out of him. He just flat would not tell us anything. I assume that mom promised not to talk about it, because she gave the same vague answers he did. She did tell me once about the nightmares he used to have and finally, after I was about 30, she told me a story about Dad killing some Germans in a barn. I think she was trying to shock me into leaving it alone. But I always wanted to know, because I was proud of my father for serving in such a hard time for our country.

When Ramuar got home after the war, he burned his copy of *Wingfoot* and his uniform. His wife saved the ribbons and some of his clothes, insisting he could wear those for work. His daughter thought these things must have represented a part of his life that he wanted to forget.

He just didn't want to remember. Not all of the guys were proud of what they did over there, and they just wanted to forget. He did not want to remember. I know he had others to talk to about it. When he enlisted, one of his friends and one of his cousins enlisted too. They all went to basic together and must have been together for a while. I would hope that dad talked to them when he needed to vent about it. They were known as the 'Three Roys,' because they were all named Roy.

And now with both my parents gone I have little recourse to get the information I want. This is where the Internet has come in. I started looking almost from the time I plugged into it. I had been writing posts on a message board about seven years ago. But the web site no longer exists. I never really got much there anyway. I did get dad's medical records for the time he served, and they told me about the fire that took out the service records. In the medical records is how I found out about a fight my dad had with a group of Marines.

After the service, Daddy went back into construction, and he, along with both of my grandfathers and some of my uncles, helped build the Plant Industries here in the Lake Area. I was six months old when they moved us from Welsh to Lake Charles so that Daddy could work here on those plants. He did that for several years. Then after that he was building houses. That was his downfall. He fell off of a roof and became disabled because he severely hurt his back. He had five back surgeries before he was 50.

In your interviews with the men, would you mind asking if they remember the Cajun who loved to dance. I am almost certain that if there was a dance hall near the base that Daddy would have gone dancing every chance he got.

࿏

"My dad was a loner, and he had hard memories from the war," said Cheryl Kashuba, Charlie Kashuba's daughter. "He spent years going around and visiting the men he served with. Visiting the other men was a catalyst for him to discuss the war. He wanted to be with people who understood his sadness. He'd have terrible nightmares about things he couldn't — or wouldn't — share with us."

Kashuba told his family that he was one of the first men from the 101st to discover the concentration camps around Landsberg.

"He and a man from Green River County found a camp," Cheryl said. "He could not believe it. He didn't know what kept those people alive. There were bodies stacked like cordwood, and some of the people were moaning, barely alive. It was one of his worst memories. After the war, when he'd see a freight train, he'd freeze, turn around and go the other way."

࿏

Not only children of American soldiers wondered about their fathers' war experiences.

Anne Cummings sent me an e-mail after finding photos of her aunts, Anna and Regina Levasier, on my website. Buck Fuharty had sent me the photo, which he had taken in 1945 while billeted in their home.

Cummings' father, Valentin Levasier, was a German soldier who fought on the Russian front. He was captured by the Russians in Poland and didn't return home until 1948 or 1949. He died in 1992, leaving her with questions.

"I think it's everywhere the same," she wrote. "My father only talked once about his experiences when I had asked him directly. I remember all through my childhood the visits to his war comrades. At least once a month we would drive somewhere and visit them. They were all very close throughout the years, and I can still remember their names and see their faces. I never heard them talk about their war memories, but we were children and maybe that's why we didn't hear anything. It was when I went to Israel in my 20s and saw all the memorials in Jerusalem and later the Concentration Camps in Poland that I started to ask questions."

Stan Majcherkiewicz's father, 2nd Lt. Seweryn Majcherkiewicz, was a prisoner of war liberated by the 101st Cavalry. Majcherkiewicz wrote that his father defended Fort Modlin on the outskirts of Warsaw in 1939, was wounded there, and was eventually captured by the Russians and transported to Murnau in Bavaria. He, too, wished he knew more about his father's service. He and his brother, Przemo, wrote about their father and what little they knew of his history.

Valentin Levasier, who served in the German Army on the Russian front. Buck Fluharty was billeted with Levasier's mother and sisters after the war.

Photo courtesy his daughter, Anne Cummings.

We grew up in a special period of Polish history. It was forbidden to talk about things like the slaughter of Polish officers and intelligentsia in the forests of Katyn by the Soviets ... . This was also a time when a simple and obvious thing like listening to Voice of America or Radio Free Europe was strictly forbidden. Maybe that is why our father was hesitant in sharing his war and camp memories with us.

Our father never showed us too many keep-sakes, but we remember several: a leather belt, a hat, a cigarette box, his officer side bag, and a statue in his likeness carved by a friend in the prisoner of war camp.

And this was it. We knew not much more. Our father did not talk, and we did not ask.

After our father's death, we kept finding documents here and there. That's how we found his military ID card, some letters, and other documents.

Seweryn Majcherkiewicz, prisoner in a POW camp liberated by the 101st.

Photo courtesy his son, Stan Majcherkiewicz.

Some of these sons and daughters felt their fathers' silence came from a desire to protect their families from the horror of war and from the pain of too much understanding. From what I have heard, it seems the greater pain is caused by not knowing.

Map 5
March 29, 1945

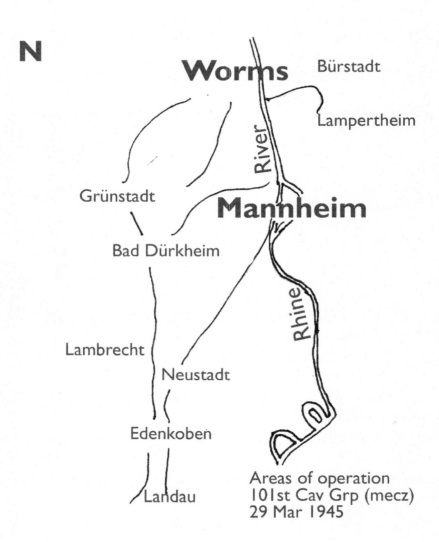

N

Worms

Bürstadt

Lampertheim

River

Grünstadt

Mannheim

Bad Dürkheim

Rhine

Lambrecht

Neustadt

Edenkoben

Landau

Areas of operation
101st Cav Grp (mecz)
29 Mar 1945

Last Days of March 1945

Lampertheim

Germany and American soldiers had maintained a more-or-less eastward drift for the past several days. Their movement had been confined to the secondary roads and densely wooded mountain areas, which were difficult to keep under constant surveillance.

On March 25 the 101st Cavalry Group was patrolling all the roads in the area, mopping up the remaining German units, establishing roadblocks, and taking responsibility for lines of communications in the XXI Corps zone. In addition to all of this, they were also directing the movement of people, basically transporting all non-German nationals, whether prisoners-of-war or displaced people found on the road, to centers in Pirmasens, Kaiserslautern, Neustadt, or to the nearest town with the capability to care for them.

March 28-29, 1945

On March 28, the 101st arrived at the Landau-Neustadt line, an abrupt division between the mountains and the flat, fertile valley of the Rhine. The assault gun troops and tank companies of both squadrons created a screen along this line, and the remaining troops of each squadron moved out on foot from a second line about 10 miles west. Their job was to thoroughly comb the wooded, mountainous areas and drive the German soldiers into the trap set by the assault gun troops and tank companies that were waiting like a giant net between Neustadt and Landau.

At about noon, the Group received word that the next day they would go to Lampertheim, about three miles east of the Rhine. They were given a to-do list not much different from what they had been doing the last few days: protect the XXI and XV Corps' line of communications, mop up enemy resistance, control movement of civilian traffic, and divert or transport all non-German prisoners of war and displaced persons to centers established by the corps. The zone in which they were working covered a broad area near Worms, where they were preparing to cross the Rhine. It was a huge order, especially as it related to the displaced people.

After the rapid retreat of the Germans, the countryside was filled with hundreds of prisoners of war from every Allied nation, including Americans. Added to these were people from every country that the German Army had overrun — Poles, Ukrainians, Lithuanians, French, Italians, etc. – who had been brought to Germany as slave labor. After breaking out of the camps abandoned by the retreating Germans, these people had existed by hiding and looting. This situation continued throughout Germany until the end of the war and for weeks after.

One of the platoons adopted an Italian cook, and Group Headquarters inherited two Ukrainian sisters as maids, with

Map 6
March 29-30, 1945

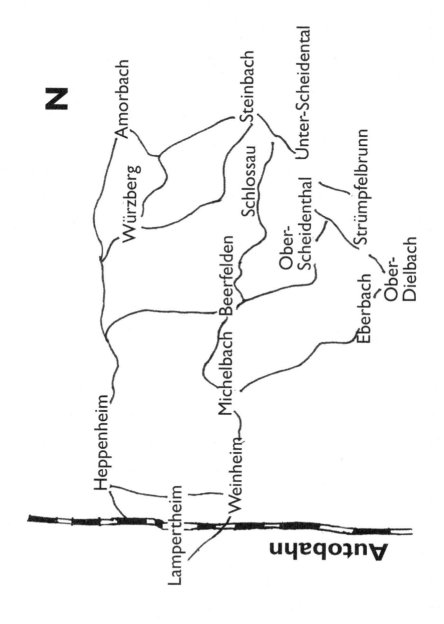

a strict understanding among the men, wrote Col. Graydon in his history, that there would be no "hanky-panky."

"We got acquainted with the people, and they accepted us pretty well," said William Pierce. "Two French kids used to do the dirty work for us. They stayed with us for awhile, then left. A lot of people did that – a lot were sent to relocation camps after the war. The whole country was in pretty bad shape. When these two French kids had the opportunity to leave, they did. I had a camera and a dagger disappear the same day they left. I don't know if they took it, but I always suspected that maybe they did. I hated losing all the pictures that were in that camera."

"A little Russian boy took up with us," said John Almond. "He'd sit in the back of the armored car playing his accordion. He spoke several languages. He'd go down into the towns and tell us where the Germans were. He was one brave little old boy. He was in his early teens. There was an Italian boy in another platoon – I don't remember in which town – but he was killed by a sniper. The Russian boy sneaked through the woods and shot that sniper. He was real brave. When he had to leave us, he hugged our necks and squalled. He didn't know much English, but when the commander made him leave, he called him 'Commandant SOB.'"

Clair Becker said that it wasn't uncommon to recruit these refugees to help patrol, since they knew the roads and local areas. Some of the troopers thought the refugees worked out okay; others felt they couldn't be trusted.

"Some of our own people were shot at by these refugees," Becker said, "and we didn't have time to teach them our weapons, so we stopped recruiting them."

The 116th Squadron left Sarnstall at 10:23 on the morning of March 29, and by late afternoon the cavalry was at Worms, with Lampertheim just a few miles away. All that stood in their way was the Rhine. The infantry threw up a screen of billowing smoke to hide their movement from the Germans as tanks, armored cars, guns, and men started across the river on pontoon bridges.

"I remember crossing the rivers on those pontoon bridges that were like upside down canoes with boards running across them," said Almond. "I'd see those white caps with water running so fast the weight of the cars would push it down and it was like you were driving right on the waves. I didn't like that."

As the Germans pulled back, they were blowing up bridges to slow the advance of the Allied troops, so Army engineers were constantly repairing bridges, or the cavalry would cross on whatever was handy, like railroad bridges.

"Once the Germans blew up the regular bridge right in front of us," said Almond, "so we took the railroad bridge. I can still remember that bumpety-bump driving along the railroad tracks."

Once the various units of the 101st Group had crossed the river, they came together at Lampertheim, and by 7 p.m. they had orders that put them on the move again. This time they were headed 30 miles to the east, where they were to establish contact with the 10th Armored Division, which was operating north of the Neckar River.

The Neckar ran along the south flank of the XXI Corps and on the north side of the city of Heidelberg. Because of its long cultural history, Heidelberg had been declared an "open city" by the Allied and German high commands. This meant it was exempt from shelling and occupation by either side.

One of the cavalry columns advancing up the north shore of the river ran into a small contingent of German soldiers and needed to fight its way through a roadblock opposite the city. A trooper quoted in *Wingfoot* described it as "a weird feeling, to be fighting like mad while across the narrow river, hundreds of men, women, and children lined the banks and rooftops to watch as though they were seeing a Saturday afternoon sports event."

When I was in Heidelberg, I struck up a conversation with the young man at the desk in my hotel, one of the few people I had met who spoke English. He asked what brought me to Heidelberg, and I told him why I was there. Then I told him the story of the battle across the river. He told me that he knew that story. He had been taught about this event in school, about how the Americans and the Germans had fought it out across the river during the war. As I climbed the narrow stairs to my room, I was struck by the fact that a schoolboy in Germany had known about this event in my father's life long before I did. And it saddened me.

B Troop, 116th Squadron, enters an almost deserted Heidelberg.

Photo courtesy Joseph Borkowski.

"Our troop was sent into reserve in Heidelberg," said Robert Klein. "While there, we got an alarm one night that the Germans were surrounding us in the hills around the city. We headed up there and looked for them all night, but we never found anyone."

Once past Heidelberg, the Cavalry Group broke into six task forces in an effort to uncover the German forces hidden in the forest and drive them back. At the same time, Group Headquarters, reinforced with tank and assault gun platoons, formed a seventh task force. Sometimes, to cover all the roads, it was necessary for the troops to break down even further into platoon-size task forces. The 116th Squadron formed three: Task Force Joe, composed of Troop A's 1st platoon, Troop E's 3rd platoon, Company F, and a squad of engineers; Task Force Sam, which included Troop C, plus one squad of engineers;

and Task Force Feagin, composed of Troop E's 3rd platoon, Troop C's 1st platoon, Company F, and one squad of engineers. Troop B went into Group reserve.

This mission would take the 101st through the steeply wooded slopes and narrow valleys of the legendary Odenwald Forest. All columns were forced into the valleys, an extremely rugged terrain ideally suited for the delaying tactics so popular with the Germans: roadblocks, destroyed bridges, mines and other obstacles. Here for the first time the cavalry columns were subjected to strafing by enemy aircraft, as the small, but determined, rear guard of the German defense began to slowly tighten up. German airplanes were constant pests to all columns of the 101st throughout the day. One of them flew right into the crosshairs of the headquarters task force – a Messerschmitt, ME109 – in the vicinity of Beerfelden, and soon there was one less plane to harass the troops.

At midnight, headquarters, headquarters troop, and the first platoon of the 116th's B Troop followed the 101st Squadron as they moved out in two columns and entered the mass of hills east of the Rhine River at Weinheim. The rest of the 116th entered at Heppenheim.

March 30, 1945

The composition of XXI Corps had changed significantly since leaving the Rhine: the 63rd, 70th and 71st Infantry Divisions had been replaced by the 4th and 42nd Infantry Divisions and the 12th Armored

Sgt. Robert Klein during the war.
Photo courtesy Robert Klein.

Division. Troop A, 101st Cavalry Squadron, still remained with Headquarters Sixth Army Group.

Trying to follow the movements and attachments of the various troops and squadrons at this point is difficult. As William Pierce said, "We — the Cavalry — were up for grabs, attached to several different outfits throughout the war."

As the Group approached the valley of the Tauber River, the units spearheading the march began to meet increasing German resistance. Sometime during the day, Pfc. Bennie Gonzales, C Troop, 116th Squadron, was killed in action.

"They say when a soldier dies, he hollers for his mama," said John Borotka. "Well, they shot Gonzalez in the head, and he was calling for his mama. There wasn't a single thing we could do for him."

Enemy air attacks became more active, and here, for the first time, the Cavalry were attacked by Luftwaffe jet fighters. Hitler had expected to turn the tide of war with these jets, but trained pilots were in short supply, and the Allies had heavily bombed the factories. The jets would typically reach the battlefields too late and in numbers too small to be effective. The untrained German pilots, unaccustomed to the high speeds of the jet aircraft, often overshot their targets, a lucky break for the Allied troops in the area.

It was here, also for the first time, that the troopers encountered the hated "nebelwerfers," which consisted of up to 48 6.2mm rockets mounted on tanks or trucks that could be fired simultaneously or in tandem with devastating effect.

By late afternoon on Good Friday, March 30, the various troop headquarters were situated in the following towns:

> Troop C, 101st, Oberdielbach
> First Platoon, Troop C, 101st, Strumpfelbrunn
> Troop A, 101st, Oberscheidental
> Troop B, 101st, Unterscheidental

> Headquarters and Headquarters Troop, 101st Cavalry Group, and Troop B, 116th Squadron, Schlossau
> Task Force, 116th, Steinbach
> Troop C, 116th, Kirchzell
> Troop A, 116th, Amorbach
> Additional members of the 116th, Worzberg

By the end of the day, the group had taken 244 prisoners, secured the Seventh Army bridgehead line in the XXI Corps zone, and were headed toward the Hochstadt-Neustadt-Rothenberg line some fifty-five miles to the east.

At this point, the 101st had moved almost one hundred miles in eight days with varying degrees of opposition. At times the German Army seemed without spirit, and the troopers dreamed of the war ending soon. They didn't know that some of their worst fighting was yet to come.

March 31, 1945

On the morning of Saturday, March 31, the 101st Cavalry was continuing east with reconnaissance elements of the 12th Armored Division.

At noon the task force under the command of Major Robert D. Feagin Jr., 116th Squadron, was ordered to seize the small towns of Grunsfeld, Ippensheim, and Neustadt. The task force included Headquarters troop; B Troop's first platoon; and, from the 101st Squadron, Company F's first platoon and Troop E's first platoon. They were told to proceed aggressively, and whenever necessary to complete their mission, to go around enemy resistance rather than confronting it.

The task forces headed east. The 101st Squadron, strung out for thirty-five miles along the Sindolsheim-Boxberg-Tauber River line, was trying to reach the 63rd Infantry Division, just south of Bad Mergentheim. Heavy fire slowed the squadron to a crawl, and by nightfall they were only able to progress as far as Eubigheim, ten miles from the river.

Troop A of the 116th Squadron was operating in the extreme northern part of the zone, just a day away from Giebelstadt. Task Force Joe, made up of platoons of the 116th that had not been included in the other task forces, was between the Tauber River and Ochensfurt (near Bad Mergentheim) and heading north. They reached the Tauber by nightfall.

In the late afternoon, Task Force Feagin was approaching Grunsfeld from the west when it was stopped by heavy resistance. It fell back to defensive positions on the high ground to the northwest for the night.

Sgt. Andrew Lakitsky, Cpl. Glenn Eanes, Andre Patterson, and other members of tank crew.

Photo courtesy Bill Hart.

At 8:55 that evening, Task Force Sam had arrived in Essel-brunn, approximately 15 miles south and west of Grunsfeld, where they remained for the night. Command posts were established in the area at Distelhausen (101st Group), Kupprichhausen (101st) and Zimmern (116th).

Map 7
March 31-April 1, 1945

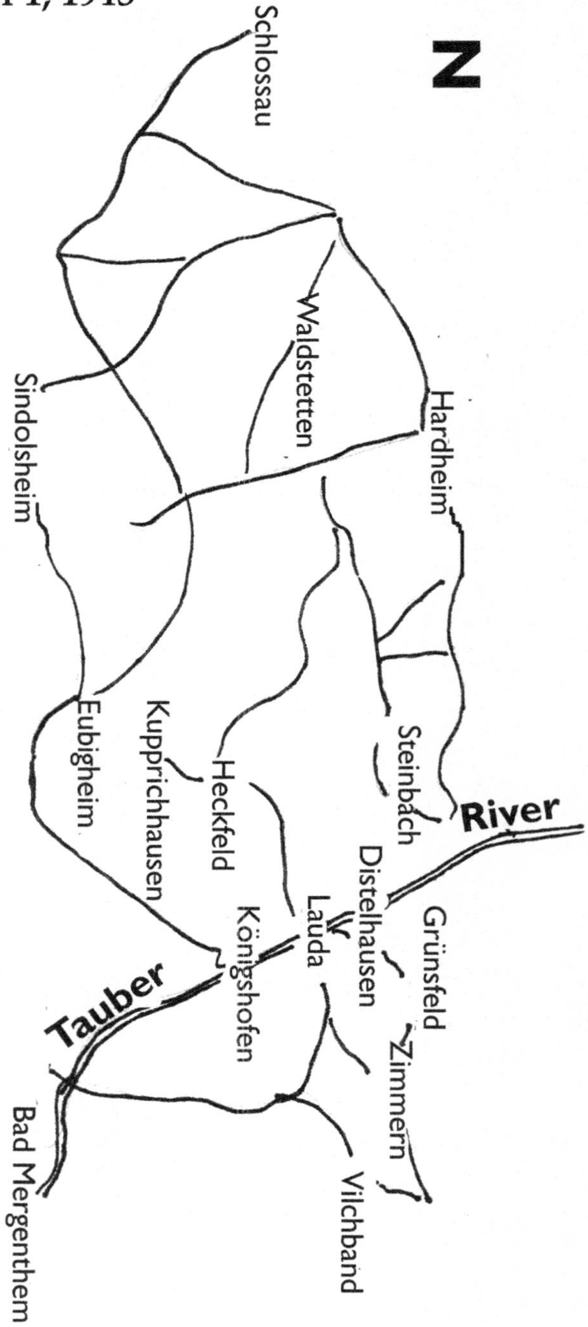

N

Schlossau

Waldstetten

Sindolsheim

Hardheim

Eubigheim

Kupprichhausen

Heckfeld

Steinbach

Distelhausen

Lauda

River

Königshofen

Grünsfeld

Zimmern

Tauber

Bad Mergenthem

Vilchband

Tauberbischofsheim

Tauberbischofsheim 2006

The 101st arrived in Tauberbischofsheim on Easter Sunday, approximately two weeks after getting through the Siegfried Line. Ted and I made the trip by regional train from Saarbrucken in four hours.

We might have chosen any one of a hundred places for our next stop – the 101st passed through an endless array of small towns and villages – but our figurative dart landed on Tauberbischofsheim.

Tauberbischofsheim isn't a large city; nearby Bad Mergentheim would have been a better choice for the average tourist. Tiny Tauberbischofsheim, located in the northeast part of Baden-Wurttembergon on the Tauber River, population 13,000, was a refreshing change from industrialized Saarbrucken and more like the picture-postcard Germany I had expected.

Small hills rise all around the town, and our hotel, Hotel am Brenner, sat at the top of one, giving us a great view of the valley. Once settled, we saw most of what the town offered in one afternoon: a church, part of the original city wall, and a castle. The "bischofsheim" part of the name means "bishop's place," which was given to the town because of its close relationship to the bishop Saint Boniface. In the 8th Century, his relative Lioba had been the abbess of the town's monastery. Since Germany had several "Bischofsheims," the Tauber part was added later to avoid confusion.

When we were there, the city was exploding in brightly colored eggs and flowers for Easter. Red and yellow, blue and green bloomed everywhere. I doubt it was the same on that Easter Sunday when the Cavalry arrived. Pink, lavender, yellow, blue, and green eggs looped around fountains; Easter trees covered with decorations greeted people entering the town square, and chicks, bunnies, and spring flowers brightened the entrance of every shop. The troopers would have passed through a nearly deserted town center and crossed the Tauber River, a tributary of the Main, with little to show it was a holiday.

We found the square peaceful, filled with late-afternoon shoppers. The only sound was the hum of traffic at the main

Tauberbischofsheim store display for Easter

Tauber River

intersection. Each time we left the square and crossed the small bridge over the Tauber, I tried to picture troops crossing this same river 60 years earlier.

Church bells ringing all across the valley woke me the morning we were going to leave for the countryside. We would spend the day in search of the hills and villages where several battles had taken place. Standing in the window of our hotel, I could see those hillsides in the distance, shrouded in mist. It was there the cavalry had fought its way by foot and jeep, mile by mile into Tauberbischofsheim. We would go by train, and our first stop was Lauda.

Lauda, although not large, was still a bigger town than I had expected. As we walked around, we tried to identify pre- and post-World War II buildings. We knew the town had seen heavy fighting, but we assumed that a few of the buildings we were seeing had survived the war. We also carried with us the pages from *Wingfoot* that dealt with the days spent in Lauda,

Bad Mergentheim, Tauberbischofsheim, Zimmern, and other small towns in the area. We tried to connect the reports in the book with where we were – a treasure hunt of sorts.

When we noticed a square door leading into the cellar of an old, half-timbered building, we quickly thumbed through the pages of the book. There was a story about a cellar door. I made Ted go over and push the door open just a bit more, as I read from *Wingfoot* about an anonymous soldier's adventure in Lauda.

> I had been talking to the boys in the command post half-track and was just about back to my own vehicle when the screaming 'gobble gobble' of nebelwerfer shells came overhead. I hit a pile of potatoes in a cellar with three men on top of me. After a respectful wait, we surfaced and saw that the shells had hit near the half-track. I searched through the dense cloud of smoke and dust fearfully. Not a man was scratched. No one will ever convince us that the prayers of the good folk at home were not working full force at that moment. It was Easter Sunday.

Who could say if the cellar that Ted and I had found was even a potato cellar; all we could see through the open door was a ladder leading down into the dark. Whether it was or not, my imagination was fired, and I could see the four soldiers rolling through just such a door, each one falling on the man below, praying that this Easter Sunday was not his last. I saw them as they climbed up the wobbly wooden ladder leading back to the light, and watched as they brushed away the cellar dust and laughed in fear and relief. I wondered who they were. So far, no one remembered this event.

On the way back to Tauberbischofsheim, our train sped through brown hills covered with plowed fields and groves of orchards, not yet filling out with the leaves of spring. Villages with no more than two dozen houses and a church, nestled in the low places where the hills came together. I looked for signs to indicate we were passing Grünsfeld or Zimmern, places mentioned in the reports, and as we approached Zimmern, I snapped a few blurred photos before our train sped past. The clouds that had been with us all day began to separate, allowing a few rays of sunset to brighten the towns red roofs and the teal and yellow houses. It was a lovely sight, but seen through the window of the train, we could only hold onto the image for a matter of seconds. My father had probably forgotten the names of these villages before I was born, if he ever knew them. But I knew he had bivouacked there, maybe caught a few hours rest, and I was glad I saw them, even if only for a moment.

Map 8
April 1-7, 1945

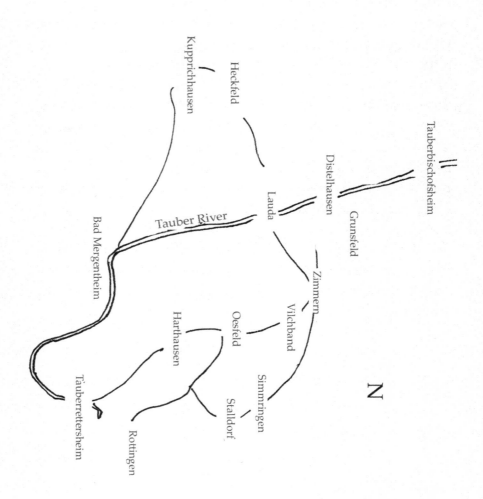

Kupprichhausen

Heckfeld

Tauberbischofsheim

Distelhausen

Grunsfeld

Lauda

Tauber River

Bad Mergentheim

Zimmern

Vilchband

Harthausen

Oesfeld

Simmringen

Stalldorf

N

Tauberrettersheim

Rottingen

Easter Sunday 1945

First light of Easter morning, April 1, 1945, found the troopers scattered throughout an area south of Wurzburg, bordered roughly by Tauberbischofsheim in the north, Heckfeld in the west, Lauda in the south, with the Tauber River to their east. On their way to the Tauber, they had experienced only light resistance, but as they drew closer to the river, the German defenses intensified.

Several men were killed when the cavalry ran into some trouble in a valley south of Distelhausen and near Lauda.

"It was the toughest day I saw in the war," said Frederick Altizer. "It was Easter Sunday and we had just had a German jet pass over us, strafing us. Those planes went by so fast that it was gone before any of us could react, but I fired my machine gun at it over a surprised Sgt. Giza's head anyway. We – Grover Cleveland Wilson and me – just knew it wasn't ours and didn't know what it was. We had never seen anything move so fast. Occasionally we saw our own planes strafing the retreating Germans ahead of us. When we advanced, there would be dead horses and cows and soldiers and wrecked vehicles along the road for miles."

The new jet-propelled planes appeared to move faster than their new and peculiar roaring sound. In his history, *With the 101st in World War II*, Col. Graydon wrote, "The jets came back again and again, until the nerve centers of each and every man reacted on a split-second basis, as animal instinct thrust aside the slower processes of reason."

Task Force Sam – Troop C, 116th Squadron, and one squad of engineers, under the command of Captain Louis V. Bossert – had started out early near the town of Heckfeld, where they had convinced the entire civilian population to surrender. They then moved north to Dittwar and Steinbach, both of which were free of German soldiers, and joined Task Force

Zimmern 2006

Feagin in an attack on German positions. By noon, the German resistance in that area had been reduced to nothing more than scattered sniping.

Task Force Feagin followed Task Force Sam east toward Grünsfeld, also in the company of the headquarters troop for the 116th. A battle had developed on the other side of Grünsfeld between the infantry and the Germans, and the infantry had suffered several casualties, who were evacuated through the 101st's medical aid station. Joining the infantry, the troopers fought their way into Zimmern, about three miles away. They remained there for the night.

As Task Force Feagin and Task Force Sam were pushing their way east, the headquarters task force turned south to Lauda, but was halted there by heavy German automatic weapons, small arms, and nebelwerfer fire from the high ground across the Tauber to the east, where the Germans had dug in.

Eventually, the pressure the Cavalry exerted from the north and the fire power of the headquarters force drove the enemy off the slopes facing Lauda, enabling the headquarters force to quickly move north along the east side of the river.

Task Force Joe had gone through Tauberbischofsheim against light resistance early in the morning, crossed the Tauber River, and turned south along the east bank. By 10 a.m. they had arrived in Gaubuttelbrunn, 13 miles to the east.

Later in the day, when the remaining troops crossed the river, they crossed under a canopy of nebelwerfer fire, which exploded in great clouds of smoke pierced by thousands of fragments, from the size of a pinhead to large gouging chunks.

Killed in battle that day were Pfc. Stanley Gawlak and Sgt. Johann Hinck, both from B Troop, 116th Squadron; George Gardner, 101st Headquarters, who was killed by sniper fire; and T-4 William Kornblum.

"We were engaged with some German troops," said Altizer, "and some tanks with the outfit came charging across the field with some guys riding on the back, firing on the

Germans. Pvt. Gawlak was riding on the back of one of those tanks, and the Germans shot him right off. Our lieutenant saw what happened, and he ordered us to drive out in our jeep and pick him up. Before we could, the tank commander, jumped out of the tank and ran back to try and help Gawlak, and the Germans shot him, too. They shot Gawlak a second time and he died on the field. The tanks finally drove the Germans off, and we got the wounded tank commander out of there."

"In the village where Gawlak and Hinck were killed," said Lt. Joseph Borkowski, "women came out and screamed at us, called us killers. There was nothing we could have done any differently."

Not every German civilian called them killers. "A lot of the German people were good people," said Carmickle, "nice to us. We'd been going all day and all night with nothing but C rations when we entered a village one morning right after the German soldiers had pulled out. An old man invited us into his house for breakfast. It was a good breakfast, too."

Tharp tells of another house where the family had a ham baking in the oven. "They invited us in and fed us," he said.

In one village, a family even protected the Americans from German soldiers.

"The girl of the house went to the barn, which was alongside the house, to feed the cows," said Tharp. "When she went up to the loft to kick down some hay, she found a German soldier asleep there. The girl promised the soldier that she wouldn't tell the Americans, but she came back in and told her daddy, and he told us. Two of us went out to get him. We shot through the loft and thought we had him; however, when we went up to the loft, he was still standing. We took him prisoner, questioned him, and turned him over to Pvt. Morris White."

Tharp goes on to say that White had the German dig a grave and then shot him. I had heard similar stories about a man called "Killer" and a man who shot several prisoners of war when one spit on a lieutenant. Lt. Borkowski insists that incidents like this never happened, but I had heard too many to doubt they ever happened. It was war.

In one of the small towns the troopers passed through that Easter Sunday, Captain Walter Kohnle and the entire Group Operations and Intelligence Sections could have been wiped out if not for a joke made by Kohnle. They were riding in a half-track named "Gilhooly," when the column was held up by fire on the town's main street. Captain Kohnle mentioned that, according to the Field Manual, they should disperse the vehicles. Even though he had been joking, since they rarely referenced the Field Manual, they took his advice and backed into a side street. Not more than a minute later the men heard the characteristic "gobble, gobble" of nebelwerfers as they crashed into the street exactly where the half-track had been, leaving nothing but a large hole.

Corporal Douglas Cupp, Company F, 116th Squadron, from Long Island City, New York, earned the Silver Star that day. One of his officers was out on patrol when he radioed Cupp that he had been wounded. Sniper and mortar fire were so heavy, no one could go to his assistance, but Sgt. Cupp volunteered to go to the rescue. He reached the lieutenant, administered first aid, and then called for his tank to come forward and evacuate the wounded officer.

Staff Sergeant Vincent Kelly, Troop F, 116th, Brooklyn, New York, also earned a Silvert Star. Kelly was wounded and under heavy sniper fire near Distelhausen when he voluntarily faced the snipers to give first aid and evacuate seriously wounded comrades.

At 7:26 p.m. word was received from Troop C, 116th Squadron, that Pvt. Willis Hammond and Sgt. James Donlon had been injured. Also wounded that day were Second Lt. Joe Dees of Troop E and Pvt. James Hodge, John Allen, and Joseph Kuzniewski, all of Troop B, 116th.

"We had just taken a little town and were passing a hill heavily covered with large trees," wrote Allen. "There were snipers in those trees just waiting for us. One of them picked out our jeep as a target and opened up with a machine pistol. The lead was flying all around us, and my friend, Sgt. Hinck, right beside me, was killed."

Sgt. Hinck was a native-born German, whose parents had immigrated to the United States years before the war started. He was killed within 10 miles of the village where he was born.

A bullet bounced off Allen's machine gun, and when he pulled back, he lost his balance and fell off the road.

"We were going about 45 miles per hour, and how I kept from breaking something, I'll never know," wrote Allen. "My knee was busted up and bleeding pretty bad. I had a concussion out of it, and I will always have a scar on my right knee. I was taken to the hospital, and it was 15 days before I could walk. It was no fun, except the rest and sleep were wonderful after being in action for so long. No sleep and always fighting, or standing guard every night with nothing but cold rations to eat, shaving in cold water, and being dirty, wet and cold most of the time – it was hard on everybody. I know why young men come back old. It was nothing to laugh about, and I don't ever want to see a war movie, or even a scary one, again. I want to throw my gun away and never see it again either."

Map 9
April 8-13, 1945

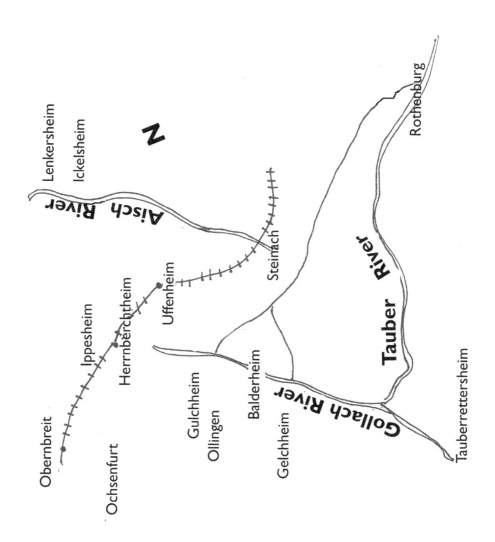

Lenkersheim

Ickelsheim

N

Aisch River

Steinach

Rothenburg

Tauber River

Uffenheim

Ippesheim

Herrnberchtheim

Gulchheim

Balderheim

Tauberrettersheim

Obernbreit

Ollingen

Gollach River

Ochsenfurt

Gelchheim

The Bloodiest Month

Tauberbischofsheim

Landsberg

A pril proved to be the most highly concentrated period of combat faced by the 101st Cavalry. When not actually exchanging fire with the Germans, the men were on the move, pushing through the German lines, finding shelter at night in towns and villages, often with the nearest infantry divisions 12 to 30 miles to their rear.

"[Infantry] officers writing after the war heaped praise on the men who rode the point jeeps and armored cars," wrote Sweeney in *Wingfoot*, "carrying the assault through unending miles of resistance. Even the men in the heavy armored units had sincere respect for those 'crazy cavalrymen.'"

April 2, 1945

At 6 a.m. on April 2, the troops of the 116th Squadron had their command posts established: Squadron Headquarters was located at Zimmern; Troop A command was at Gaukoniger-hofen; Troop B, Tiefenthal; and Troop C, Harthausen.

The 101st Squadron was deployed between Bad Mergen-theim, the Tauber River, and Ochsenfurt. After running into strong resistance west of Bad Mergentheim, Task Force Feagin was dissolved, and its members returned to their own troops.

Around 11 a.m. that day, Captain Bossert's C Troop, along with first platoon of Troop E and first platoon of Company F, 116th Squadron, was attempting to penetrate the German defense line when it ran into a hornet's nest at the little town of Oesfeld.

"As we approached Oesfeld," said John Borotka, "I was in the front jeep. Directly behind me was an armored car, then another jeep. The whole outfit was behind me as we entered the town. A panzerfaust fired, and it just missed me. I turned around and saw I was all alone. No one was there protecting the rear."

Borotka quickly returned to the rest of his troop

"We set up our mortars on a little ridge outside the village," he said. "The Germans set off a round of mortar fire. We had light tanks, and they didn't hold up well against the panzer-fausts. As we were going forward, the Germans would aim for the gunner's side on the left side of the tank."

Sometimes, the Germans got a direct hit.

"That's how my friend Theodore Evanko was killed," said John Borotka.

The next day was the same: the Americans moved forward, and once again the Germans beat them back.

"We were moving forward through a freshly plowed field, and we couldn't see the Germans who were hiding between the rows. We rolled right over one guy, and he stood up and tried to throw a grenade into my car. Sgt. Martin grabbed his gun to shoot the guy, but it jammed. He tried a couple of times to shoot it, then he started screaming 'My gun is jammed! My gun is jammed!' and hitting the German in the face with the butt of the rifle."

Lt. George P. Langton, Jr., from squadron headquarters, was on patrol in the area, and as he made a call for air cover, his jeep ran into a booby trap: a wire stretched tightly across the road. He was talking on the phone with an airplane overhead when he was killed.

"You can imagine what happened," said Erwin Perkins. "That's when we started attaching the upright T-bars on the front of our jeeps to break those wires."

Captain Bossert and the men under his command were pinned down by a rain of fire, so he hurried forward ahead of his troop's front lines to a vantage point where he could observe the enemy. From there he was able to direct artillery fire, saving the lives of his men and permitting the evacuation of wounded troopers. A native of New York, Captain Bossert earned a Silver Star for his actions that day.

John Rothengast

John Rothengast, Troop B's 26-year-old supply sergeant, was a popular figure with the other men. Raised in the Bronx, Rothengast came from a family of New York City police officers and had passed the examination for appointment to the New York City Police Department before the war.

Rothengast had left Fordham University in 1941, his junior year, to join the Army. He planned to join his brothers on the force as soon as the war was over: Conrad, the acting deputy chief inspector and com-

John Rothengast

manding officer of the Third Detective District; William, a detective on the Simpson Street Squad; and Joseph, a patrolman on the Emergency Squadron (*New York Times*, April 16, 1945).

"Our platoon had surrounded a little town, and he had gotten in and out safely," said Clinton Thompson. "I don't remember why, but he went back in and was shot by a sniper."

"We were short of ammo or something," said John Gorski. "Sgt. Rothengast went back to get some, and when he returned, they shot him in the head. His driver reached back to him, and when he looked at his hand it was covered with blood. It was pretty bad for him. Rothengast was one of my closest friends."

"Sgt. Rothengast was well-liked by the men," said Lou Gergley. "As supply sergeant, he always complained we used too much toilet paper. He said we should use both sides before we threw it away. He was a funny guy."

"He was a great story teller," said Gorski. "His whole family had been in law enforcement; he knew some great stories. Everyone missed him."

In a story written in the April 16, 1945, *New York Times*, Rothengast was credited with "designing and developing an important fire-control device for a cavalry weapon," an achievement that, according to the *Times*, earned him a Legion of Merit medal, although I was never able to confirm whether or not this was true.

April 3, 1945

April 3 was a deadly day for the 101st. Troop C and the 22nd Infantry Regiment tried once again to fight their way into Oesfeld. The troop managed to break through the outer defenses on the north end of town at about 10 a.m. Rockets hit two of Troop C's armored cars, and one man escaped. The others, however, were listed as missing.

The battle continued throughout the day, and shots from German and American guns echoed from the hills around the Tauber River. At the small town of Vilchband, about two miles from Oesfeld, a barrage of automatic weapon, small arms, panzerfaust, mortar, artillery and nebelwerfer fire forced the troop to withdraw to high ground just south of town. Some members of the 4th Infantry Division came up on the troop's right flank, but they were turned back as well. Several men were wounded in action that day: Tec 5 Samuel Berkowitz, S/Sgt. Nicholas Foley, Tec 4 Joseph Stepp, Tec 4 Donald Brown, all of Troop C; S/Sgt. Gordon Elder, Sgt. Harold Wilson, Tec 4 Charles Brown, all of Company F; and Tec 5 Rowell McHatten of Headquarters and Service Troop. First Lt. Raymond Paquette, attached to the 116th, was wounded, and he later died from his wounds. In addition to Paquette and Rothengast, Tec. 5 William Elliott and Tec 5 Theodore Evanko, both of C Troop, 116th Squadron, and PFC Ira McCarty, Company F, were killed in action.

In spite of the casualties and heavy fighting, the 116th Squadron was able to determine the outline of the German's main line of resistance between Gerlachsheim and Gulchsheim and force the Germans to reveal the presence of their artillery, mortars, and anti-tank weapons. This was a small victory.

In January, while still in England, Lt. Col. Leonard had written to his wife about the "great lovers," Capt. Francis Bages, 1st Lt. Raymond Paquette and 2nd Lt. Robert Schafer, who were away in London on a three-day leave. By the second day, Leonard wrote, they were broke and probably "raising whoopee." Now, of those three, only Bages remained alive.

Troop C was ordered to keep a lid on Oesfeld until the 12th Infantry Regiment had passed through the area, and Troop B had similar orders: keep the Germans contained in the vicinity of Simmringen until other units of the 12th Infantry Regiment (Combat Team 12) went through.

The day turned into one of moves and countermoves, as the troops provided reconnaissance or engaged in combat. The names of the towns — Simmringen, Ochsenfurt, Gerlachsheim, Gulchsheim, Stalldorf, Ollingen — pile onto one another in retelling the activities of the day. It requires a map and patience to sort out the troop advances and retreats.

By the end of the day, 75 prisoners of war were taken by Troop C, and a conservative estimate placed German dead at approximately 100.

Clinton Gosnell wrote that Troop C was up for a presidential citation for making the Germans at Oesfeld think there were more of them than there were and for keeping the Germans from counterattacking. But since their officer had been killed, and the rules state that an officer must be present to verify the action, no citation was allowed. Troop C would later receive a citation for another battle: Merkendorf.

Borotka said that the troop never did learn why the Germans had so violently defended the small town of Oesfeldt. They never got into the town, but they thought possibly it had supplies of munitions. It was the best reason they had.

April 4-6, 1945

For the next few days, the mission remained unchanged. Troop B was pushing eastward, then south toward Stalldorf, but because of the extremely difficult terrain and the strength of German resistance, progress was slow. At least one trooper, PFC Donald Brumfield, Headquarters, 116th Squadron, was killed in action on April 4.

On April 5, about 4:30 a.m., members of Troop C confirmed that one member of the missing tank crew, Tec 5 Irwin Thomas, had returned. He had spent more than a day hiding in a hay stack before he was able to get back to his unit.

Thomas reported that approximately 150 German soldiers were directly in the path of the 101st. He also said that he had seen 2nd Lt. Orville Hughes and Tec 4 McCarty, who had also been reported as missing. Unfortunately, they had been taken prisoner by the Germans and moved from the area.

During combat that day, Tec 5 Seymour Farber, Tec 5 John Lutchko, and PFC Roy Dryden, all of Troop C, 116th Squadron, were wounded in action.

Second Lt. William Andrew from Northfield, Vermont, had led a reconnaissance patrol of one platoon of mechanized cavalry into the German-held high ground west and southwest of Bad Mergentheim, trying to get a sense of the Germans' armored strength. He completed checking his assigned area and continued still deeper behind enemy lines to locate the bulk of their forces. Lt. Andrew discovered the German main line of resistance and learned that all approaches to it were impassable and all the bridges had been destroyed. By nightfall, he was also certain that the German Army still occupied the entire area in great strength.

As Lt. Andrew began to lead his platoon back to the line, German soldiers tried to close their withdrawal routes and, in the ensuing fire fight, Andrew was seriously wounded. For

The 116th Squadron enters a German town.
U.S. Signal Corps photo. Courtesy the National Archives.

leading his men back to camp, even though wounded, Lt. Andrew received the Silver Star.

By that night, the forward American units had reached the Unterbalbach-Harthausen line and broken it. Troop B, 116th, had moved through Stalldorf and Nassau by early morning of April 7, and by 11 p.m., the 116th Squadron was occupying the line Riedenheim-Gelscheim-Bolzhausen-Hopferstadt-Gnodstadt in sufficient numbers to prevent the Germans from breaking through. The Group now served as a moving screen and as the liaison between two units of the 4th Infantry Division: Combat Team 12 on the right (south), and Combat Team 8 on the left (north).

April 7, 1945

Working with the 92nd Cavalry Squadron, the 116th Squadron was ordered to conduct aggressive reconnaissance in the zone Waserndorf -Herbolzheim-Windsheim on the north and Waldsmanhofen-Grossharbach-Geslau on the south. Troops A and C of the 116th, each with attachments of one platoon of medium tanks, one platoon of light tanks, one platoon of assault howitzers, and one squad of engineers, found German resistance in their assigned area was strong, limiting the amount of reconnaissance they were able to do.

By nightfall, patrols from Troops A and C, 116th Squadron, had cleared the towns of Aufstetten, Lenzenbrunn, Baldersheim, and Ollingen. The Squadron Command Post of moved to Gelscheim at 1 p.m.

April 8, 1945

While attached to the 12th Armored Division, Troop C of the 101st Squadron was ordered to patrol up to the Aisch River, some thirty miles to the southeast in an area bounded on the west by Schaftersheim and Unter-Ostheim and on the east by Obernbriet and Lenkersheim.

Tec 5 Manuel Jimenez was seriously wounded in a battle that stopped the 116th Squadron from reaching the Gollach River, and the squadron ended up spending the night along a line that ran through Gulchsheim, Rodheim, Herrnberchtheim, and Ippesheim.

Later that night, when other units reached the Tauber and Gollach rivers, they found that all the bridges over the Tauber had been destroyed, delaying them even more. The Germans had not given up the fight by any means, and the cavalry now entered a race with the Germany Army, hoping to prevent them from getting far enough ahead to establish another line of resistance. Practically every one of the dozens of towns in the zone of advance had to be fought for, and the Germans frequently counterattacked with tanks and assault guns. Resistance was particularly strong along the lines of the Gollach, the Aisch, and the Zenn rivers.

In combat like the Cavalry now faced, they had to depend once again on their speed and agility. Their thin-skinned light tanks and armored cars were completely vulnerable to the tank guns of the Wehrmacht, and the 37mm guns mounted on their vehicles could not penetrate the thick plates of the German tanks. But the fast moving cavalry forces could dart in to locate the enemy and, if they could, overcome the resistance. If they could not, the heavier and more powerful 12th Armored Division Combat Commands' medium tanks and armored infantry could be called on to help.

April 9, 1945

Early in the morning of April 9, all units of the 101st Cavalry were back in action. Troop B, 101st Squadron, forded the Tauber River near Tauberretersheim and penetrated about a mile southeast into German defensive positions, including a strategically important hill, Hill 394, which was reminiscent of Hill 283 on the Saar River. Taking Hill 394 required fighting every step of the way.

Troop C of the 101st Squadron was putting pressure on the Germans at Burgerroth and Baldersheim, but were stuck, unable to move. Struggling in their own area, the 116th overcame stiff resistance to clear the towns of Gulchsheim, Rodheim, and Herrnberchtheim.

It began to look as if the German resistance would prove an insurmountable obstacle to the 101st, so the 12th Armored Division command decided to commit its Combat Command R to attack toward Ippesheim, Weigensheim, Pfaffenhofen, and Gattenhoffen, and from there to the northwest. The division's Combat Command B was also called in for a similar action.

The 101st Squadron withdrew from its position along the Tauber River and assembled in the vicinity of Geisslingen, where it would prepare to follow Combat Command R and continue on the reconnaissance mission.

The Germans were still mounting a strong defense along the Gollach River to the south, and the men of the 116th Squadron were sent to put as much pressure as they could on those positions. By nightfall on April 9, they were attacking Lipprichhausen and Geckenheim, a fight which continued all of that night and into the morning of April 10. That overnight struggle included counterattacks by the Germans against Gulchseim and Ollingin, which the 116th pushed back with minimal damage to their own equipment and no casualties.

April 10, 1945

On the morning of April 10, the 116th Squadron was stopped at Ippesheim by fierce resistance from the town and by German positions in the wooded hills to the east. Again, the troopers fought throughout the day and night, but made no headway.

Private William J. Harding, Troop B, 116th, from Johnstown, New York, was on a reconnaissance patrol in the vicinity of Lipprichhausen, when a few platoons of Troop B were held up by small arms fire. Although he opened himself up to increasing enemy fire, Private Harding stood at his machine gun and fired into the German positions, which gave a 10-man patrol of Troop B a chance to seek cover. For his actions that day, which undoubtedly saved the lives of members of the 116th, Private Harding received the Silver Star.

Also awarded the Silver Star for action on the same day was another member of the 116th's B Troop. PFC Theodore Price, who entered military service in High Point, North Carolina, was on patrol when he came under small arms fire. Price drove a machine gun bantam right into the line of fire, allowing the gunner in the car to cover a foot patrol as they ran for cover. It also gave the platoon time to reorganize, so that they could continue with their mission.

April 11, 1945

With barely any time for rest, all units of the 101st Cavalry Group renewed their attack at dawn on April 11. The 101st Squadron moved forward to protect the left flank of Combat Command R as it broke through at Ippesheim and moved southeast against continued strong resistance. At 10 a.m. the Group commander ordered a coordinated attack against Gollhofen, where the Germans were blocking the Cavalry's principle route south.

As units of the 116th Squadron continued to press the Germans at Baldersheim and Aub, just north of the Gollach River, the infantry stepped in to offer relief. Troop B continued its fight in Lipprichausen and Gollachostheim, and some time during the battle, Tec. 5 Morton Rodgers, B Troop, 116th Squadron, was killed in action. Troop A was pushing against Gelscheim as they moved toward Hemmersheim. Both troops were under heavy mortar fire throughout the day.

By 4 p.m., Troop C, 116th Squadron had reached the northern edge of Gollhofen. Entry from the northeast was blocked by destroyed bridges and German resistance. The commanding officer of Company F, 101st Squadron, moved his tanks and a platoon of B Troop to the northwest to help stop the attack from that direction. He maintained a base of fire with the remainder of his force, giving C Troop and platoons from the 101st Squadron the ability to enter the town. By 6:30 p.m., they reached the town center of the town in spite of increasing enemy fire.

"The main street of the town ended in a 'T' intersection," said David Levitas of C Troop. "When we got to the end, we had to turn left or right. Two Germans came running out of a building with their hands up, and we had been told that if any of them wanted to give up, to let them, so we did. At the end of the street, we came to this garden wall, and I jumped over it. I remember Carmine Garafano jumped over the wall and said, 'Hey, come on, let's go.'"

The men all started running, but at about the same time, the Germans fired a panzerfaust in their direction.

"We didn't even know what happened," said Levitas. "But that anti-tank shell hit Carmine. Some of the guys said they had just seen him laying back there on the ground and that he was dead."

Unable to hold the town through the night, the cavalry withdrew before dark.

"We had to leave Garafano's body there," said John Borotka. "We were afraid the body had been booby trapped."

"Three guys used to come to my house when we were stationed at Ft. Mead," said Levitas, "and my mom would cook for them: Johnny Boyorek, Theodore Evanko, Carmine Garafano. Only Johnny and I made it through the war."

During the night, the men in the command post were awakened by incoming fire from German tanks. In an instant they had moved from sleep to fighting for their lives in the dark. Eventually they were able to beat back the attack, but there would be little sleep the rest of that night.

April 12, 1945

At dawn the attack on the command post was renewed, this time by German jets. The troopers woke after a brief, restless sleep to bombs falling and a plane strafing the town.

As soon as possible, the 101st Squadron moved out, heading south through Neuherberg and toward Morlbach. They were now on the left flank of Combat Command R, 12th Armored Division, which had just broken through the German defenses in the area. At Morlbach, the 101st turned west and resumed patrols in the area. By dark, platoons in the front had reached the general line between the towns of Burgbernheim, Ottenhofen, and Wiebelsheim; however, German soldiers to the rear of the cavalry had been harassing the squadron supply route, making it difficult to get necessary supplies. The cavalry had to move back to Buchheim for the night and wait.

While the 101st Squadron was in Buchheim, the 116th was launching fresh attacks against Gollhofen, Lipprichhausen, and Hemmersheim, and by 2 p.m., these towns had been captured. A combat patrol from Troop C penetrated to within 400 yards of Uffenheim, but was driven off at dark by enemy small arms, mortar, and panzerfaust fire. Sometime during the night, Sgt. Charles Vacek, F Company, 116th, was killed in action.

A patrol reported that a lot of German vehicles were still moving into and around Uffenheim, and from their observation posts, Troops A and B saw that the enemy in the pocket formed by Combat Command R and the 116th Squadron were withdrawing and headed toward Uffenheim. The cavalry and

Map 10
April 13-17, 1945

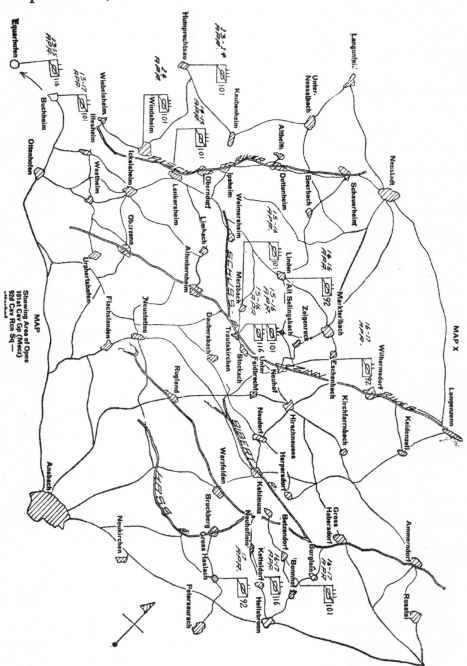

Combat Command R spent the night firing artillery into the town, as well as along the roads leading out of town.

April 13, 1945

Beginning at first light, the 101st Squadron, still firing into Uffenheim, had begun aggressive reconnaissance to the southeast against stiff enemy resistance. At 8:30 a.m., the burgermeister of Uffenheim sent word to the squadron that the German garrison had retreated more than six hours earlier. Elements of Troop C, 116th Squadron, entered the town at once, and headquarters troop, 101st Cavalry Group, quickly moved its command post from Ober-Ickelsheim to Uffenheim. The town was completely occupied by 11 a.m.

Near Illesheim, patrols of the 116th Squadron reported a concentration of German self-propelled guns and tanks at a camouflaged airfield, while in the vicinity of Pfaffenhofen two companies of German infantry supported by Mark V tanks attacked the 116th's squadron command. Again the men spent the hours of darkness engaged in battle.

As soon as they were able, men from the 116th Squadron moved rapidly southeast to the Adelshofen-Steinach line, but were unable to penetrate enemy defenses beyond that point. Troop A of the same squadron fought its way into Adelshofen, but was forced to withdraw, and Troop B was repulsed in every effort to by-pass enemy resistance at Steinach.

At 11 p.m. on April 13, verbal orders were received through the 12th Armored Division for the 101st Squadron to change assignment once again, this time with an attachment to the 4th Infantry Division. This would be effective April 14 at 4 a.m.

Between April 8 and 13, the 101st Cavalry had been responsible for reconnaissance of an area 19 miles wide and 16 miles deep. The German Army had not made this an easy mission for the men to achieve, and the troopers had needed to fight for every mile, capturing 384 prisoners of war and destroying large amounts of German materiel in the process. These successes had come with a cost, however. Five of their own had been killed during these few days and 21 had been wounded.

April 14, 1945

At 4 a.m., all elements of the 12th Armored Division and attached troops were alerted that they would be pulling out, starting at 6 a.m. It wasn't much notice for the 116th Squadron. They were to provide reconnaissance in an area bounded on the west by Highway 13 (Uffenheim-Ansbach-Gunzenhausen-Weisenberg) and on the east by Highway 8 (Langenfeld-Neustadt an der Aisch-Langenzenn). They would by-pass Nurnberg to the west and eventually head south on the autobahn.

Troop B of the 116th Squadron was attached to Combat Command R of the 12th Armored Division, and it headed in another direction.

The rest of the 116th Squadron, now minus Troop B, was attached to the 92nd Cavalry Squadron, 342nd Armored Field Artillery Battalion, and two platoons of medium tanks from the 43rd Tank Battalion. Their objective was the Ellingen-Hil-postein line, and they had orders to destroy any of the enemy who got in their way. The units moved forward with squadrons abreast: the 116th Squadron on the right, the 101st Squadron in the center, and the 92nd on the left. In order to avoid problems with the 12th Armored Division's Combat Commands, the main effort of these squadrons was directed to the center of the zone.

No serious resistance was encountered north of the Aisch River,

Earl Carmickle

Photo courtesy his daughter, Jeanette Carmickle Walsh.

but all the bridges had been destroyed. At 5 p.m., after a careful and detailed reconnaissance of the stream, members of the squadron forded near Lenkersheim and then over a bridge near Ippesheim that had been repaired by civilian labor. German automatic weapons fire from the high ground southeast of the river showered on the troopers as they continued their patrols on the south bank. By dark, forward units had reached Weimersheim and Ickelsheim, but withdrew to Lenkersheim for the night. Tec 5 Preston Kurth, A Troop, 116th Squadron, was killed sometime during the day.

Carmickle remembers one night on the push south through Germany when they were sent to hold one of the few bridges that the Germans hadn't already destroyed.

"We were told to hurry," he said. "We had to go through enemy territory and weren't to waste any time. We took two armored cars and two jeeps. We passed one German soldier who was asleep. We woke him up and took him prisoner. He said there were 20 other soldiers nearby, but we didn't want them. We wanted the bridge. When we got there, to the bridge, it was so cold that Sgt. Schnalzer wanted to build a fire. This one boy from Chicago told him, 'Don't you dare strike one match. I didn't come here to get captured by the Germans.'"

April 15, 1945

Except for Troop B of the 116th, the two squadrons of the 101st Cavalry Group resumed their attack at daylight on April 15, meeting strong resistance along the line between Weimersheim-Ickelsheim.

At 1 p.m. Troop A of the 92nd forced an opening in the enemy defense north of Weimersheim and pushed through the wooded areas, capturing the city of Linden at 3:30 p.m.

For most of the day, the 116th Squadron had been trapped northeast of Ickelsheim, unable to penetrate the enemy defenses along the high ground, but at 5 p.m., they managed to break away. They followed the 101st Squadron through the gap north of Weimersheim that had been opened by the 92nd.

From there, both squadrons moved rapidly southeast against light resistance and by night were scattered along the north bank of the Zenn River.

Abe Friedman

At some point after the Group broke through the gap at Weimersheim, Capt. Abe Friedman, Troop A, 101st Squadron, was ordered to take some men and find a place where the troops might bivouac for the night. One of the men with him was Lt. Erwin Perkins, who was a good friend. Theirs was an unlikely friendship, Perkin's wife told me. Friedman was born and raised in the Bronx and was Jewish. Perkins grew up as a Christian on a farm in the Midwest. But they became close friends during basic training, and stayed friends the rest of their lives.

On this particular day, Perkins took one vehicle and a couple of men, and Friedman had a driver and a radio man with him in a recon car.

After driving a while, they came to a fork in a gravel road. "I told Abe I'd go left and he could go right," said Perkins. "I didn't see him again until several years after the war."

An Army engineer was working on the road that Friedman took, so Friedman asked him if the road ahead had been cleared of land mines.

Capt. Abe Friedman
Photo courtesy his son, Lev Friedman.

"The Germans didn't put any mines here," the engineer said.

Capt Friedman didn't believe him, so he and his men proceeded with caution. It had been raining, and Friedman hoped the rain might have created depressions where mines were buried. As their truck crawled along the muddy road, Friedman watched for any sign of mines and occasionally raised his binoculars and scanned the fields and hills for German patrols.

About a mile and a half from the fork in the road, he spotted a farmhouse. Outside, a farmer about 60 years old and two children about 10 and 12 were working. This domestic scene convinced Friedman that the engineer had been right about the mines. He climbed back into the truck, confident the way ahead was clear. After traveling just a few minutes, a mine exploded under the truck, blowing Friedman out through the canvas roof and onto the ground.

In shock and temporarily blinded in one eye by gravel, shrapnel, and blood, Friedman began limping toward the farmhouse.

"I'm sorry about what happened," he told his men. "I'm going for help."

Capt. Friedman desperately needed to get to headquarters to find help for his men, but about halfway to the farmhouse the intense pain of his injuries brought him to his knees. He didn't realize it at the time, but he had suffered a compression fracture that merged the fourth and fifth vertebrae in his back and both legs were broken. Shrapnel was embedded throughout his body.

On his hands and knees, he continued toward the farmhouse until one of the children spotted him and got the farmer to help him go the rest of the way. The farmer put Friedman in a chair and washed off the blood and dirt, while Friedman struggled to communicate by speaking Yiddish. He asked the man to take him back to the American lines, but, afraid the Americans would shoot him, the farmer said no.

"I'm a captain," said Friedman. "They will reward you." He hoped the man would cooperate, but he was ready to draw his pistol if necessary. He had seen evidence that civilians were shooting captured American soldiers, so he was prepared to kill the farmer if he had to. In this case, the farmer cooperated; he got his horse and wagon and helped Capt. Friedman climb in.

"The bumpy ride in that wagon was agony for him," wrote Friedman's son, Lev Friedman. "After the farmer dropped him at headquarters, he took off like a shot, still afraid the Americans would kill him. My father never got to thank him."

The other two men, both severely injured, were quickly rescued. All the nerves had been severed in the leg of the driver, and the radio operator died of his wounds in the ambulance.

Following this event, Col. McClelland wrote to Friedman: "The officers here were distressed when word of your accident came in ... we were still in the town of Windsheim, I believe. I have never been informed definitely of the extent of your injuries, but understand that they were most serious and have led to your discharge. We have attempted to recognize your services by recommending you for the Bronze Star award which, we sincerely hope, will be approved by higher authority. You certainly deserve it, and the entire Group joins me in recognition of your courage, proficiency, and ability to do a job."

April 16, 1945

April 16 was a warm, clear day, and the troopers resumed the search for crossings over the Zenn and Schussenen rivers. The troopers dodged a hale of fire from the south bank as they moved along the north bank of the Zenn, hoping to find a bridge intact or one that could be easily repaired, or even a spot where fording might be possible.

At Trautskirchen they found one bridge across the Zenn that, although damaged, looked as if it would be the easiest to repair. The squadron concentrated on establishing a bridgehead there, and by 2:30 p.m. the strong enemy resistance south of Trautskirchen finally ended and a treadway bridge was constructed without delay. Troop C, followed by Troop A, both of the 116th, crossed the river and moved southwest to Danbersbach, capturing the town at 3:30 p.m. Both units then turned southeast and fought their way to Neudorf, where they broke through several defended roadblocks and arrived at 8:30 p.m.

∾ঙ৯

Lt. Col. Hubert Leonard

Lt. Col. Leonard was checking the recently repaired bridge near Trautskirchen, when he noticed Major Edward French, Captain Louis Bossert, and four enlisted men of Troop C heading downstream along the river bank.

His attention returned to the bridge, and after a short time, a barrage of small arms fire broke out, coming from the place around the river bend where the group of men had vanished. Leonard asked if anyone knew the source of the fire, but no one at the bridge knew anything about it. By that time, troops of the squadron had begun to cross the bridge, but none were moving in the direction of the firing. Lt. Col. Leonard attempted to call both Captain Bossert and Major French by radio, but couldn't reach them. Nor could he reach anyone who knew where they were.

He became increasingly certain that the men he had seen moving down the river were now the target of the firing. He immediately ordered the senior officer at the bridge to send him whatever troops were available, and he moved on foot and alone toward the firing until he could see what was happening.

Before he had gone far, Lt. Col. Leonard discovered Major French, Captain Bossert, and their men pinned in a ditch by heavy machine gun and small arms fire from a wooded hill a few hundred yards across the river.

Alone and easily seen by the Germans across the river, Col. Leonard checked the enemy position, attracting much of the fire to himself as he did so. A few minutes later, when a platoon of light tanks arrived, he went out to a point completely exposed to enemy fire and pointed out the enemy position to the tank platoon leader, directing the tanks into a firing position. He took charge of each additional element of his command as it pulled in, placing each one where its fire would be most effective, although he remained in the open, in full view of the Germans.

Leonard did not leave his position until he was sure they were finally overpowering the Germans, and the trapped reconnaissance party could escape from the ditch where they had been pinned down. His actions that day earned Leonard a Silver Star.

Lt. James Bobo and PFC Olaf Lupardus, Troop C, 116th Squadron, were killed the same day.

"Lt. Bobo was shot in the head," said Borotka. "When we came under fire, I got out of my armored car – I often elected to get under my car in such circumstances – and a round landed right where I was planning to lay."

Tec 4 Jack L. Swanson from Troop B, 116th Squadron, died around the same time. Lt. Borkowski remembers lying along the side of a road that day and watching a shell arc through the air and land on a half-track. "I saw Swanson get killed," he said. He tells this story at least once whenever we speak. Sometimes, in the middle of another story, he will just say, "I remember the day Swanson was shot."

෴

April 17, 1945

German strength in the vicinity appeared to be disintegrating, and, on April 17, the men met resistance only at certain crossings over the Bibert River. When the 116th Squadron crossed the river at Leonrod, they received heavy fire from the woods to the west. In their attempt to side-step the attack, the squadron shifted to the east, but was hit again at Kleinhaslach as they attempted to cross the Hasel Branch. Finally they were able to cross unopposed at Kehlmunz, less than a mile northeast.

At 5:30 p.m. the squadron attacked Heilbronn and, after entering the northern outskirts, was forced to withdraw by intense enemy automatic weapons, panzerfaust, and mortar fire.

Troop A was clearing towns in the area around Burghausen, Dornhausen, and Obersulzbach, and Troop B was patrolling toward Ansbach. Troop C blocked the line along the south edge of the wooded area from Anfelden to Horndu. They were hoping to cut off the retreat of German forces driven south by the attack of the infantry coming through the woods.

Since Oesfeld, pitched battles had continued day and night over a zone twenty miles wide and thirty-five miles long. Troopers who were there may have forgotten the names of Gulchsheim, Baldersheim, Uffenheim, Gelchheim, Aub and Burgeroth, if in fact they ever knew the names of the villages they were passing through, but they remember the fighting that took place there.

It was standard procedure, upon entering such towns, to summon the Burgermeister and have him be the one to tell all the town's citizens to turn in their weapons and cameras for confiscation.

Pierce said that they destroyed some of the most beautiful carved weapons he had ever seen. That was their assignment.

"We busted them against the back of trucks and threw armloads of them into trucks," he said. "Some of them had been in German families for generations. It was a shame."

If the unit was to remain overnight, the Burgermeister was told to arrange for billets in private homes, gasthauses, chateaus or whatever was available. The Group's interpreter, a German-speaking sergeant, was eventually wounded and evacuated, so it became difficult to transmit instructions to local officials. On one occasion, the Catholic chaplain, Father Powers, was called upon to converse in Latin with the local German priest.

The reaction of the German people varied considerably from a sullen attitude to one of friendliness (whether genuine or not). Rarely was there outright belligerence. Most were glad that the Americans and not the Russians had come. No one would admit to being a Nazi, although it was well-known that all the cities and towns were run by them.

Since spring was coming on, local farmers had more to think about than the war. It was plowing and planting time. "There was one old man out plowing in his field while a skirmish went on all around him," said Gay. "He didn't stop to look or even pause in his plowing."

For some time the troopers had been reporting the disintegration of not only the Wehrmacht, but of the entire German nation, as the Allies closed in on the German heartland from both directions. Hitler's divisions, with few exceptions, were down to less than one-third strength, wrote Sweeney in *Wingfoot*. Added to their ranks had been thousands of school-age boys and old men unfit for battle.

Factories had been destroyed and supply lines cut. Many of the troopers held a grudging respect for the way the soldiers in the German army continued to resist with as much skill as they did, even though it was also apparent that many others were losing their will to resist. The exception was Hitler's SS Troops, many of whom continued the fight with zeal.

April 18-19, 1945

At 4:30 a.m. Headquarters 12th Armored Division, to which the 101st Cavalry Group was attached, ordered a change in the direction of advance from southeast to the southwest, a change

Map 11
April 18-19, 1945

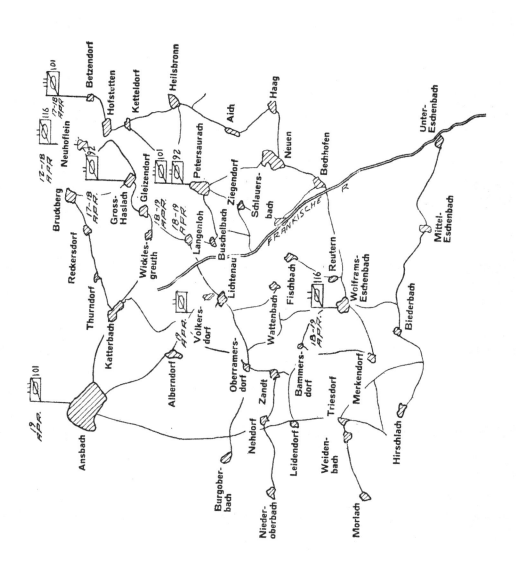

of ninety degrees. The new axis of advance was to be Ansbach-Feuchtwangen-Crailsheim. Twelfth Armored Division's Combat Command B was directed to move to the southwest and seize and secure Feuchtwangen, while Combat Command A was ordered to follow Combat Command B and occupy Ansbach. The 101st Group moved on all available routes to protect the south flank of Combat Command B and assist it in the attack on Feuchtwangen.

Beginning at first light on April 18, the 116th, operating on a southeasterly axis, had passed through Petersaurach and Ziegendorf against light enemy resistance. The bridge over the Frankische River at Schlauersbach was seized intact by Troop A of the 116th. Following the seizure of the bridge, Troop A, followed by Troop C, moved rapidly south until it got as far as Wolframs-Eschenbach, where it won a determined fight for that town. Troop A then moved southwest, bypassing Merkendorf and entering Triesdorf without opposition.

By nightfall, things changed, and the 116th Squadron ran into strong resistance along the high ground north of Berbersbach in the vicinity of Buch a Wald-Jochsberg.

To avoid another battle, Troop A and C bypassed this area and continued to the southeast, only to be stopped again along the railway line from Ansbach to Crailsheim by defensive positions of Germans supported by mortar and artillery fire.

Meanwhile, Troop C of the 101st Squadron ran into trouble at the small town of Schoffloch and could not break through. The medium tanks and armored infantry of Combat Command A were called in to help, and they quickly overran the German defense. The 101st moved on, but soon hit another wall at Wildenstein. Troop C slipped around the town and came up on the German rear. Lt. Col. Kendall formed Task Force Brock (Maj. Henry Brock, executive officer), consisting of his B Troop (101st Squadron) and B Troop of the 116th. After a three-hour attack coming from both directions, the resistance was finally broken.

By now, forward units of the 12th Armored and the 101st were approximately sixty miles from the Danube River. It had become clear from Intelligence sources that the Germans planned to leave strong delaying forces north of the river while using the main force to build up well-placed defensive positions south of the river. It was anticipated that bridges over the river would be prepared for demolition. Under the circumstances, speed was critical. If resistance held up the advance, they would bypass it when possible. It wasn't always possible.

A drawing of the events in Merkendorf, reprinted from Wingfoot. *The caption on the drawing read: "Merkendorf ... the CP door was blown in with panzerfaust fire and then they came through the windows screaming, 'SS' ... the darkened room lighted momentarily from the muzzle blast of a roaring 'grease gun' ...*

Illustration by Captain Crozier Wood.

Merkendorf

In the territory of the Tauber and Danube rivers, the battle grew in intensity. Sometimes it took the cavalrymen three or four days of steady fighting to break through the German defenses. The violence peaked in the small town of Merkendorf, where the SS made a night counterattack.

Troop C of the 116th Squadron; first platoon of Company F, a tank company; and third platoon of Troop E were assigned to hold the town of Merkendorf, located astride the German supply route southeast of Ansbach.

The town was an important target for the Americans, as it was meant to serve as protection for the operations of the 12th Armored Division near Nurnberg and Ansbach. Even though the troopers had advanced fifty-five miles in the past sixteen days, fighting in six major engagements while doing so, they still pushed forward aggressively against nearly constant fire from German artillery.

"Merkendorf was a railroad hub," said Tec 5 David Levitas. "When we got there, the Germans had nothing left. They had been falling back faster than we could keep up. That's why we were so surprised when they came back at Merkendorf."

Entering Merkendorf, Troop C ran headlong into SS troopers of the 17th Panzer Grenadier Division and the SS Totenkopf Division, and their progress slowed to a crawl as the men fought for one house at a time. As night came, the Americans had control of the town and were billeted for the night in houses and barns. The SS withdrew to the surrounding woods, settling in to protect their supply route and to harass the cavalry with artillery fire on all the roads into town, as well as on the town itself.

Sometime during the night of April 18, the civilians in Merkendorf let the German soldiers know where the Americans were billeted and pointed out the strong points of the American command. Then, in the darkness of early morning, around 4:30 a.m., April 19, 150 SS troops overran the town, screaming "SS" as their battle cry. They surprised the unit outposts on the southern and eastern edges of the town and fired panzerfausts and machine pistols into vehicles and houses where they believed the troopers were resting. Fortunately, the troopers had considered just such a possibility and had changed billets after dark.

"I woke up and looked out the window to see German helmets going up the street," said Levitas. "They were burning our vehicles as they went. They had just been waiting for us to tuck ourselves in, I guess."

"I was out on watch in a foxhole from 2 to 4 a.m.," said John Borotka. "We felt something was going on, but we didn't know what it was. We were just glad to be relieved and able to go to bed. I had just gone upstairs and taken my boots off when I heard a commotion down the street. I saw a panzerfaust firing from up on the top of one of the houses. I heard someone call out in German, and then the bottom of a house blew out. We saw a jeep coming down the street and we challenged it. The men in the jeep didn't respond, so we fired and hit it.

John Borotka

Thank goodness no one was hurt; it was one of ours. The jeep was destroyed. We lost a lot of vehicles in Merkendorf."

"About nine of us walked out and went the wrong way and ran right into them," said Levitas. "Borotka and his guys were across the street – they went the right way. I was wounded in the foot and several of us were captured. I'm Jewish, so I buried my dog tags in the sand."

"Buck Weaver and me had our rifles shooting, shooting," said Borotka. "Must have cut the German soldier in half I shot so many times."

Trying to organize an effective battle plan under the circumstances was impossible, so the men did what they could in

Map 12
April 20-22, 1945

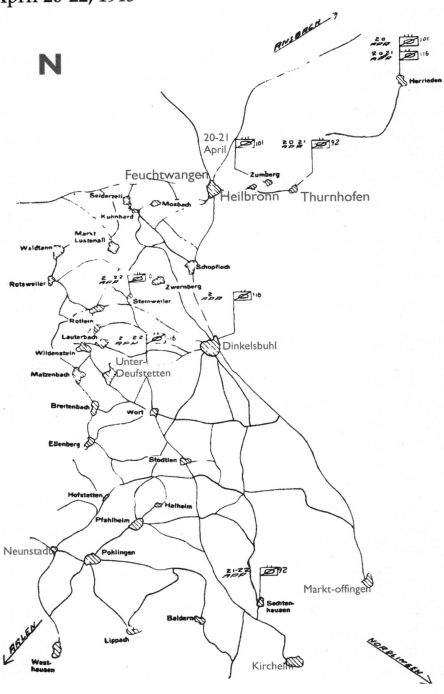

N

ANSBACH ?

20 APR | 101
20-21 APR | 116

Herrieden

20-21 April

101

20-21 APR | 92

Feuchtwangen

Zumberg

Heilbronn

Thurnhofen

Seiderzell

Masbach

Kuhnhard

Markt Lustenall

Waldtann

Schopflach

Rotsweiler

2 22 APR | 0

Zwernberg

Steinweiler

2 APR | 116

Rotlein

Lauterbach

2 22 APR | 116

Dinkelsbuhl

Wildenstein

Unter-Deufstetten

Matzenbach

Breitenbach

Wort

Ellenberg

Stadtlen

Hofstetten

Halheim

Pfahlheim

Neunstadt

Pohlingen

21-22 APR | 92

Markt-offingen

Sechtenhausen

AALEN

Baldern

Lippach

Westhausen

Kircheim

NÖRDLINGEN

small groups. The outnumbered survivors of the attack seized their weapons and defended themselves in what was described later as "fierce and bloody fighting." Running quickly out of ammunition, the men resorted to using knives and bare fists against the SS, struggling for their lives in hand-to-hand combat inside pitch dark rooms and in narrow streets strewn with rubble. Some men were wounded as they dove for cover in the streets.

"One of our men was out there," said Borotka, "and I went to find him. He was hiding behind a wood pile, so I brought him in. He was okay, but he was real scared. There was a German machine gun across the street."

The men in the command post were out of ammunition and surrounded by the SS. They had nothing they could do but surrender. They tossed their weapons to the ground and raised their hands. As they stood there defenseless, the SS shot them all.

Along with Levitas, the Germans also captured Tec 5 David Petras, PFC Clarence Leonard, Pvt. Michael Doolittle, and Harold Huddleston.

Levitas, who had been wounded in the foot, was carried out of town on a stretcher, with a German soldier at one end and another captured cavalryman at the other.

"The guy carrying me had been hit in the helmet and had a huge lump on his head," said Levitas. "He had been knocked out at first, but he kept saying he was okay."

Many of the men who had fallen in the street were only wounded, but stayed where they were, feigning death in the hopes the Germans would not check too closely.

"They asked me where my buddies were," said Levitas, "and I told them that they were all dead. 'See them laying there in the street,' I told them."

One man, however, couldn't stay down.

"Carl Moore was an extremely pleasant guy," said Levitas, "but he didn't have the sense to just lay still. He jumped up and ran, and they shot and killed him."

Around 7 a.m. the next morning, as daylight broke, the troopers slowly came together from their scattered locations around town.

"In the morning I saw the German soldiers that we had killed laying there in the field," said Borotka.

As the cavalrymen regrouped and searched the town for SS, German reinforcements counterattacked from the southeast. This time, however, by rapidly forming their ranks, the troopers had greater success. In spite of the severe losses in comrades and equipment – or perhaps because of it – Troop C pushed forward with renewed energy, sending artillery fire everywhere they knew the German soldiers to be and holding on to the small, but strategically important, village of Merkendorf.

Approximately 150 Germans had attacked that day, and of that number, 80 were killed and 26 were captured. The remainder fled. In addition to Carl Moore, Tec 5 Harold L. Turk died in Merkendorf. Among the wounded in Troop C were 1st Lt. Louis Mayes, Sgt. William Claxton, PFC Lonnie Weaver, PFC Edward L. Moss, PFC Clarence Leonard, PFC Morris Winick, and PFC Frank Terrell. Company F's 1st Lt. Francis Reale, PFC Herbert Summers, PFC Edward Garbarski were also wounded in action.

In addition, six armored cars, three quarter-ton trucks, two assault howitzers, one half-track, and four light tanks were destroyed in the battle at Merkendorf.

Troop C was decimated by this loss of men and equipment, and Lt. Col. Leonard reorganized it into two platoons instead of the normal three.

In recommending the unit for a Presidential Unit Citation, Brigadier General John Willems wrote, "The gallant performance of these men under the constant and at times intense enemy pressure and against great odds coupled with the conspicuous heroism and courageous determination of each member are in keeping with the highest traditions of military service."

For their actions on April 19, two men received the Silver Star: Sgt. William Claxton of Columbia, Missouri, and Cpl. Louis Peele from Chicago.

Sgt. Claxton was seriously wounded, but when he saw some of his men were in danger, he crawled more than 200 yards under heavy fire to save them.

Cpl. Louis Peele, Troop E, 116th Squadron, and two other men were attacked by about 30 SS troops, who were undetected to within an arm's length of the cavalry under the cover of the dark night and the explosive noise of the burning town. Cpl. Peele refused the German's repeated demands to surrender, and while engaged in hand-to-hand combat in the darkness, he mounted a self-propelled howitzer and fired back. Making use of a carbine, grenade, and 50-caliber machine gun, Peele was going to throw everything he had into the darkness.

Louis Peele
Photo courtesy his son, Bruce Peele.

Finally a panzerfaust hit his howitzer and destroyed it. Although wounded in the right shoulder and in the leg, Cpl. Peele continued to hold his post under repeated attacks and small-arms, machine gun, and panzerfaust fire until reinforced by the remainder of his platoon. Together the cavalrymen forced the enemy to withdraw and abandon their attack.

෴

After the attack on Merkendorf, Levitas spent several days in a hospital in Speert.

"It was an old beer garden," he said. "First they had put us in a little barn-like structure for about three days. Then they said they'd put me in the hospital, but they were taking Eddie, who'd been hit in the helmet, with them. I told them he'd been hurt, but they said there was nothing wrong with him."

Levitas spoke to the Germans in Yiddish, which he said he could make sound more like German. It worked. They were pleased that he could speak their language.

"My mother is German," he told them. He believes that getting rid of his dogtags and speaking to them in German may have been what saved him.

At the hospital, food was scarce. "We ate carrot soup and moldy bread," he said, "but one of the nurses did bring me some milk. It was the first glass of milk I had had in a long time."

Levitas was liberated a few days later, and by May 5, he was in a hospital in Paris.

Troop B, 116th Squadron : April 14-20, 1945

For six days, the history of my father's troop, Troop B, 116th Squadron, veered off from the rest of the outfit. Attached to Combat Command R, 12th Armored Division, they headed toward Ansbach, following the main highway from Uffenheim. The troop's advanced patrols operated toward the south on the highway about six miles east and slightly south of Habelsee.

Their job was to watch the enemy, so observation posts were set up by day and listening posts by night from Steinach to Endsee. On April 16, they received orders to move to an area near Illesheim and secure the flanks and rear of both advancing columns of the Combat Command, which had left the highway and were advancing on Ansbach from the north, parallel to the main north-south highway.

At one point during their advance, the men came under fire. Charlie Kashuba jumped into a foxhole, followed closely by Borkowski, who landed on top of him.

"That's okay, Lieutenant," Kashuba told Borkowski, who was making a nice cover, "you just stay right there."

"Sometimes," he said, "we were as frightened as all get out. One night I dug a hole under my armored car so I could get some sleep. It offered some protection."

Although the men joke about the fear they were feeling, it was still a part of every day, and it made some men take extreme measures to avoid facing it.

Borkowski remembers one man who shot off his finger, hoping that would be his ticket home. He doesn't condemn the man. "It wasn't easy," he said. "We were frightened a lot of the time."

Several men have told me about a lieutenant fresh out of West Point who shot himself in the foot so he could go home.

One night, Borkowski and about a dozen of his men were sleeping in a barn when a low rumbling woke them up. Borkowski looked outside and saw a column of Germans passing by. The equipment shook the ground as the roar of engines became louder and louder. "We were afraid all right," he said, "but all we could do was wait it out."

One thing that helped ease their fear a little was knowing they could trust their leaders. This wasn't always a comfort.

Eugene Tharp and the rest of his platoon were spending the night in a house on one side of a field; a number of German soldiers were in the woods nearby.

"We saw a bunch of U.S. soldiers heading toward us across the field," Tharp said. "We didn't know what unit they were with, but they had four-leaf clovers on their shoulders. If they came into that field, we could see they were going to get it from the Germans, so my captain and lieutenant told me to go across and tell them to stay out of the field. If they came in, they'd lose men."

Tharp made it to the Americans – most likely members of the 4th Army – and delivered his message to the officer in charge.

"Then I made it back across the field and into the house just in time to hear my captain say, 'Here they come. That smart boy is bringing them across.' Sure enough," said Tharp, "the officer had disregarded the warning and was bringing his men into the field. They lost a lot of their men that day."

"Some officers were good; some were bad," said John Gorski. "We had one first lieutenant, Lt. Mann, who was so good. I don't know why he was just a lieutenant; for crissakes, he should have been at least a captain."

Tharp tells a story about both kinds of officers. "We were supposed to spend one day on point, and I had been out for two days and nights. This second lieutenant who was new and right out of basic training told me I had to stay for another day. I told him no, that I'd been out there for two days already."

He said, "Do you know that you are disobeying orders?"

"Yes, I do," Tharp told him. "So he took me to the captain, who asked me, 'What did you do now?'"

Tharp explained to the captain what had happened, and the captain paid attention to what he had to say.

"Then he chewed out that lieutenant and told him, 'You better listen to this kid,'" said Tharp. "That lieutenant didn't last long – four or five days. Some of those guys, they didn't know anything."

One officer was relieved of his command in front of a group of men that included Robert Klein.

"A bunch of Germans were hiding in some caves on the side of a hill," said Klein. "Instead of calling for a more heavily armed unit, our task force commander ordered us to attack. We had no business attacking them, and we were in trouble. We heard a roar of airplanes and, luckily for us, we saw the scarlet tail of the French planes. They were diving right into the hill. Then a general's jeep pulls up next to us, and a two-star gener-

Ted Welch and Lusher.
Photo courtesy Frederick Altizer.

al asks me who was in charge. I pointed to the task force commander, and the general relieved him right there. I had never seen anyone relieved of their command right on the spot."

April 21, 1945

At 12:45 a.m. on April 21, the 116th Squadron moved to Dinkelsbuhl, and the 101st Squadron, whose advance wasn't going so well, was spread out slightly south of there. From the moment the squadron had crossed the road between Neustadt to Dinkelsbuhl on its southern march, it had been challenged.

The squadron struggled unsuccessfully to penetrate the enemy defenses at Wildenstein or Lauterbach, so to help them, Troop C slipped to the west and then turned southeast to Unter-Drefstatten, putting them behind the enemy line.

Task Force Brock was formed (Troop B, 116th Squadron and Troop B, 101st Squadron) to eliminate the troublesome resistance in the hole that Troop C vacated. The combined pressure of the task force from the north and Troop C from the south broke the German centers of resistance. By nightfall on April 21, the squadron had finally advanced about six miles to the west, near the Matzenbach-Unter-Deufstetten, line.

The 116th Squadron – except for Troop B, which was still near Unter-Deufstetten – remained at Dinkelsbuhl in reserve throughout the day, leaving around 5 p.m. for Unter-Deufstetten and arriving before dark.

At 11 p.m. that night, the Danube River became the main target of the cavalry. The 12th Armored Division ordered an advance of more than 20 miles along a broad front – approximately 50 miles wide – to secure the bridges over the Danube between Markt-Hustenau and the line of the main highway.

April 22, 1945

The 101st Squadron had been clearing German resistance from the woods south of Unter-Deufstetten, and it was now directed to move south through Lauchheim and mop up enemy resistance along the Lauchheim-Bopfingen Road, then continue south to the Danube River and seize crossings in the vicinity of Lauingen.

Hurrying to reach the Danube while its bridges were still intact, the squadron ran into trouble near Lauchheim, but they received help from Combat Command R. Once the area was clear, they began a night march, and by 11:30 p.m. they occupied Lauingen. None of it mattered. The German soldiers had destroyed all bridges over the Danube just moments before they arrived. They actually heard the blast that destroyed the bridge at Erlinghoffen, which was only two miles away.

As they tried to reach the bridge in Dillingen, the men of the 101st Squadron became embroiled in a strong battle to keep them away. While they fought the Germans just outside of town, the 12th Armored Division's Combat Command A

Map 13
April 22-23, 1945

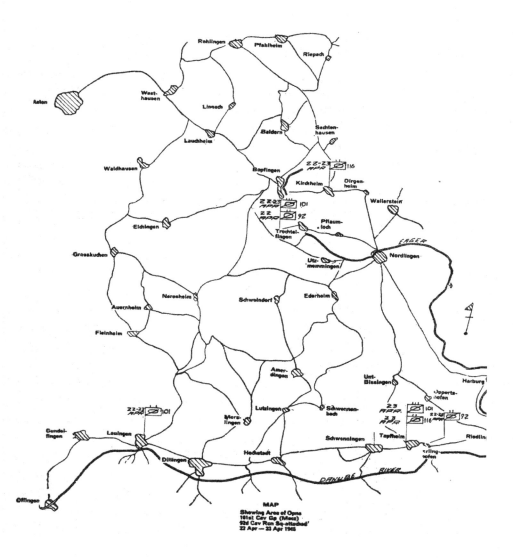

MAP
Showing Area of Opns
101st Cav Gp (Mecz)
92d Cav Rcn Sq-attached'
22 Apr — 23 Apr 1945

entered Dillingen, and, to their surprise, were able to capture the city's main bridge intact.

April 23, 1945

The 101st Squadron stayed in Lauingen throughout the cold, rainy day of April 23, except for one task force that left at 10 a.m. hoping to seize the bridge at Offingen about six miles to the southwest. The task force moved along secondary roads as quickly as possible, but the bridge had been destroyed by German bridge guards before they could get there.

Troop B, 116th Squadron, was deployed near Oppertshofen, and its progress was impeded by undefended roadblocks and demolitions, which could be cleared fairly rapidly. The German rear guard did all they could to keep the cavalry from reaching the plain of the Danube River, while at the same time covering the withdrawal of the Germans across the river at Erlingshofen. The Americans countered this defense with artillery fire directed at the retreating German columns. The 116th Squadron finally fought its way into Tapfheim and Erlingsofen around 8 p.m. The cavalrymen weren't going to get much rest; the boom and roar of artillery kept them awake and on edge throughout the night.

April 24, 1945

On April 24, Troop B, 116th Squadron, was relieved of its duty to Task Force Brock and rejoined the squadron, which was now on the north side of the Danube.

One cavalry squadron was now moving southwest along the south bank ahead of Combat Command B, and the other squadron was leading Combat Command R along the north bank.

At 4 p.m., the 101st Squadron was on its way to the Mindel River, again to capture bridges before they could be destroyed. At the same time, they searched for additional crossings on the

Danube. They ran into a group of German soldiers west and southwest of Gundelfingen, slowing their progress even more. The flat and marshy nature of the terrain would have made maneuvering armored vehicles extremely difficult even without the added problem of an aggressive enemy.

Troop C of the 116th Squadron had fought its way into Burgau and seized the causeway and bridges that spanned the Mindel River there. Troop A continued south and seized the autobahn crossings over the river less than a mile away. Both units held their respective crossings through the night, even though the Germans continued their attempts to sneak demolition parties through the cavalry lines.

It was here along the autobahn that the 116th squadron made one of many remarkable discoveries they were to stumble across over the next few days. Hidden in a large, wooded area were several hundred jet aircraft in various stages of completion. The men suspected that the airplanes had been moved from aircraft factories in the vicinity of Munich to avoid Allied bombing. Several of the soldiers stopped long enough to snap a photo, and then they were on their way again.

The 101st Squadron, moving to the left of the 116th, encountered dug-in enemy defenses supported by the dreaded 88mm anti-aircraft guns used effectively as anti-tank guns. At the same time the 63rd Infantry Division on the right flank of the 12th Armored Division was fighting off a day-long German counterattack. It was apparent that the Germans were building up another main line of resistance along the general line of the autobahn.

April 26, 1945

Reveille sounded early on April 26, and the 116th Squadron moved out at 6 a.m. They probably would have moved out even earlier if a major traffic jam of heavy equipment hadn't been blocking the road. It took some time before an orderly progression for the march was created, and the platoons were able to march out according to plan: first was Troop C; then Headquarters followed by Medical Detachment; then Troops A, B, E, Company F, and the Rear Echelon. German planes strafed them as they moved toward the bridge over the Danube, where, still under fire, they crossed at 7 a.m. and assembled at Aislingen. Four men from Troop B were wounded by mortar fire during that time: Tec 5 Lee Rest, PFC Charlie Frazier, PFC William Campbell, and PFC Hal Strange (Troop C).

The cavalrymen discovered German airplanes hidden in the woods.
Photo courtesy of Edith Holloman.

"A lone German fighter plane was flying over our line on a wooded ridge we were holding for a day," said Clair Becker. "He was flying at tree top level, and I could see his face in the cockpit. I was standing by the ring mounted .30-caliber machine gun on an armored car. By the time I got the gun around to fire, he was gone with one of our own P47s after him."

At 7:30 a.m., Troops A and B of the 116th relieved the 92nd Squadron from its positions on bridges crossing the Mindel River at Burgau and on the autobahn about one-half mile to the south. Troop C moved east along the autobahn, meeting resistance in the wooded areas about two miles east of Scheppach.

The 101st Squadron moved forward between Glott and Zusmarshauen, and at 8 a.m. scouts in the lead encountered determined resistance along the Zusam River at Baiershofen and Ellerbach. After a long fight, the enemy positions were reduced and the squadron slipped to the east bank of the Zusam River and turned south. They made good progress until fierce opposition from entrenched German soldiers, who were supported by 88mm guns and 40mm anti-aircraft guns, stopped the squadron's progress north of the autobahn near Zusmarshausen. After a prolonged and bitter battle, the enemy was driven from this position. Units to the front of the squadron moved southeast against continuing opposition, and they reached Kutzenhausen at dark.

At 9 p.m. the 101st squadron was directed to continue to the south and seize the bridges over the Wertach River at Gross-Aitingen. They continued until they were stopped by enemy small arms, automatic weapon, mortar and artillery fire from positions on the wooded high ground southeast of the line Fischach-Diedorf.

At 2 p.m. that afternoon, a combat patrol of the 116th Squadron, operating east of Ziemetshausen, intercepted a courier from the 17th SS Corps. He was carrying classified documents and a map marking German locations. He was also carrying the plans for a coordinated counterattack by three divisions against the Leipheim-Gunzburg bridgehead and had information that a fourth division was in the area. The courier was taken to headquarters, where he told the Americans that the Germans' left boundary along the Mindel River was not clearly defined. On the chance that the boundary might not be strongly defended, the 92nd Squadron headed down the river valley, followed by the 116th Squadron. The hunch paid off. They broke through the German line there with relative ease. Soon both squadrons were operating behind the German front.

At 3 p.m. Troop A, 116th Squadron, was relieved of its mission near Burgau and moved east to Rosshaupten, then south, joining forces with Troop C at the autobahn. The two troops cleared the heavily wooded area of German soldiers, uncovering hundreds more German airplanes and even an underground airplane parts factory.

Led by Troop B of the 116th, the race resumed to the Wertach River at Hiltenfingen and Siebnach in order to secure the bridgeheads there. At 8 p.m. the bridge near Hiltenfingen was seized intact, and the squadron pushed on into the town against disorganized resistance. By 9:20 they had secured two additional bridges over smaller streams and captured the town.

As the 101st Squadron continued to fight off counterattacks southeast of the Fischach-Diedorf line, the 116th began its move to the Lech River ten miles to the southeast, hoping to capture the bridges in the vicinity of Landsberg. Both squadrons reached the Lech in record time, only to have all bridges along the river blow up in their faces.

Map 14
April 24-27, 1945

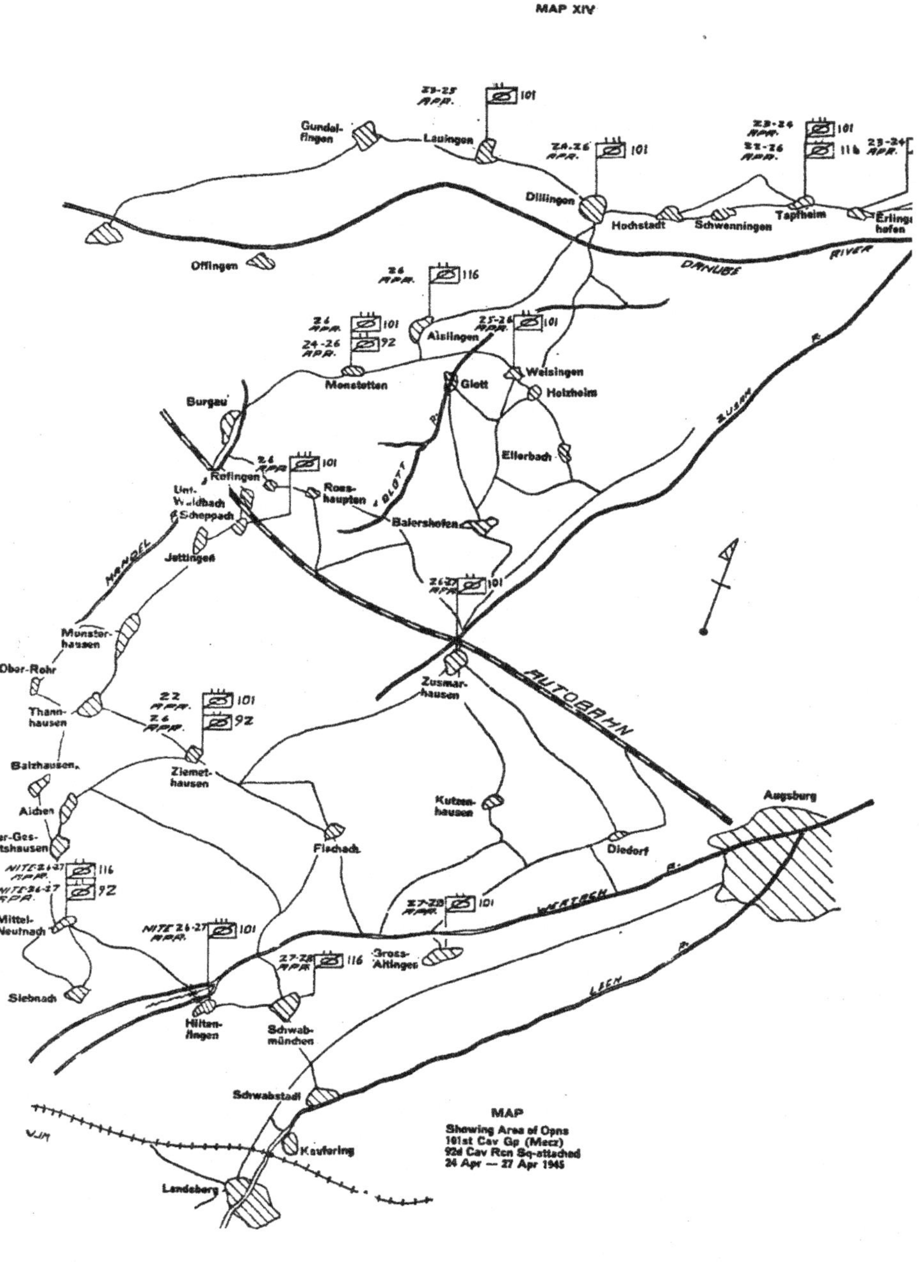

MAP XIV

23-25
APR. 101

Gundel-
fingen
Lauingen

24-26
APR. 101

23-24
APR. 101

22-26
APR. 116

23-24
APR.

Taptheim
Erling-
hofen

Dillingen

Hochstadt
Schwenningen

Offingen

24
APR. 116

DANUBE RIVER

24
APR. 101

24-26
APR. 92

25-26
APR. 101

Aislingen

Weisingen

Monstetten

Glott
Holzheim

Burgau

Ellerbach

24
APR. 101

Refingen

Roes-
haupten

ZUSM R.

Unt-
Waldbach
Scheppach

Baiershofen

BLOTT

Jettingen

26-27
APR. 101

AUTOBAHN

Munster-
hausen

Ober-Rohr

MINDEL

Zusmar-
hausen

Thann-
hausen

22
APR. 101

24
APR. 92

Balzhausen

Ziemet-
hausen

Kutzen-
hausen

Augsburg

Aichen

Ober-Ges-
sertshausen

Fischach

Diedorf

NITE 26-27
APR. 116

NITE 26-27
APR. 92

WERTBACH R.

Mittel-
Neufnach

NITE 26-27
APR. 101

26-28
APR. 101

27-28
APR. 116

Gross-
Altingen

Siebnach

LECH R.

Hilten-
fingen

Schwab-
münchen

Schwabstadt

MAP
Showing Area of Opns
101st Cav Gp (Mecz)
92d Cav Rcn Sq-attached
24 Apr — 27 Apr 1945

Kaufering

Landsberg

Landsberg 2006

Landsberg am Lech

Landsberg is a small Bavarian town west of Munich famous for its prison, where, in 1924, Adolph Hitler wrote *Mein Kampf*. Following the Nazi Party Congresses of 1937 and 1938, the town became a pilgrimage site for Hitler youth, who staged "Adolph Hitler Marches" to visit Hitler's prison cell and receive copies of his book.

Most members of the 101st Cavalry Group couldn't have imagined what they would discover in Landsberg. Even after two months of watching mines and bullets shred the bodies of their friends, a new horror was waiting for them. All my father had said of those camps was that he couldn't believe people could do such things to each other. Other men I talked to tried to describe what they saw, but often found they didn't have the words. I wanted to visit the site of these camps, but it was hard to get much information about them. Unlike Dachau or Auschwitz, no tour buses go to the cluster of camps near Landsberg.

It helped when I learned the camps were more familiarly known by the name of another nearby village: Kaufering. Once I began searching for camps using that name, I found a website commemorating the 20th anniversary of a memorial at Kaufering VII. I sent an e-mail to the contact listed, and several weeks later received a response and an apology from Anton Possett, who wrote that he spoke no English, so had needed time to translate both my e-mail and his response.

Herr Possett suggested Ted and I meet with him in Landsberg, his hometown, and he would show us around. This became the most eagerly anticipated part of the trip for me. I hadn't been able to learn much about the camps, except for what was written on Herr Possett's website, and I was eager to hear more. Ted's ability to translate would be extremely useful now.

Members of a 101st Calvary recon mission were among the first to discover these camps, with their charred and emaciated bodies smoldering in the ruins of prison barracks.

While walking through the woods on a scouting mission, members of Troop B stumbled on a freight train loaded with the dead and dying and released about 2,400 of those who were strong enough to walk. This wasn't the only such train they found, but many of the others had no survivors. They were filled only with the dead, beyond hope of rescue. Ted and I were bracing ourselves for a difficult visit.

We called Herr Possett as soon as we arrived at our hotel. At first we agreed to meet the next day, but then he suggested that he just drop by that evening, show us some pictures and discuss what we would see the next day. We were tired, but agreed. The next four hours were fascinating, educational, and horrific, and Herr Possett would contribute personally to all three.

"He seemed okay on the phone and he seemed okay again for the first few minutes of the car ride," Ted wrote in his journal, "and then as a sort of icebreaker, I thought it would be nice to tell him I thought Landsberg was a pretty town. That's when he started yelling at me."

Ted doesn't overstate Possett's demeanor. He did start yelling, and he didn't stop yelling for four hours. I still see him, a tall man with wavy gray hair, a short gray mustache no wider than his nose, and sky blue eyes, stabbing his finger repeatedly toward my son, shouting. Our plan had been that Ted would translate, but, even though I kept saying, "What, what," Possett never paused. I would pick up words here and there that I understood – numbers, references to places or to my father's unit – but it was still difficult to follow. When we compared notes later, Ted assured me that I had gotten the gist of the message. He wrote about the experience in his journal.

> Herr Possett would not shut up. I never could get a word in edgewise to translate for Mom. As near as I could tell, he hit the same few subjects in cycles of 10 to 15 minutes:
>
> 1. The Holocaust as a moral system was primarily about power relationships, not necessarily about German hatred of Jews, but about one human being allowed to command another to march in the snow.
>
> 2. Your average German citizen knew damn good and well what was going on in this camp and others like it. He pointed out to us on several occasions how close the road was to the camp and how close the camp was to the railway line.
>
> 3. He obviously had plenty to say about our current stateside president, who in his opinion will never measure up to other great American presidents like Eisenhower and Clinton.
>
> 4. Nobody – especially the city of Lands-

berg or the Jews – helped him out with the bills or helps him mow the lawn. In all fairness, he has clearly put a lot of work and money into the memorial, but of all the subjects he wouldn't shut up about, this is the one that he wouldn't shut up about the most. Nobody pitched in for the €100,000 field or the €10,000 headstones and he had to dig holes for the foundations and pour the foundations for the headstones.

Like Ted, I was uncomfortable with the way Possett was shouting, but how he talked about the Jews went beyond creating mere discomfort, especially considering where we were standing. His grandfather had died in Dachau, so I asked if he were Jewish. He told me no, his grandfather had been a political prisoner.

About two hours into our time with Possett, we were both ready to call it a day. While he shouted at Ted, I wondered how a man could put all this passion into preserving a site like this and show this much anger toward one of the groups of people who had been slaughtered here. Or how he could claim to be doing all this in order to teach the world tolerance, when he showed so little tolerance.

Twenty years ago, Kaufering VII, where he took us first, was in ruin, forgotten, except for the local youth who used its abandoned huts as a place to throw parties, drink and have sex. Possett purchased some of the land on which the camp had stood and began to repair the crumbling huts. He contacted heads of state from 15 European countries whose citizens had perished there, and now stone pillars from each of those countries stand amid the huts in this snow-covered field. Beyond the trees surrounding the memorial is another part of the camp, which is now owned by the city; bulldozers have razed all the huts that were there, and nothing remains.

Memorials from several European countries and the remains of a hut at Kaufering VII.

As we stood inside a hut where more than 300 women had been imprisoned in a space that would have been crowded with 150, Possett said he had done all of this so that people wouldn't forget that the Holocaust happened here, not just at the better-known sites of Dachau and Auschwitz. The fact that those other sites attracted more fame and money could be added to Herr Possett's list of complaints.

After a couple of hours, we climbed back into his car, hopeful we were finished and could go have a quiet dinner. But Possett pulled up in front of his house, and, after he told us what it had cost and complained about property values in Landsberg, he invited us in. At the door, he introduced us to his wife, who warned him to be civil and told us in English that he sometimes turned people off with his passion. I could see how this might happen.

For the next hour or more we watched a video about his project and heard about how he had helped Steven Spielberg when he made *Band of Brothers*. The camp featured in that movie is supposed to be Kaufering IV. (My father's unit was attached at the time to the 101st Airborne Division.)

In his journal, Ted noted two other things that Possett began to lecture on – although in a less strident tone – once we began watching a slide show of photos taken by a U.S. soldier at the site of the camps:

> 1. The city of Landsberg is selling photos for $90 each and making money off of them and won't share the cash.
> 2. Steven Spielberg used the pictures for the concentration camp episode of *Band of Brothers,* then didn't share any cash.

Possett also mentioned the fact that Spielberg was Jewish, "but," Ted wrote, "by that point I had pretty much stopped paying attention."

It began to look as if Possett meant to keep us all night, so I thanked him, told him was getting late, and we had taken too much of his time. He must be hungry, and his wife probably had dinner ready. He seemed flustered, as if he was prepared to go on for hours more, but he returned us to our hotel and told us he would return at 10 o'clock the next morning.

Walking to a restaurant down the street, we began to plan how we might excuse ourselves from another day with Herr Possett. We thought the surreal nature of our day was over, but not quite.

"As if we weren't creeped out enough by our day so far," Ted wrote, "we wandered into a restaurant filled with Bavarians in lederhosen with an honest-to-God oompah trio playing traditional German music."

It was too much after what we had been through, so we left. We had just closed the door behind us when a woman in a dirndl and platinum blond crewcut ran out and told us we could sit down. She seated us at a table with a German couple, and we ordered some food. I was starting to relax, and Ted had ordered another beer when our waitress came back to tell us that someone else would be needing our table, which was fine with us. As we were leaving, the oompah trio launched into "Hava Nagila," and the crowd laughed and began to sing along. This was just too much. At that point we were both ready to leave Germany and never come back.

Normally, a beer hall and an oompah band might be a welcome piece of the tourist experience, but in this town where *Mein Kampf* was written and celebrated, and where people turned blind eyes to the camps in their midst, the playing of a Jewish folk song for a night of Bavarian entertainment was the last straw. I could only hope that we had misread the moment.

Remains of a hut at Kaufering VII.

At 9:00 o'clock the next morning, Ted called Possett's house to cancel our plans for the day. He and I were in agreement that we couldn't take another day like the one we had just experienced. When Frau Possett answered the phone, however, she told us that he was on his way. Apparently this Sunday was the day that Germany went to daylight savings time.

On our way to Kaufering IV, which we believe is the camp my father's platoon discovered in the woods, Herr Possett was strangely subdued. He was more informative and less volatile. He had no particular time or financial investment in this camp; this land was owned by the city. Unlike Kaufering VII, no memorial stands to honor those who died here. Nothing is there but a gravel pit and a field where deer feed.

"This was the typhus camp," he told us as we walked toward the gravel pit. "When your father first saw it, it was strewn with hundreds of dead bodies." His estimate is corroborated by *Wingfoot*, which states that the soldiers saw about three hundred bodies littering the ground when they came through the wire fence surrounding this camp. In some of the other camps, the numbers were much higher.

In the days after the camp was liberated, U.S. Army commanders forced people from town to put on their best clothing out of respect for the dead, come to the camp, and place the bodies in mass graves. When the city began to dig the gravel pit in the 1950s, bones were unearthed, said Possett, but nothing was done to preserve the remains or stop the digging.

Anton Possett shows Ted Moisan the gravel pit at the site of Landsberg IV, the camp where members of the 101st Cavalry found hundreds of bodies.

We stood at the rim of the gravel pit, filled now with water, and talked about what it must have been like for the soldiers the day they came here. Awful, I thought, it must have been awful. I had seen the photos, and I can't imagine what my father thought when he saw it. How it may have changed his life, I'll never know.

We drove by a small memorial marking the site of Kaufering I, and Possett only commented that it would have been impossible for the people in Landsberg or Kaufering not to know about this camp. "Look," he said, pointing to the train station across the highway. "There they were unloaded and marched into this camp. The trains went by every day. Look how close. It's not possible they were unaware."

I could see he was right. It was not possible. The train passed within a few feet of the edge of the camp, marked now by a small stone with an inscription about sorrow and suffering, words that made Herr Possett angry.

"Murder," he shouted. "They were murdered. Here, look! Their bodies were here." He sweeps his arm over the empty field in front of us. "Thousand of corpses littered the fields when the Americans came through those trees."

He asked us to imagine something very different from what he had asked of us at Kaufering VII. Yesterday he had kept saying, "You must imagine how much this cost, how hard it was for me." Today his tone had changed as well as his words: "You must imagine what this must have looked like, what it smelled like, what those young soldiers thought and felt."

I tried, but it was impossible. And the veterans I talked to were understandably silent on this topic, more so than any other subject relating to the war.

On our way back to the hotel, just a few miles from Kaufering IV, a little church glowed baby pink in the morning sun. A stone fence surrounds the cemetery in the church yard, and evergreen trees, yews, and white birch grow among copper crosses in tidy rows in the neatly groomed grass.

The church at Landberg prison, where war criminals are buried.

The State of Bavaria pays for the upkeep of this cemetery, Possett told us. It is a protected historical site and the final resting place for the unclaimed bodies of war criminals who had died in Landsberg prison. This was one time I needed to be absolutely sure I had understood him correctly. I asked him twice if these were really the graves of war criminals.

"Yes, yes," he said in English, nodding his head fiercely, "war criminals."

When I returned home, I was sure I must have misunderstood, so I looked for information about this church, the prison, and the tidy cemetery with its rows of crosses that rests between the two. I learned that among those buried in the cemetery are Oswald Pohl, head of the SS fiscal administration; SS Standartenführer Wolfram Sievers, who oversaw human genetic experiments; SS Hauptscharführer Otto Moll, head of the crematoria of Birkenau, and SS Sturmbahnführer Martin Gottfried Weiss, Commandant of Dachau.

Landsberg is a tourist town awash in pastel yellow, pink, green, blue and gold. Filled with restaurants, boutiques, and historic buildings, its centerpiece is the Lech River, churning through town over a series of falls. Under different circumstances, it is the kind of town I might want to see again, maybe in the springtime – late April maybe – when the flowers and sunshine return to Bavaria. But when I think about what my father experienced there in April 1945, I can only see death, and when I see a cemetery for those who made the camps and a gravel pit as the memorial for those they tortured, I see injustice. As we checked out of our hotel, I knew I wouldn't be coming back.

Possett took us to the station and put us on the train, complaining now about people who don't take the time to see the camps properly, who, like us, just come in, take a few pictures, and leave. But he is kind, almost sad, and not shouting. He waves as the train begins to pull away, and I am left feeling that the human heart is truly complicated, and I will certainly never understand Anton Possett's.

Landsberg am Lech

Survivor

Henry Dressler was a survivor of the Landsberg camps. I was able to find him through his son, Murray Dressler, who had written a note about his father on a website dedicated to keeping the memory of these camps alive.

On the phone, the first thing I noticed about Henry Dressler was his voice. It is deep and strong, a serious voice, with no hint of the softness that often accompanies age. It carries just a hint of his native Poland, and, as he speaks, there is a sense that he has told this story many times. He speaks without emotion; it is recitation.

Interviewing someone who survived the Holocaust is more difficult than I thought it would be. "What was it like? How did you feel?" We don't need to ask anyone these questions. We know the answers. How can we ever expect someone to put the unspeakable into words?

"I was born in Lodz, Poland, in 1925," Henry Dressler began.

> The Germans walked into my city in 1939 within months of my Bar Mitzvah. They marched in on a Friday, right after the candle-lighting. From the day they first arrived, we couldn't walk on the main streets. We had to go to the back streets. We couldn't go to school.
>
> We were moved into a ghetto in 1940. Things were very bad there. There was no food. People were starving, dying in the streets. The ghetto had its own government – police, fire, distribution of food, even its own currency.
>
> Mordechai Chaim Rumkowski was chosen to run the ghetto. He thought he was a king. He'd go to the cemetery and talk to his wife: 'I'm the king of the ghetto,' he'd tell her. He had been the head of an orphanage before the war. He had done a lot of good, but after the war started he came under the influence of the Germans. In the end, he went to Auschwitz like everyone else.
>
> In the ghetto we had no wood, no heat. In the winter the walls were covered with snow.
>
> Beginning in August 1944, every second day people would be called away. Trucks took them to Auschwitz.
>
> One of my two sisters died in the ghetto, and my father died of starvation. In 1944, my brother, my other sister, my mother, and I were sent to Auschwitz. It took three days to get there. During that time, we had no food and no sanitation.
>
> At Auschwitz, my brother and I were separated from my sister and mother. They went straight to the ovens. We had heard that if you had the

same last name, you would be separated, so I used my mother's maiden name. That way my brother and I were able to stay together.

My brother and I didn't stay long at Auschwitz. Within days we were transported to Landsberg to work: Landsberg, where Hitler wrote *Mein Kampf*.

We were working every day in Landsberg. We worked on the railroad, fixing the rails. Some days they gave us just worthless work to keep us tired and busy.

What food there was there was bad; everyone got sick. Later on we didn't work – it just became a death camp. That was about two months before liberation. My brother died in April, the month we were liberated, beaten by the capos and the Germans.

The German citizens, the people who lived in Landsberg and Kaufering, they saw us each day.

A small memorial at the site of Kaufering I. It sits next the railroad track that runs between Kaufering and Landsberg. "This is proof," said Anton Possett, "that people knew what was happening."

They watched us go to work and called us bad names. We would see them standing in front of their houses laughing. They knew. They saw it. And they just stood laughing and making jokes. They knew exactly who we were: "Juden," they called us. Everyone knew. After the war, no one knew anything.

It wasn't easy to deal with it all. But we were so hungry, we only thought of food. We were sick and isolated. We had a little watery soup. Everyone ate it and everyone got sick. The Germans were afraid of our sickness, so they would stay away from us. The capos did everything.

We didn't know the Americans were coming until the day they came. One day in late April the Germans gave us a piece of bread and lined us up for our "last march." Then a high officer came and said it was too late, that we couldn't leave. That night we heard shooting and bombardments, and the next day the Germans were gone.

When we woke up on the morning of April 27, we went out like we always did to be counted, and the camp was empty and the gates were open. We were free. The Germans had left their tanks, trucks, everything. We started to grab bread, but it made us sick.

Some of the Germans who had been guarding the camp changed out of their uniforms. They just disappeared, they ran away so fast. But most of them were caught.

In camp Number 1, they didn't have time to run. A Russian Christian in that camp took a shovel and opened the head of one of the Germans. The Jews didn't do that.

The Americans helped us by transporting the very sick to hospitals, by giving us food. Still, after the war many more people died.

Lt. Col. Edward Seiller, 12th Armored Division, ordered civilians to clean up one of the Landsberg camps.

We were put in a displaced persons camp for four years after the war. We had classes in the occupational trades. I worked in a metal workshop. Some people worked in the kitchen. Everyone did something.

I met my wife in 1946 in the displaced persons camp. The Nazis had her working in an ammunition factory during the war. She lost everyone. Like me, she was from Lodz. She had her mother with her. Her sister, brother, and father had left for Warsaw, thinking it would be better. Once they got there, they planned to send for the rest of the family. Of course, they couldn't.

All we thought about were our families. I was alone. I knew what happened to my mother and one sister, but not my other sister. Not what happened to all my aunts, uncles, cousins. I had one friend from our city, and he and I went back to

Poland in 1945 to look for our families. When we walked into a market, the Poles saw us and said, "Look at how many Jews are left."

I couldn't find any of my family, so I returned to Germany. We didn't want to go back to Poland. No one accepted us. They didn't accept us before the war or after.

Everyone was gone. It was hard, very painful. I am the only surviving member of my family, except for two uncles who left Poland in 1916; one went to America and one to Switzerland.

I was in Germany until 1949, then I went to Israel until 1961. I finally found my uncle in America, and he sent for me. My wife and I have two sons and four grandchildren. A small family. I don't talk much about the past. One son reads a lot, and he knows what it was. I don't like to talk about it; it makes them upset. The thoughts are with myself. Not a day goes by that I don't think about my family that is lost.

Dressler lets me know the interview is over with an expression he had used whenever I interrupted his story with an occasional expression of shock or horror. This time his words had a note of finality: "It was what it was," he says. "It was what it was."

Landsberg 1945

Landsberg am Lech

From April 24 to 27, the 101st Group had been providing security for both flanks of the 12th Armored Division. The Danube River was now behind them, and the cavalry probed the German main line of resistance to the south until they finally found a weak spot. That gap in the German defenses was all the Americans needed; they poured through it as if the dam had broken.

At 4:30 a.m. on April 27, the order came for the Cavalry to move southeast and seize the bridges over the Lech River near Landsberg. Although the 101st made good time, reaching the Lech by 8:30 a.m., it was too late. Just moments before they arrived, the Germans had destroyed the bridges.

Reconnaissance was immediately extended about three miles north of Landsberg to Kaufering and to Dornstetten, six miles to the south. Results of these patrols were equally disappointing. After carefully searching the west bank of the Lech River for possible crossing sites, the best that the cavalry patrols could offer were locations where engineers might repair blown bridges or construct new ones. Whatever they decided, they needed to move quickly to get across the Lech.

Large numbers of the German Army were congregating near Munich, 20 miles to the northeast, which seemed to confirm what Allied Intelligence Services had reported about Hitler's plan to build up a "National Redoubt," a fortress of final resistance high in the Bavarian Alps. It was there, the reports stated, that Hitler hoped to hold off the Allied armies until he could come to favorable terms with Eisenhower and the Russians. Allied commanders concluded that the German Army congregating near Munich would soon head to this "National Redoubt." The XXI Corps, which included the 101st Cavalry, was to head as quickly as possible to the Alps to prevent this.

To reach the Alps in time to block the German Army in the passes, the 101st would need to cross the Lech soon and get

Near the Alps in Bavaria.
Photo courtesy of Edith Holloman.

through the towns of Wertheim, Penzburg, and Bad Tolz to the south. One squadron of the 101st would screen the long, exposed left flank of the 12th Armored Division, and one squadron would move out in front of the 12th's Combat Command A to capture the those three towns. But first, the 101st had to wait for a bridge to be repaired.

During those damp and chilly Bavarian nights, the troopers could usually find some kind of shelter where they could bed down. They commandeered farm houses, barns, gasthauses, and even schlosses (castles). In the middle of the night on April 27 in Hiltenfingen, 14 miles north and west of Landsberg, Col. McClelland had found shelter in a gasthaus and had gone to bed quite late. At dawn, Major Leo Nawn woke the colonel with a message from 12th Armored Division. While waiting for McClelland to get ready, Nawn asked who the colonel's roommate was, pointing toward the bed where McClelland had just been sleeping. The two men stooped to check under the bed and found a dead German tucked into the small space.

Because so many towns were destroyed during the war, such stories, unfortunately, were not uncommon. Earl Carmickle tells of a similar experience shortly after he crossed the Saar.

"One night when it was real cold," he said, "we entered a village that had been bombed pretty bad, and the buildings were still burning. Our sergeant told us to go into one of the houses — the roof had been blown off — and sleep. 'At least,' he said, 'the four walls will keep the wind off of you.' We bedded down on the floor. We never slept in a bed, since there were a lot of booby traps left in the villages: mines, trip wires, that kind of thing. We woke up in the morning and saw a woman was in the bed. She was dead, probably killed in the bombing."

All through the night of April 27, men from the 12th Armored Engineers worked feverishly to repair a partially destroyed railroad bridge near Landsberg, chosen as the most feasible crossing site. By 6 a.m. the next morning, the bridge was ready for traffic. Since the 101st Cavalry was to cross ahead of the division, they took off as soon as it was repaired and finished crossing by afternoon; the 12th Armored Division followed, with Combat Command A in the lead. The use of only one bridge demanded that units cross on a tight time schedule, and Group Headquarters and Headquarters Troop spent an embarrassing fifteen minutes stalled on the bridge when one of the "liberated" German vehicles broke down halfway across. It finally had to be towed across the bridge by a tank.

While waiting near the bridge for everyone to cross, the men began to notice wraith-like figures who were wandering aimlessly along the roads and through the fields. In *Wingfoot*, Sweeney described them as "hollow-eyed, living skeletons wearing striped pajama-like garments hanging from their protruding bones."

These men and women had apparently broken through the barbed wire of one the nearby camps when they learned of the approaching American troops. Once outside, the prisoners began looting and foraging for food in the nearby countryside. Some of the troopers heard stories of prisoners who had killed

Photo taken inside Kaufering IV by Richard Bischoff, Troop C, 101st Squadron. On the back of the photo he wrote, "Quite a photo, isn't it?"

Photo courtesy Frances Lerner.

their German guards. Other camps were abandoned by the guards, and still others were burned to the ground as guards fled ahead of the Americans.

Troops A and B of the 116th Squadron had been the first to cross the river, and as they moved through the woods they encountered wire enclosed camps with hundreds – by some accounts thousands – of bodies scattered around the grounds.

Robert Klein had two radios on his half-track: one to the platoon, which was primarily a voice radio, and a larger radio that was continuous wave – Morse Code – and voice. It went to squadron headquarters.

"Most of our messages came through coded," said Klein, "but one day we got an uncoded call from the colonel. 'Let me talk to Ulmschneider,' he said. I asked him for the password, and he just yelled, 'Klein! I said let me talk to Ulmschneider.' I recognized his voice and his tone, so I gave the phone to Ulmschneider.

The colonel gave Klein's crew directions and told them to hurry.

"We pulled up in front of this large fenced area and saw men hanging on the fence in striped suits," he said. "They were starving, so we shared some of our K rations, but it made them sick. Some of the people were eating grass they were so hungry."

In 1990, Klein gave testimony on what he saw for Yale University's Holocaust collection.

"No one can exaggerate the horror of that place," he said.

Although the Cavalry had been able to release about 2,400 from the freight train near Landsberg, at least one of the concentration camps in the area was captured too late to save those whose burned and emaciated bodies strewn about the still smoldering ruins of their prison barracks.

The sight of those people in their blue and white striped rags, which barely covered their protruding bones, and all

Inside one of the camps near Landsberg in April 1945.

Photo is courtesy of Robert Klein.

those charred bodies clarified for many men in the cavalry exactly why they were fighting.

The barely living still inhabited Kaufering I and VII, but more than 300 bodies covered the ground in Kaufering IV, the typhus camp. It was here that the fleeing Germans set fire to the huts still filled with prisoners, and where American soldiers walked into a hell of smoldering wood and humanity. In Kaufering I, where mostly Lithuanians and Russians were imprisoned, according to some who where there, the Germans hadn't escaped fast enough. The dead and dying included both prisoners and guards, who lay together like twigs blown about in a wind storm.

Several miles beyond Kaufering IV, near Penzberg, troopers found a stalled railroad train with a string of cattle cars all filled with dead prisoners. Evidence indicated that they had been machine gunned down while trapped inside the cars.

This was the horror that Cheryl Kashuba said her father lived with for the rest of his life.

"People were starving," said Lt. Borkowski, who was able to communicate with a few of the captives in Polish. "We offered them something to eat, but they were too hungry to eat. They were afraid it would make them ill. A few told us that all they wanted were guns to kill the Germans."

Lou Gergley, also in B Troop, said, "We were about the eighth or tenth car in line going by one of the camps. I remember the people were all bald and so thin. We tried to give the people C-rations, but they didn't want any. Lt. Borkowski put a handkerchief on one of the men there and designated him as a leader. He got the people cleared off the road so we could go through. We heard some of them had murdered the guards, but we don't know if that was true."

Earl Carmickle remembers a big deer ran through one of the camps, and he shot it. "The people were so hungry they just fell on it," he said, "and they started skinning it. I thought I might be in trouble, but no one said anything."

"My sergeant, Sgt. John Schnalzer, had six brothers in the German Army," said Carmickle. "We were approaching one of the camps, and the Germans guarding the camp started running away. One of our men raised his rife to fire, and Sgt. Schnalzer said, 'Don't shoot. One of those men could be my brother.' Our corporal said, 'Don't ever say that again. If you are so worried about your brother, you might just want to and join them.'"

Fluharty remembers that it took a bulldozer to shove a path through the rubble to get through the camp. "It is hard to describe," he said. "When we rode in, the Germans were gone. We threw one man some food, but they really needed medical attention. There were big ditches and a row of steel ovens. We could see bones inside. One soldier fired his rifle into the ashes he was so angry. A prisoner who told us he was Polish said they had put people into the ditches, threw in oil and lit it. His job was to throw people into the ditch. He said that one man couldn't stand it, so he jumped in."

Tharp remembers seeing several camps. "We went in one big camp and saw people who were just skin and bones. A bunch of people were just laying in the yard. There were some German guards there, but they didn't get far. We stopped them at the gates. The soldiers just threw their guns down and put their hands on their heads. At one camp, they had pushed a bunch of people into a trench right before we got there."

"I don't want to remember the camps," said Gorski. "One of the priests with us came up to me and said, 'John, I want to show you something. You're never going to forget this.' And he took me to one of those camps. He was right; what I saw, I never forgot. I'm sorry I went with him."

"I didn't want to see it," said Charles Covey. "I tried to duck it. Some couldn't walk or talk. It was pitiful to treat a human like that. I couldn't treat anybody that way."

Covey summed up with a comment that reflected how most of the men felt: " I don't know how a human being could do it."

Two Polish brothers from one of the camps, teenagers about 17 or 18 years old, rode with Gorski in his jeep for the rest of the war. "One of them played the accordion," he said. "He could play it real good. When the war was over, he gave it to me. I thought I'd bring it home to my dad. He played the accordion."

Gorski took care of the accordion all the way home, across France and then across the Atlantic.

"But when we got to the U.S.," he said, "someone threw it off the ship and smashed it all up. That was a shame."

Once through Landsberg, the men continued quickly toward Austria, trying hard to put the horror of the camps behind them. Three men from Troop B, 116th Squadron, were wounded in action that day: Cpl. Ernest Gallego, Cpl. James McAlister, and Pvt. Charles Crowe.

"We just went in and out of the camps," said Fluharty. "It wasn't our job to do anything. Another unit cleaned it up."

"We didn't stay long, maybe about half an hour," Klein said, "then had to head off on another mission."

End of April 1945

Leaving the horrors of the Lech River behind them, the squadrons fanned out to the east on new missions. The 101st Squadron followed the 116th, moving to seize the causeway over the northern tip of Ammersee, one of Germany's five largest lakes. Located west and slightly south of Munich in upper Bavaria, the Ammersee is fed from the south by the Ammer River, a tributary of the Neckar, and drained to the north by the Amper River.

Progress was delayed by frequent demolitions, and the squadron was forced to detour south through Unterfinning and then north by the main road paralleling the west shore of Ammersee.

Just west of the northern tip of the lake and 12 miles east of Landsberg is the town of Greifenberg. From the woods southeast of there, the Germans launched an attack against those who were leading the squadron's column. Using four tiger tanks and a substantial number of infantry, the Germans fought a short, sharp battle, and then retreated to the northeast toward the causeway. The cavalry followed close behind until stopped by a series of explosions. The last few Germans to cross the causeway over the Ammersee left demolition charges in their wake, stopping the cavalry on the Amper River line.

The 116th, followed by Combat Command A, turned south toward Weilheim and Bad Tolz the next morning, while the 101st Squadron continued east toward bridges at the north of Ammersee and Wurmsee.

Until they arrived at the town of Rott, the 116th experienced only scattered resistance. Troop B of the 116th was still clearing roadblocks and occasionally taking German demolition parties by surprise, capturing them before they could blow up bridges necessary for the cavalry's advance.

About 600 yards from one bridge they needed desperately if they were to reach Weilheim, the troop was once again stopped by a road block. As they worked feverishly to clear it, they saw a group of Germans working just as feverishly to demolish the bridge before the cavalry could break through. A few patrols from Troop B left their work on the road block and rushed forward. After a short, intense struggle, they overpowered the Germans just in time to save the bridge. The way was now clear to Rott and Weilheim.

Rain had begun to fall during the night, making for a drizzling, morbid morning when the cavalry arrived in Rott. From inside the walled town, the Germans launched their defense, forcing Troops A, B, and C of the 116th Squadron to spend most of the day in a battle that was not helped by the weather. The early rain soon turned to freezing sleet and finally to snow. Troops A and C bypassed Rott and kept heading south toward Diessen, leaving Troop B to deal with the German Army that evening.

In the morning, the men of Troop B renewed their attack near Rott, and by 10 a.m. they had broken through the German defenses there and moved toward the western outskirts of Weilheim, capturing a bridge there that spanned the Ammer River. Pushing ahead against sporadic sniper fire, they had secured that town by 11 a.m.

Before daylight the next day, Troops A and C were back on the march to the Alps, now visible in the distance, after a short night's rest. Troop A reached the main highway between Diessen and Mitterfishen by sunrise, and Troop C moved into Diessen, capturing the town. There they found a military hospital with about 400 convalescent German soldiers.

Meanwhile, the 101st Squadron had raced east as fast as the men and equipment could go, hoping to surprise the Germans defending the bridges over the Ammer River at the foot of Ammersee. They were stopped by demolitions along the only access road and took a wide detour to the south. Within a few miles, the leading task force was again stopped by an attacking force of German infantry, which was supported by several tiger tanks equipped with 88mm guns. The battle continued until the arrival of the 342nd Armored Field Artillery Battalion, which forced the Germans to withdraw. By late morning the bridges had been taken intact.

When the 101st Group Headquarters got word that elements of the 116th Squadron had captured bridges near Mitterfischen, they directed the 92nd Cavalry to relieve the 101st Squadron at the north end of Ammersee so that squadron could move south to the bridges at the southern end. This would ease the full responsibility for these vital bridges that had so far been shouldered by the 116th. The 101st Squadron moved down the west shore of Ammersee, mopping up scattered resistance en route and entered Diessen at about 1 p.m.

Around 2 p.m., in the midst of all this movement, two representatives of an anti-Nazi group from Munich appeared at the Group Command Post in Diessen and reported that the

Nazi authority in Munich had been overthrown. They requested that American troops enter right away to restore order. They
promised that there would be no German resistance. Accordingly, Col. McClelland ordered the 101st Squadron to move
into Munich, about 35 miles away, and they headed toward the
city down Highway 12. Halfway there, however, at 7:30 p.m,
the squadron came under fire from Ober-Seefeld, and a strong
German force could be seen attempting to outflank it. Fierce
German attacks blocked all attempts to bypass the area, and
it became apparent that the information about taking Munich
without opposition was false.

At the same time, word came from XXI Corps, advising
the 101st to stay out of Munich, since General Milburn, corps
commander, had "promised" the city to General "Iron Pants"
O'Daniel, one of his division commanders. So for these rea-
sons, the mission was canceled, and Lt. Col. Kendall, squadron
commanding officer, stated later that he was "mighty glad" he
didn't have to try to capture a city of more than one million
people with his eight hundred men.

"We were on our way into Munich," said Lt. Borkowski,
"and the outskirts of the city was filled with dead people and
dead horses. We had done a lot of bombing."

While Borkowski and his men waited to see if it was okay
to enter the city, they noticed a big building on the side of
the road.

"There were three or four guys inside, all in uniform and
with guns," said Borkowski. "I could mumble in German, or
sometimes I got a guy who spoke Polish, so I talked to them.
These guys weren't going to fight. They didn't want to fight.
They surrendered. Strictly luck. They were not soldiers; they
were conductors. They just turned their guns over to us. That
was strictly luck."

After its mission to Munich was cancelled, the 101st Squadron was sent to block the line between Mitterfischen and
Seeshaupt. By midday they were spread out all along the line,

Map 15
April 28-May 3, 1945

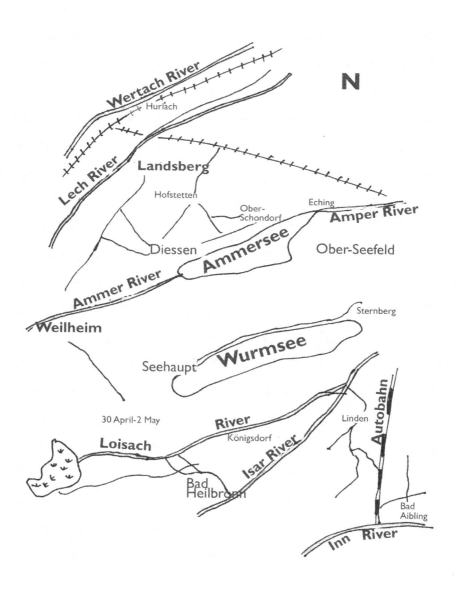

N

Wertach River

Hurlach

Lech River

Landsberg

Hofstetten

Ober-Schondorf

Eching

Amper River

Diessen

Ammersee

Ober-Seefeld

Ammer River

Weilheim

Sternberg

Wurmsee

Seehaupt

30 April-2 May

River

Königsdorf

Linden

Autobahn

Loisach

Isar River

Bad Heilbronn

Bad Aibling

Inn River

but by late afternoon they were called to Seeshaupt. Plans had changed once again.

At first light on April 30, the 116th, except for Troop B, moved south to find a crossing over the Loisach River, as the bridges at Rain and Sindelsdorf had been destroyed. They advanced against sporadic German resistance and reached the river in the late afternoon.

One of the forward units fired on a German officer, a courier who, apparently unhurt, abandoned his vehicle and escaped into the woods. In his haste, he left behind official maps and documents, which the troopers found in his dispatch case. The papers revealed plans for a counterattack against infantry units on the cavalry's right flank. The cavalrymen also learned that the Germans were using a key highway along the Mindel River as a boundary between units, offering possibilities for swift penetration. This assumption was correct, and the cavalry moved to spearhead the 12th Armored Division deep into enemy territory, cutting the 13th SS Corps' main supply routes, seizing bridges over the Wertach River, and generally disorganizing enemy communications and other installations. Ultimately, they forced the SS to break off their counterattack and withdraw in confusion.

The cavalry moved forward so swiftly that they caught the enemy off guard time after time. German airports with hundreds of planes were captured intact, including the jets which had harassed the men every step of the way for days.

"One could almost feel the moment when the heart went out of the German troops," wrote Sweeney.

The collapse of the German units came as more of an anticlimax than a surprise. Prisoner-of-war pens began to bulge with men. Some were downcast and others were happy just to be alive. Thousands more began to pour back along every road.

Dejected as they were, however, the cavalrymen could see that the German prisoners of war didn't have anything close to the horrible hopeless look in their eyes or the haunted slouch that had characterized the released men and women of the Nazi concentration camps seen a few days earlier, and after that experience, I can only imagine that pity for the German Army was in short supply.

Troop B of the 116th, still attached to Combat Command A, 12th Armored Division, had only been in Weilheim for one hour when they were ordered to move through the mountain passes in the Alps and capture Innsbruck some seventy miles to the south. At about 1:15 p.m., they began reconnaissance for that mission along the main highway from Weilheim through Oberau, along with one platoon of medium tanks from Co. F and one platoon from Troop E. They had gone about five miles when enemy fire rained down on the leading platoon from both sides and from the front. After a 30-minute engagement, the Germans on the left withdrew, and the troopers forced the Germans in the front and to the right into the open, where they suffered heavy losses while trying to escape.

Near the German-Austrian border, Charlie Kashuba is on the right.
Photo courtesy of Joseph Borkowski.

Munich 1945.
Photo courtesy of Joseph Borkowski.

After traveling only a few more miles, the troopers encountered another group of German soldiers defending a road block constructed out of upright logs. They quickly ran off the German guards, and in about 40 minutes a bulldozer had pushed down the road block. Once again the cavalry was on the move, this time the Alps and the Austrian border was its destination.

Murnau 2006

Looking south from the vicinity of the train station, the main street in Murnau curves down a hill, giving the foothills of the Alps even more room to stretch out and fill the scene in front of you. From where Ted and I stood, they seemed to cut the sky into jagged halves. Snow still clung to the stream banks and along the side of less-traveled streets in Murnau, and when the 101st arrived there on April 29, 1945, snow still covered the ground. You had to be patient here in the mountains as you waited for spring.

My father had grown up where the rounded hills crested at around 1,050 feet. These Bavarian foothills, all sharp edges and angles, rose to more than 5,000 feet, with mountains behind them rising to more than 9,000 feet. I live with Mt. Hood and the other Cascade peaks right outside my window, and I was still impressed. I can't imagine what my father thought as he stood in the shadow of these giants. Maybe in war you can't see the beauty around you. Maybe that comes later, when the shooting stops.

In Murnau, the 116th's B Troop was credited with liberating Oflag VIIA, a prisoner of war camp for Polish officers. When I began looking for information about this camp, I found the

Murnau 2006

website, "Les Photos Oubliées," (The Forgotten Photos) which has become a meeting place for other children seeking information about their fathers, this time children of Polish prisoners of war.

"My father was one of thousands of young Polish Officers to stay at Oflag VIIA in Murnau," one woman wrote on the website. "He did not speak much about his time there so I don't have many stories to impart, but I would be interested to hear from any survivors if there still are any. My father recently died at age 93."

These inquiries from Poland, Australia, and Canada express the same longing as similar letters written by the sons and daughters of American war veterans: Can anyone tell me about my father or what happened to him in the war?

I contacted some of those listed at this site, and I was surprised at the gratitude they expressed for the men from the 101st who had liberated their fathers, some even telling me they owed their existence to what my father and others had done.

Stan Majcherkiewicz wrote from Canada that his father, Seweryn, was a Polish officer who spent five years of his life behind the barbed wire of Oflag VIIA. He didn't have many other details; his father, like mine, died in the 1970s.

George Jurand's father, Vlodzimierz Jaszczuk, was at the camp from 1939 until liberation. He was a 2nd Lieutenant in the 64th Infantry Regiment, 16th Infantry Division, Army Pomorze, and he lived in Barracks F at Oflag VIIA. He and some other prisoners attempted to escape in 1943 or 1944. They did manage to get out through a manhole cover, but were recaptured several days later.

Second Lt. Jaszczuk had been awarded the Virtuti Militari, a Polish medal, for his role in capturing the town of Lowicz during the Bzura offensive in September 1939. After liberation he was transferred to the Polish Second Corps in Italy.

My trip to Germany had been an enlightening experience, but it didn't compare to my other journey: the one I had been on since I went to that first reunion in 2004. I had met so many other people, all connected directly or indirectly to the story of the 101st Cavalry. Just trying to learn all I could about this one city, I met a man who served in the Army in Murnau in the 1950s, three people whose fathers had been imprisoned in Oflag VIIA, and a French photographer, Alain Rempfer, who found hundreds of photos in an attic in his house and felt they should be shown to the world.

From Murnau, the cavalrymen crossed the Alps into Austria. They didn't know it at the time, but the end of the war was only days away. Ted and I had an advantage over them in that regard. We knew the war was winding down, as was our trip. Instead of following them through the Alps, I would pick up their trail as they headed back north to Lorsch and Heidelberg. I wanted to see where they spent the summer before they went home, and Ted wanted to see Prague.

Oflag VIIA 1945

Oflag VIIA

"When we finally got into Murnau," Altizer wrote, "we found that the delaying tactics, which had held us up on the outskirts of town, had given the Germans enough time to escape. They had pulled out in such a tearing hurry that when we entered their deserted barracks, we found their still warm dinners on the table. They'd left so quickly, they hadn't had time to eat. We were afraid of the food, even though it looked hot and palatable, since it might have been poisoned."

Eugene Tharp had mentioned sleeping in the snow one night after a long march, because the barracks where they could have slept had been booby-trapped. After days of marching fueled only by cold rations, tired and hungry, how disappointed the men must have been to sleep on the cold ground when hot food and warms beds were so close.

Approaching the town of Murnau on April 29, the 101st Cavalry rounded a bend in the road and saw, directly in their path, a German military prisoner of war camp still under full guard with sentries in their elevated guardhouses and walking the perimeter. The camp was Oflag VIIA, home to approximately 5,000 Polish officers and about 300 regular soldiers.

Oflag VIIA Murnau was used principally for officers in the Polish armed services, though other nationalities were present in smaller numbers (Russian, Serbian, French, English, and, towards the end of the war, Italians). A small number of non-commissioned Polish troops were also housed in the camp.

Oflag was short for offizierslager (officers' camp), as compared to stalag (mannschaftsstammlager, troop camp) and dulag (durchgangslager, transit camp). From 1939 to 1945 Germany had 62 oflags and 112 stalags. Oflag VIIA was officially described as a "musterlager" or "workcamp," and it came under the German Munich military region (VII Wehrkreis).

Seweryn Majcherkiewicz, a Polish officer who spent five years of his life behind the barbed wire of Oflag VIIA.

Photo courtesy his son, Stan Majcherkiewicz.

The camp, which was originally built in 1939 to house German tank units, included three one-story barracks, a number of administration and service buildings, eight garages and a sports hall. It was turned into a POW camp on September 25, 1939. Because it was originally built for soldiers of the German army, its facilities were far superior to those in other oflags and stalags. The closeness of Murnau to Switzerland made it more accessible to the Red Cross than most other POW camps, so the Germans used it as their model POW camp for propaganda purposes. Although the barracks had been designed originally to accommodate between 800 and 1,000 German soldiers, between 1939 and 1945 they housed more than 5,000 prisoners by using the basements, attics, and garages.

Lieutenant Konrad Siekierski entered the camp in early October 1939, soon after it was commissioned as a POW camp. He was 29 years old and had been married for one month when he was taken prisoner during the defense of Warsaw in September. Poland was already involved in a quiet mobilization, preparing for what many feared was coming, and Siekierski had to leave his young bride just one day after their August 25 wedding.

On that Sunday in 1945, almost six years after his capture, Siekierski, along with the other prisoners, awoke to the sound of gunfire from the direction of Munich, about 40 miles to the north. An American plane circled overhead and dropped its wings a number of times, signaling those held in the camp.

Lieutenant Konrad Siekierski

Photo courtesy his son, Maciej Siekierski

Often during the war, from behind the fence, the prisoners had seen examples of America's air power as hundreds of planes at a time would fly overhead, unaware of thousands of cheering prisoners in the camp below. This time the plane was acknowledging them as well.

"The Germans had some idea the day before," Siekierski had told his son, Maciej. "They gave us back our personal items." Lt. Siekierski had a dagger, a type that was given to officers, and when the Americans entered the gates, he gave that dagger to the first man to enter. Maciej Siekierski said the memory of that act meant as much to him as if he had his father's dagger.

In the early afternoon, on the orders of Captain Pohl, a German officer, the 40 or so camp guards relinquished control of the watchtowers and handed in their weapons. This was not a sign the Cavalry would get a free pass as it traveled past the camp. At around 3:00 p.m., as the American Army approached Murnau from the north, a small group of SS men approached the camp from the opposite direction. When the SS and the Americans met just outside the front gate of the camp, gunfire erupted. Most of the SS turned their cars around and fled back to town, but the lead car opened fire, which brought even heavier fire from the medium-tank platoon and their 76mm guns. Two members of the SS, Colonel Teichmann and Captain Widmann, were killed in the exchange of fire, as prisoners in the camp climbed on the front fence and watched the proceed-

A confrontation between the Americans and the SS in front of Oflag VIIA brings cheers of encouragement for the cavalry from the prisoners. Two of the German officers are killed.

Photos courtesy of Alain Rempfer, "Les Photo Oubliés."

ings, cheering the Americans on. Also killed by a stray bullet during the exchange of fire was 2nd Lt. Alfons Mazurek, one of the prisoners.

Two of the American tanks pursued the SS cars, which were fleeing toward Murnau, while another tank entered the camp through the main gate. One of the first Americans to enter the gate was Corporal Richard Pawlowski from Chicago; another of the soldiers was from Kalisz, Poland.

Members of B Troop, 116th Squadron, were involved in the brief firefight outside of Oflag VIIA.

Photo by Lt. Edward C Newell, U.S. Army Signal Corps. Courtesy of National Archives.

According to the official 12th Armored Division records, Troop B, 116th Cavalry Reconnaissance Squadron, and Combat Command A of the 12th Armored Division, XXI Corps of the American, 7th Army, are recognized as the official liberators of Oflag VIIA at 4:55 on the afternoon of April 29.

It was just another short stop for the cavalry. They quickly continued past the camp to the outskirts of Murnau. A small detachment with Sgt. Feist in charge was sent to check what appeared to be a hospital of considerable size on the right side of the road. When the sergeant arrived at this "hospital," he received the surrender of a general officer and his staff and several hundred men. Because of the rapid rate of advance, this information did not reach troop headquarters until it was some miles past the spot, and engaged in yet another fight.

Only about 1,500 yards past the southwestern outskirts of Murnau, the cavalry encountered 20 German infantrymen, who blasted the troopers with panzerfaust fire for about 10 minutes. Three or four of the Germans were killed and the rest withdrew. The troopers only made it another 400 yards before they were stopped again, this time by an upright-log road-block. It was undefended and only took about 35 minutes to clear it enough for the troopers to continue.

At 5:30 p.m., about two miles below Murnau and headed toward the Bremmer Pass, the point platoon and the second platoon came under German rifle and panzerfaust fire from both sides. The troopers killed the four men firing the panzer-faust, but had trouble seeing the riflemen. It was clear that the only way to get rid of them completely would be to leave their tanks and jeeps and, on foot, try to locate them: a time-consuming operation. Therefore, they decided to "run the gauntlet," or speed through as quickly as possible and hope for the best. The troopers got to the other side, but not without losing one soldier, Tec. 4 Anthony Ivinski.

Cavalrymen taking a German guard from the first tower at Oflag VIIA in Murnau.

Photo taken by 2nd Lt. Edward C. Newell, U.S. Army Signal Corps. Courtesy National Archives.

Photo courtesy Frederick Altizer.

"I could see a German," said Gergley, "and I fired my 50-caliber at him. I hit him, and he was still crawling toward me when my 50-caliber jammed. I dropped down to get out of the line of fire, and I was shot. The sniper got three others. The mess truck driver, Anthony Ivinski, was hit in the stomach. I crawled out and told Kashuba to take over."

The rifle unit had been stronger than they thought at first, and it kept the entire column under constant fire along a three-mile stretch of road all the way into the town of Eschenlohe.

"They put us on a jeep," said Gergley. "There were three litters: two on the back and one on the hood. Snow was coming down so fast that it was slow going to the evac hospital in Dillingen, 100 miles back behind the lines. It took us several hours.

"The next morning, when they started to unload us, I told them to check Ivinski, that he was hurt bad. The nurse said that he was dead. He had died during the ride to the evacuation hospital. The doctor checked me out to another hospital. Two days later, we heard that Hitler had committed suicide."

Map 16
May 4-11, 1945

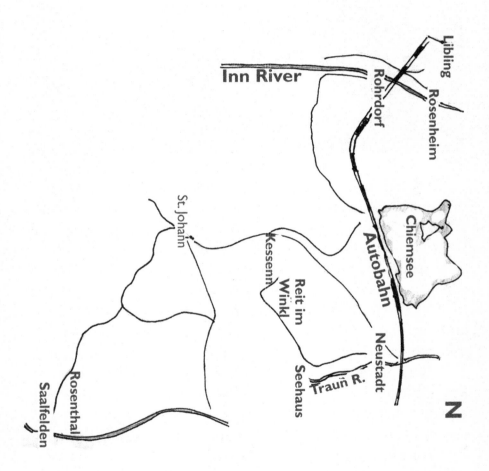

Inn River

Libling

Rohrdorf

Rosenheim

St. Johann

Kessenn

Chiemsee

Autobahn

Reit im Winkl

Neustadt

Seehaus

Traun R.

Rosenthal

Saalfelden

N

The War is Over

For two days, Troop B of the 116th had been attached to the 12th Armored Division headed for Austria, and Troops A and C had been guarding bridges in an area between Diessen and Mitterfischen. On April 30, they were ordered to assemble near Weilheim once again and secure the bridges over the Loisach River.

On the night of April 30, while posting the situation map, Sgt. Jack Langridge, group operations sergeant, made the observation that the American and German units in southern Germany seemed to be headed off in every possible direction. It was, he noted, "the damndest can of worms" he had ever seen.

The German Army seemed to be in a state of complete disorganization, with some units fighting to get into the Alps, while others were fighting desperately to prevent the Americans from crossing the Alps.

"They were without sufficient supplies and ammunition and had little or no communications left," wrote Sweeney. "One captured German staff officer told us that the only way they knew where their forward units were was to intercept our messages reporting enemy contacts. By that time most of our messages were being sent in the clear because things were moving so fast there was little time to encode and decode them."

During April, units of the 101st Cavalry Group had suffered 126 casualties and had taken an amazing total of more than 17,000 prisoners. This large number of prisoners had become more of a problem than a blessing. The cavalry could no longer provide escorts to take them to the rear. All they could do was direct them to turn themselves in at the nearest corps or division collecting point.

German defenses appeared to have lost all coordination, but here and there enough isolated SS units continued to defend road blocks and strong points, so life for the cavalrymen in the lead was still uncertain. Hour after hour in those final days, they walked into the unknown and the special kind of fear that existed there. No one knew where, when, or how they would next find themselves under fire. They expected machine gun fire from behind the next knoll, hill or river line. Panzerfaust rockets might be fired from the next farmhouse or clump of woods. An 88 could still pick off the lead vehicle from a village wall a thousand yards away, or they could

Joseph Coccia
Photo courtesy Joseph Coccia.

be caught in crossfire. They had learned that anything could be waiting around the bend in the road or over the next hill.

"The most amazing thing I saw," said Hawkins, "was when we were going through the mountains. We saw a stack of wood in the front of a house, and an 88 was sticking out of that pile of wood aimed right at us. We were sure scared, but we were never fired on."

"We were at the bottom of the Alps, going into this house where we were supposed to be billeted," said Joseph Coccia from Baltimore. "This lady started screaming. We didn't know anything, so we figured she was pregnant. We called a medic, told him this lady was screaming and screaming. We didn't speak German; she didn't speak English, but we figured she must be pregnant. He checked her out. 'She's not pregnant,' he told us. 'She just wants you out of her house.'

"'It's our house now,' we told her. "

Coccia said it was clear by then the war would be over soon. "The Germans were coming out of the mountains by the thousands to surrender. If they had charged us, we'd have been done for, but they didn't want to fight anymore."

The month of May found the cavalry partly in the foothills of the Bavarian Alps and partly in the plains adjacent to the Chiem See, headed down the autobahn in pursuit of the remaining elements of the SS thought to be hiding in the mountains just above the Austrian border.

The various units of the Group had missions that took them down the valleys to the west of Berchtesgaden and into the Austrian Tyrol, where, in the mountain passes, fighting was only sporadic.

May 1

During the first days of May, the direction and nature of the Group's advance changed several times. Sometimes they were advancing in front of the 12th armored Division and sometimes protecting its flanks. The 101st Squadron, which was attached to the 4th Infantry at the time, was assembled at Seehaupt, awaiting assignment to a new mission. At a few minutes past midnight they were ordered to Starnberg at the north end of Wurmsee to look for a route across the Loisach and Isar rivers. Nearly impassable secondary roads caused a delay in their mission. While they were delayed, the 36th Infantry Division gave the cavalry permission to cross the bridge at Rain at 1 p.m.

At 4 p.m. the 116th Squadron turned north, hoping to seize the bridges over the Loisach-Isar Canal, which remained intact around Konigsdorf and Wolfratshausen. Their search was often interrupted by a few isolated pockets of German resistance, and by the time they reached the bridges in the area, they had all been destroyed. That much hadn't changed; even though the Germans were surrendering in record numbers, they were still doing all they could to thwart the advance of the American Army.

May 2, 1945

Time estimates for the construction of a new bridge at Bad Tolz indicated a long delay, and at 1:40 a.m., May 2, the commanding officer of the 101st Cavalry Group ordered all units to move north on a route running east of Wurmsee. They would cross the Isar River through the 4th Infantry Division bridgehead at Wolfratshausen, where Combat Command A, 12th Armored Division, had crossed during the night of May 1. They were then to proceed to Rosenheim and then south through the Inn River Valley.

May 2

At 6:45 a.m., May 2, the 12th Armored Division ordered the 116th Squadron to follow the route of Combat Command A,

Cavalrymen heard from civilians that 30 or 40 American prisoners were held in Weilheim, so they went to see if the story was true. They found the men in this cage behind City Hall on April 28. Here cavalrymen from Troop B, 116th Squadron, open the gate to free the men.

Photo taken by 2nd Lt. Edward C. Newell, U.S. Army Signal Corps, courtesy of National Archives.

entering the autobahn at Holzkirchen and proceeding to the bridge over the Inn River. The cavalry would screen the left flank and rear of Combat Command A between Rosenheim and Ostermunchen and patrol the autobahn from Holzkirchen to the Inn River Bridge.

Troop A, 116th Squadron, moved north through Grub, then east and south to the autobahn and at 5:25 p.m. secured the Inn River Bridge. The balance of the Group moved to Bad Aibling, where a command post was established. Troop C, 116th Squadron, extended the screen north to Ostermunchen.

May 3, 1945

At 10:30 a.m. the 116th Squadron moved to the vicinity of Beitham, and their first contact with the French forces was

Dominic Stolt, Bill Olsen, and Buck Fluharty repair the tread on their tank, which was damaged when it ran into a tree near the Alps.

Photo courtesy Buck Fluharty.

made at 1:50 p.m. Two of the cavalry patrols were stopped completely by roadblocks and demolitions on main roads, as well as impassible condition of the side roads.

May 4, 1945

The Group was detached from 12th Armored Division and returned to XXI Corps control. The 101st Cavalry had spent thirty days with the division, working together as a close-knit team, in part because most of the senior officers in the Division had once been cavalrymen and knew its capabilities and how to use it.

The XXI Corps directed the 116th Squadron to proceed east on the autobahn between Munich and Salzburg, meet up with the 2nd French Armored Division, and then turn south into the mountain passes of the Alps along the Austrian border.

Troop C, 116th Squadron, assembled at first light on May 4 and headed east, meeting the French at 6:30 a.m., less than one mile west of the Traun River near Ober-Siegsdorf. The French reported that the bridge had been destroyed and that the Germans were defending from the east bank. Troop A, 116th Squadron, along with first platoon, Troop E, and first platoon, Company F, turned south along the west bank of the Traun River, overcoming a defended roadblock at Neustadl and pursuing the enemy to Seehaus, where they were stopped by another destroyed bridge and a defended roadblock. Other units of the 116th Squadron followed and assembled in Ruhpolding, where the command post was established.

At one point, as the cavalry entered the steep roads in the area close to the Alps, Fluharty's crew almost lost their tank.

"We were going down a steep hill," said Fluharty, "and there were some pretty sharp curves and deep ravines. Nick was driving, and on one corner he wasn't turning fast enough. It's hard to turn an 18-ton tank that's going 25 miles an hour. He couldn't slow down because a canteen had wiggled out of where it was supposed to be and got in the way of the lever for the left brake. He didn't make the corner and ran right into a big tree. That was lucky. If he hadn't hit the tree, we'd have gone down the ravine. No one was injured, but the tread came off on the tank."

The advance of U.S. and French troops down the autobahn was an unforgettable event to many who saw it. To the men of the 101st, it seemed that the entire Seventh Army was stampeding east along both the east and westbound lanes, while a continuous stream of German prisoners trudged west down the meridian strip.

Nat Norris, Troop A, 101st Squadron, with a sack full of wine.

Photo courtesy Robert Klein.

"It seemed that all the units of the American Army, including the Second French Armored Division, were boiling down the autobahn, Hitler's six-lane highway, at one and the same time, and all were headed for Berchtesgaden," wrote Sweeney. "Along the same highway, an equally impressive sight was the unending grey-brown river of dejected German soldiers flowing slowly to the rear."

After three months of constant movement, the cavalry had taken on a less military and much more interesting appearance. Displaced people of all nationalities had hitched rides on top of the vehicles. Now and then a black top hat or a spiked old-style German helmet appeared from a tank or armored car turret, adding a touch of GI humor. A variety of captured German vehicles were scattered along the column. For a while one troop had adopted a life-sized female mannequin wearing nothing but a fancy lady's hat as she rode along in a Jeep. Another unit had liberated a warehouse full of white sheepskin coats intended for Luftwaffe pilots. Now and then a box looking suspiciously like a case of champagne or cognac was seen tied to the back of a mud-colored vehicle.

Waiting for orders as the war draws to an end.

Photo courtesy of Buck Fluharty.

Nevertheless, according to Sweeney, the cavalry columns appeared as though they had just come off the drill field compared to the sight they saw soon after reaching the autobahn, when the entire 2nd French Armored Division came along.

The French division had been equipped by the U.S. Army with enough equipment for a normal armored division, but they had commandeered, wangled and liberated enough French, British, German, and U.S. vehicles to provide for a division twice that size, Sweeney wrote. They traveled in a variety of uniforms and with great élan, accompanied by the women of their choice who waved happily from the trucks they rode in. No matter what they looked like, Sweeney added, they were a real fighting outfit, eager to make "la Boche" — Hitler — pay for the four-year occupation of France.

Lt. Joseph Borkowski enjoying dinner in the foothills of the Alps.

Photo courtesy Joseph Borkowski.

At noon on May 4, the 101st Squadron was relieved of its attachment to the 4th Infantry and attached to the 101st Airborne Division of Ardennes Bulge fame, and they had commandeered every type of German civilian and Army vehicle imaginable for transportation. They were ordered to proceed without delay to Bad Reichenhall and locate a suitable command post for the 101st Airborne.

Col. Graydon, in his history of the war, states that at 7 a.m. on May 4, while still on the autobahn, the Group had received a XXI Corps message through 12th Armored Division that said:

"General Kesselring expected to surrender forces tonight or tomorrow. In the event he or his emissaries contact our units, they will be conducted by fastest available means to CP 503 Inf. in Munich at eight one seven five eight zero (map coordinates). Notify this Hq."

Albert Kesselring was commander-in-chief of the German troops in Italy, and the men hoped his surrender might mean they were close to receiving some very good news.

Soon after reaching Obersiegsdorf on May 4, the Group left the autobahn and turned south along the Traun River corridor leading directly into the Alps. Troop A, 116th, led the advance against stubborn SS resistance. By nightfall, the troop had gotten as far as Seehaus, where it was stopped cold by a blown bridge and SS troops heavily defending roadblocks.

The war wasn't over yet.

May 5, 1945

Early in the morning on May 5, the commanding officer of the 101st Cavalry Group directed the 116th Squadron to continue its attack south to the Austrian border, focusing on the town of Reit im Winkl. Troop A, one platoon of Troop E, and one platoon of Company F, all of the 116th, were ordered to attack the town from the east. Troop B, one platoon of Troop E, and one platoon of Company F were directed to stage their attack from the north.

Both units moved out at first light around 7:30 a.m. Troop A with its reinforcements fought its way south against strongly defended roadblocks, reaching Seegatierl at noon. The troop was stopped there by German resistance, but following a morning-long battle, cleared the town by 2:30 p.m. Troop A turned east and moved forward against an almost unbroken series of obstacles, all of which were defended by small arms and automatic weapons fire from the heights on each side of the narrow road. Progress was continuous, but incredibly slow.

Troop B, 101st Squadron, was held up temporarily by mortar fire and a blown bridge, and Troop C met no opposition until halted by a defended roadblock south of Marquartstein. The commanding officer of Troop C was contacted by a representative of the German officer, General Berger, and negotiations were undertaken that resulted in the surrender of the German command at the roadblock.

At around the same time, the 101st Squadron was reconnoitering the Crosse Ache River Valley and was in contact with Troop B, 116th Squadron. The troop, reinforced with platoons from other troops, encountered a number of undefended roadblocks and, by 1 p.m. had entered the town of Marquartstein in the Traun River Valley. The southern exit from town, however, was held by a strong contingent of the enemy, and the troopers had to fight for the right to leave. The troop then proceeded about a mile south where it was once again halted by an impassable road crater, one strongly defended by small arms, automatic weapon, and mortar fire. Some men were sent out immediately to find a way around this obstacle.

In just a few days, the cavalry had advanced to the east approximately thirty-five miles, and had turned south into the Bavarian Alps, penetrating two mountain passes against enemy resistance.

At 4:15 p.m. on May 5, the following message was received from the 101st Airborne Division: "German Army this sector has surrendered. All units remain in place." Forward units stopped, and the shooting war in the European Theater of operations was at an end for the 101st Cavalry Group.

Since the German command was out of communications with many of its forward units, some of them continued to fight. Realizing this, the 101st Airborne Division command issued instructions that all U.S. units would send out parties to inform German commanders of the surrender, advise them of the terms, and designate assembly areas for their troops. The Cavalry units were then to garrison all large towns and establish military governments. Accordingly, the two squadrons were assigned areas of responsibility for a total of approximately three hundred square miles.

"On our last day in Austria," Borkowski said, "we were on patrol to flush out some Germans. Some came out of a cottage, and we ended up in a firefight. They wouldn't believe the war was over. Some were killed; some guy about 50 feet away had me in his sights, but he got bumped off. It made me sick. The whole war makes me sad."

When asked how he felt when he heard the war had ended, John Gorski said, "Oh boy. How would you feel? All the boys were so happy; everyone was shooting their guns off. I sat down under a tank, afraid I'd get hit by a stray shell."

"When the war ended, we were all so happy," said David Gay. "But we were also cautious about whether it was really over or not. There was some fighting after the war. Captain Burgess went into a town with some troops right after the war, and people started firing at him. He fired back.

"'The war is over,' he yelled at them. A woman yelled back at him, 'Then why are you shooting at us?'

"'You fired at us first,' said the captain. There were a few incidents like that."

"I was happy as a lark when the war was over," said Hawkins. "I knew I would soon see Pidgeon Run, Virginia, the little town where I was born."

The work of disarming the Germans and attempting to establish military government in the areas just conquered now began. From descriptions given by the men who were there, the entire country was in complete chaos, particularly in the larger towns where Allied bombing and shelling had destroyed transportation and all other public utilities. Most of the Nazi officials and technicians who had governed and operated these towns had either fled or gone underground for fear of arrest. There were shortages of food and other necessities, and looting was rampant — not just by the Germans, but by Allied troops as well.

"We were a small unit (600) in the midst of thousands of Germans," said Fluharty, "many of whom did not know the war was over, so one of our men would walk guard with two SS troopers to head off any Germans coming down out of the hills. We had orders to whistle at no women, do nothing to set people off. It was a touchy situation. Nothing happened, though, and we were relieved by a larger outfit, and moved to a German town, Lorsch, to await transport home."

May 6, 1945

Road blocks of platoon strength were established along the autobahn between Ober Siegsdorf and Rohrdorf at 6 a.m. on May 6, for the purpose of collecting prisoners of war and concentrating them in the enclosure at Fraundorf. Three such blocks were established by the 101st and two by the 116th Squadron. Thousands of German soldiers were processed.

In the late evening of May 6, Headquarters, 101st Airborne Division received instructions for the 101st Cavalry Group on what to do next:

"Upon receipt of these instructions, send reconnaissance parties under officer control and with interpreters operating under a flag of truce to contact all German troops in the zone."

Reconnaissance parties were to inform German commanders of the surrender of Army Group "G." They were also told to acquaint German commanders with terms of surrender, allow sufficient time for German commanders to verify surrender, and designate to German commanders assembly areas for troops and locations of dumps for surrendered arms and materiel. When they completed these instructions, they were to move sufficient troops to garrison all large towns and villages in the sector, establish military government, and maintain law and order. The orders also laid out the area assigned to the 101st Cavalry Group. It was bounded on the north by the autobahn, on the west by the Inn River, on the south by the Windshausen-Kossen-Seegatierl line, and on the east by the Ober-Siegsdorf-Seegatierl line.

The Group sector was sub-divided into three sub-sectors, each under control of the unit noted:

> Western sub-sector: Inn River to the mountain pass Bernau-Sachrang, 342nd AFA Battalion, attached Troop A, 101st, and Troop A, 116th Squadron.

> Central sub-sector, east boundary of western sub-sector, to the mountain pass Marquartstein-Kossen, 101st Squadron, attached one battery, 342nd AFA Battalion.

> Eastern sub-sector, eastern boundary of central sector to the eastern boundary of the Group sector, 116th Squadron, attached one battery, 342nd AFA Battalion.

⇛⇝

My dear Mary,

After chasing Jerries for the past few days and chasing them over mountains, they finally quit, at least in this section. We received orders last night to cease firing and to remain in present positions and be prepared to sweep our sector for any loose elements that still think they are supermen. PWs by the thousands are coming in – out of the hills and mountains, some in small groups of ten or more and some complete companies, so the hardest part is over, thank the Good Lord. We will have many odd jobs to do for awhile which will keep us busy until things can be organized. The strain of fighting is over and this morning the only change that is noticeable among the men is that they look relieved. There is no celebrating or expression of joy in any manner, matter of fact, everything seems strange and quiet. It is hard to explain. I guess all of us have our own thoughts and wonder what we are going to do and when we are going to do it.

No mail received by us for the past few days, and I did not write for a couple of days as we were on the go. We did not get to Innsbruck, but only a few miles from it and at the moment we are not far from Berchtesgaden. This letter is being written from Austria believe it or not.

Well, sweetheart, your mind should really be at ease (I know mine is) and we can give thanks and pray that soon we can be together.

Hubert [Leonard]

Men take a break at the end of the war and do some fishing.

Photo courtesy of Frederick Altizer (shown in the foreground).

May 7, 1945

The end of the war did not mean the end of bridge repair. On May 7 the 116th Squadron began repairs on the destroyed bridge at Seegatierl.

At around 9:00 o'clock that morning, units of the 101st Squadron were stopped one mile south of Marquartstein on the main highway by an officer of the 13 SS Corps, bearing a flag of truce. The leader of that group said that the SS was not under command of German Army Group "G" and, therefore, not bound by the terms of the surrender. He said the Obergruppenfuhrer and General Waffen SS Gottlob Berger, second only to Heinrich Himmler in SS rank, wished to negotiate with our higher headquarters for the surrender of his troops.

Photo courtesy Frederick Altizer

The Cavalry had to stop while General Berger was escorted to Headquarters of the 101st Airborne Division. The principal component of his force was the 13th SS Army Corps, commanded by SS General Max Simon and comprised of the 2nd Mountain Division, Division von Donat, and the SS Nebelungen Division. It was of particular satisfaction to the 101st Cavalry Group to have been instrumental in the surrender of these troops, since they had been its principal opponents ever since the group crossed the Rhine River on March 29.

"Once the war ended," Gosnell wrote, "the soldiers stood guard together, both American and German, sometimes exchanging helmets with their former enemies and chewing gum with them."

"Most of them were just like us," said Carmickle. "They were forced to be there. Nobody really wants to be in a war. People who haven't been through it, they don't know how rough it is. But when you see your buddies killed, that's what you fight for."

"Our philosophy about the German soldiers was that they were there because they had to be, same as us," said Pierce. "Their sons and daughters had to fight, just like we did."

May 8, 1945

In accordance with the terms of the surrender, the squadrons of the 101st moved forward in their assigned sectors at 11 a.m. on May 8. By late afternoon they had occupied all enemy installations and disarmed all enemy troops in their areas. The war for the 101st was officially over.

Zell am See

Field Marshal Kesselring and the Hungarian Train

The days following the surrender became a time of celebrity hunting. Many of the high-ranking German officials had sought refuge in the Bavarian Alps, which gave some credence to the idea of the National Redoubt. Allied units seemed to be competing to see which ones could round up the most of these stars of the Third Reich.

Based on information that marshals Goering and Kesselring might be somewhere south of the 101st Cavalry zone of operations, a unit was dispatched to locate them. Headquarters for the 101st Airborne Division had provided information that indicated Goering and Kesselring might be in the vicinity of Zellersee in Austria. In the early afternoon of May 8, commanders for the 101st Airborne gave the mission to Major Edward French of the 116th Squadron, with one platoon from A Troop, which was led by Staff Sergeant Schnalzer.

"When we received our mission, I was unable to locate any-one with knowledge of the best route," wrote Major French in his report. "Therefore, we took off in the direction of Berchtes-gaden and then headed due south."

The mountainous terrain slowed the group down, and making matters worse, when they arrived at a bridge 10 miles south of Berchtesgaden, they found it destroyed, and there didn't seem to be any alternate routes.

They crossed the bridge, only to be stopped almost im-mediately by a second blown bridge. It was in worse condition than the first, but they forded the river with little trouble.

"The stream was found to be wide, but not deep," wrote Major French, "and to have a good bottom."

The men leveled the slope of the bank with shovels and removed the fan belts from all the vehicles, then the entire platoon headed across.

Zell am See, Austria

Everything was quiet at Zell am See when the platoon ar-rived around 3 p.m., but a lot of German soldiers were walking around, and the majority of them were SS.

Captain Hellman, the interpreter from an IPW team, and Major French contacted the Burgermeister who told them that the town had three large hospitals, one for the SS and the many other soldiers in the area. He also told them that a Ger-man military staff was billeted in one of the city's hotels.

"The platoon formed its vehicles in an open area near the town square and Captain Hellman and I went to the hotel," wrote French. "At the hotel, we met a Captain from the 36th Infantry Division who said he was acting as liaison officer with the German staff in contact with Field Marshal Kesselring."

French questioned the captain on the whereabouts of Kes-selring and Goering, but he didn't know. Nor did he know about the location of other high-ranking German officials.

"The only information we obtained was that he was liaison and that his headquarters were negotiating for the surrender of Kesselring and Goering through German staff at the hotel," wrote French.

Unable to make progress, French and Hellman secured a list of staff and patients from the three hospitals and learned that nearly 3,000 soldiers were hospitalized in the town.

The castle at Bruck

A Belgian prisoner of war told Sgt. Schnalzer, platoon leader for Troop A, about a large castle at Bruck, a village about three miles southeast of Zell Am See, so some of the patrol left for the castle. Once there, they discovered it was being protected by a reconnaissance platoon from a tank division of the Third Army. They questioned one of the officers, and he told them that SS personnel were being held in the castle. The commanding general of the 36th Infantry Division had just left and had given the platoon leader instructions to keep all Allied personnel out of the area.

"The whole affair seemed suspicious," wrote French.

Back in Zell am See, a German officer told French that a train with Field Marshal Kesselring and his staff on board was at Saalfelden Railroad Station. The patrol went immediately to Saalfelden and found the train.

"Captain Hellman and I reported to the adjutant and explained that we were to make sure that the Field Marshal and his staff were held in protective custody," wrote French.

The adjutant took French to Field Marshal Kesselring and explained this to him and to General Winters, his chief of staff. They agreed that no attempt to leave the train would be made by the Field Marshal or any of his staff. Guards were set up around the train, and the rest of the platoon used the hotel across the street as quarters for the night.

Goering surrenders to the 36th Division

Three reporters showed up the next morning by 9:00 o'clock. They requested an interview with Kesselring, but were denied. In about half an hour, a small patrol left for the castle at Bruck, where they found four large sedans with German markings and three German staff cars. It became clear quickly why there had been so much suspicious activity around the castle the day before. Goering and his staff had surrendered to the commanding general of the 36th Infantry Division at 10 p.m. the night before.

"We understood then that the 36th Division had known where Goering was all the time and had made negotiations for the surrender," wrote French.

The patrol returned to Zell Am See and checked in at the hotel, where French met a captain from the 508th Infantry Parachute Battalion. He was a member of an advance party sent to find billets for the battalion. French gave him what information he had, including hospital lists, as they were of no value to him at that point. They might, however, be useful in assisting the battalion when it set up a military government in the area.

German prisoners of war at a collection point.
Photo courtesy of Lt. Joseph Borkowski.

At 11:30 that morning, they returned to Saalfelden, where Major Peiper of the Field Marshal's staff again requested information as to when an American officer of rank would arrive to discuss the meeting place for negotiations.

That afternoon, around 1:30 p.m., a colonel from XXI Corps arrived and spoke to General Winters, the German chief of staff. The colonel then informed French he would probably return later that afternoon and told him to just continue guarding the train.

At about 2:30 p.m., a major from the 101st Airborne Division arrived and said he had instructions from the commanding general of the 101st Airborne to make arrangements for Kesselring and certain members of his staff to be taken to 101st Airborne Headquarters at Berchtesgaden. The major didn't make much progress. General Winters, speaking for the Field Marshal, insisted that Marshal Kesselring was entitled to meet with an American official other than a local commander.

At the end of the day, there was still no word on what to do with Field Marshal Kesselring. The three members of the press were still there, and they had not had an interview.

Finally, at 3:00 o'clock the next morning, a liaison officer from the 101st Airborne woke French up and told him that General Taylor would arrive at Saalfelden by 9:00 o'clock to meet with Field Marshal Kesselring.

General Taylor, accompanied by his G3 and interpreter, arrived promptly at 9:20 a.m. and were shown to the Field Marshal's car. Shortly thereafter, the G3 told French to move his platoon to Badgastein immediately.

Japanese Embassy

"We have information that the Japanese Ambassador, German Secretary of Economics, Secretary of Agriculture and other German officials are located there," he told French.

The platoon was on the road for Badgastein by 10 a.m. and arrived about an hour and a half later. They quickly established two roadblocks at the southern entrances to the town. Captain Hellman, Sgt. Stutzman and French went to the Swiss Embassy to see if they could find out exactly who was in town. The ambassador, his wife, and a Mr. Buchmuller, a member of the staff who spoke English, received them and arranged for the Japanese Ambassador to come to the hotel, as well as the chief of the German Foreign Office, Von Dornberg. French asked for a list of all those who had anything to do with the German government, civilian or military, and left instructions that none of those people, including their staffs, could leave their hotels.

Mr. Uchida, first secretary of the Japanese Embassy, arrived at 2:30 p.m. and explained that he was very sorry that the ambassador was not present; he was not feeling well. Uchida was told to put together a list of all members of the Embassy, down to the last child, and they were not to leave their hotels.

The Hungarian train

On the way to the Burgermeister's office, French, Hellman, and Stutzman were stopped by an elderly lady and a young man. The lady identified herself as Baroness Adele Bornemisza of Hungary. The man was a Hungarian count. The baroness told them that she needed their assistance. There was a train in the vicinity, she said, which contained valuables belonging to the Hungarian government. The items were valued at approximately $25 million, and the Nazi soldiers had made several attempts to loot the train.

"We took the baroness' name and hotel and told her we would see her later," wrote French. "Things were getting too complicated."

French met with the Franz Wagenleitner, the Burgermeister. and gave him the usual instructions on curfew, weapons, etc., and the Burgermeister assured them that he would issue instructions that no one was to leave the town. He would also provide a list of all prominent people in the town.

French also learned that the Burgermeister and others in the town were instigating a movement in Austria to free Austria of German rule and set up a free Austrian government.

"Things were really getting complicated," French wrote a second time.

Gathering up the celebrities

According to the list from the Japanese Embassy, the Japanese ambassador, Mr. Oshima, and his family, as well as members of his staff and their families – a grand total of 137 – were currently inside the Embassy.

Lists gathered from German officials revealed the following prominent people in the area:

> Secretary of State in the Reichsministry of Agriculture: Wilekens

> Reichsminister and Chief of the Reichschancellery: Harnaike

> Chief of the Reichschancellery: Dr. Lammers

> Reichsminister of Economics and President of Reichsbank: Dr. Funk

> Postmaster General: Dr. Ohnesorge

> Chief of the German Foreign Office: Von Dornberg

This information was sent to headquarters, and roadblocks were set up at all exits from the town to prevent unauthorized people from leaving.

A train filled with treasure

That night was quiet, but the next morning French was on his way back to the Swiss Embassy to learn more about the Baroness Bornemisza and the $25-million train.

"Suddenly I was approached by a man of large frame who took my arm and quickly whisked me into a nearby hotel and asked me to be seated," wrote French. "The man, who spoke little English, introduced himself as Nemeth Sandor, the Austrian wrestler. He had wrestled in the U.S.; I remember seeing a match."

Sandor said he was acting as secretary to Dr. Tobias Kornel, official of the Hungarian government. He told French that they knew the location of the train and were interested in seeing that it was taken over by the American forces, since Nazi officials were trying to confiscate the valuables.

"Things just kept getting more and more complicated," wrote French. "I couldn't figure out the relationship between the Baroness and Kornel. It seemed to me that both of them had their own fish to fry."

The Swiss Embassy couldn't help French, so he sent a small patrol to the village of Brockstein to search for the train.

"When we contacted the station master," French wrote, "he said there was a tunnel nearby, but that there were only six locomotives and nine coal cars in it and that the locomotives were inoperative. Soon after, we located a Hungarian who spoke a little English. He was questioned, and he said he knew the location of the train and its contents."

The Hungarian told French to contact an Austrian called Dr. Avar; he had papers showing exactly what the train contained: jewelry in the form of gold rings, bracelets, diamonds, ornaments, large quantities of silverware, rugs, tapestries, oil paintings, and more.

The Austrian went with French and his men into the tunnel. They walked for about three and a half miles before finding the cars, all of which were sealed. Three locomotives were deadheaded on each end. They opened one car to verify that it did contain something of value.

"The car contained oil paintings, tapestries, and rugs," wrote French. "I was satisfied that the remainder of the cars were as reported by Dr. Avar."

French didn't feel that he had the authority to open any more of the cars, so the patrol contacted the station master and gave him until 4 p.m. to get the locomotives and cars out of the tunnel. One team from Troop A were left to guard the cars once they were removed from the tunnel.

By 5 p.m. the locomotives and 25 cars containing the valuables were on a siding, and by 7 p.m., the Japanese ambassador, Mr. Oshima, and his secretary, Mr. Uchida; Mr. Wileckers; Mr. Harnaike; Dr. Lammers and his secretary, Capt. Priet; Dr. Funk and his secretary, Capt. Mahrwald; and Dr. Ohnesorge were all in custody and on their way to Corps headquarters.

At 8 p.m. the executive officer of the 101st Cavalry Group, Lt. Col. Mortenson, arrived and said he wanted definite proof that the railroad cars contained valuables. Col. Mortenson, Major French, and Capt. Wood went to the train to verify the contents, and Dr. Avar produced his papers for Col. Mortenson, explaining what the train contained. Four cars were opened and Col. Mortenson checked two cars which contained silverware and jewelry, and Capt. Wood checked two cars which contained rugs, tapestries, and oil paintings. Both were satisfied that the train contained articles of great value. Dr. Avar valued the contents of the train at $25 million.

Col. Mortenson left at 7:30 a.m. to rejoin Group Headquarters, and at 8:20 a.m. the platoon of Troop A left Badgastein to rejoin the squadron at St. Ulrich.

"Thus ending," wrote French, "a most interesting experience for all."

Map 17
May 8-12, 1945
Platoon A, 116th Squadron
Major Edward French's mission

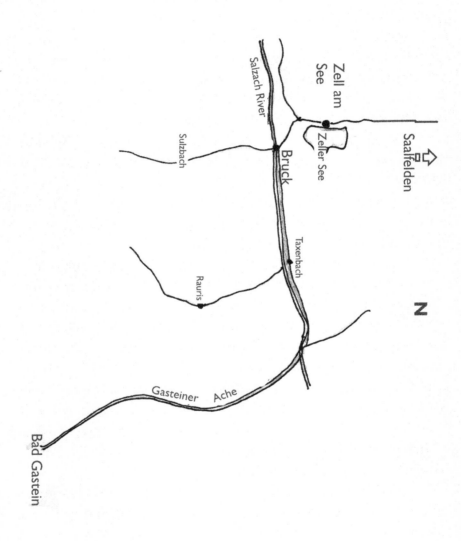

Occupation Begins

Heidelberg

Saalfelden

On May 9, the 101st Cavalry Group began to move farther south into the Alps to help transport thousands of prisoners to the various holding areas established by XXI Corps and to supervise the stockpiling of German vehicles, weapons, ammunition, and supplies.

At Kössen, Austria, the men of Group Headquarters found they were living in the same small town as the Headquarters of the 13th SS Corps. The two groups didn't exactly strike up any friendships, Sweeney wrote, but they did take the opportunity to talk and compare notes with some of the SS staff officers.

On May 10, Headquarters and other units of the Group moved to Saalfelden, Austria, to establish security around the luxurious train that had, until recently, been occupied by General Kesselring and his entourage.

Lt. Col. Leonard wrote to his sister from Austria, telling her about their occupation duties.

Austria
May 10, 1945
Dear Catherine,

Tonight for the first time since we have been on this side of the water, we have lights without any blackout restrictions. No worry about blackout curtains and blackout driving, which at times was very slow and difficult. This little item in itself is a relief to all of us. Today and for the next day or so, Squadron Headquarters is occupying a resort hotel in a valley surrounded by snow-covered mountains. The hotel reminds me of the small hotels one would find in Atlantic City or similar resorts. The troops are spread out in the nearby towns. Some have good accommodations, others not so good. In every case we had to vacate the German officers and soldiers. Our present job is to round up all the German soldiers, particular attention to the SS boys, get them in central locations, and hold them pending further orders. It's not a bad job. I have detailed various officers jobs so that I may sit and enjoy the sun and take it easy while I can.

We have no idea what is going to happen next, but I feel it will be some time before we will be back in the good old USA. There is much work still to be done and someone will have to do it. I hope it's not us. Since the shooting was over, very little or no emotions were shown by any of our bunch – just relieved that this phase is over. I wonder how people back home can raise hell and celebrate, especially those who have no good reason. Seems to me they would be doing something if they went to a church and thanked God we came through.

On May 12 the men of the 101st Cavalry turned their backs on the scene of their final combat operations. Separated from the 101st Airborne Division, they took up occupation duty in the Odenwald Forest — a familiar area. The Group's command post was initially set up at Erbach in the center of the forest, but soon moved farther west to Jugenheim at the edge of the Rhine River. Here the troops settled in for an uneasy stay — uneasy because no one knew for how long or whether their next stop would be home or the Pacific.

The Group had one officer trained in military government, Major E. L. Harris. Although he had worked diligently as the cavalry passed through dozens of towns, he was not able to handle an area as large as the Odenwald Forest. Fortunately, a small military government detachment soon arrived, providing experts in government and public utilities. Even so, the job of carrying out the everyday tasks rested with the troopers.

Throughout the war, some soldiers always had taken care of these every day tasks, and Sweeney gave them credit in *Wingfoot*:

> As the war winds down it is well to say something of the men who did so much and were heard of so little. Writers, historians, photographers, and newsmen record and glorify the front line fighting men and their commanders but are prone to neglect those who made it possible for them to fight successfully. These are the people of the medical, supply, communications, maintenance, and ordnance elements who kept the fighting machine oiled and running. With the lines of supply extended from the French and Belgian ports to the battle lines deep in Germany, it was a back-breaking, twenty-four-hour-a-day job to keep the ammunition supplied, the men fed, the wounded evacuated, and the weapons and vehicles in good repair. Our squadron sup-

ply and maintenance elements were extremely
vulnerable to ambush as they shuttled back and
forth from supply points and ammunition depots
to the front. It is right and proper that these men
as well as those who fired the weapons be given
the full credit for what they did.

The cavalrymen posted and enforced occupation regulations, restricted travel, and dealt with shortages of food and
vital equipment. One of their most important tasks was finding Germans capable of re-establishing a working government. General Eisenhower had decreed that no Nazis would be
permitted back into government, making their job even more
difficult. General George Patton had been relieved of command
of the Third U.S. Army because he had disagreed, considering
the restoration of German control to the government the highest priority. He continued to recruit the most capable Germans,
Nazi or not, to do the job.

People from various countries who have been displaced by the war wait for transport home.

Photo courtesy Joseph Borkowski.

Russians headed home after the war.
Photo courtesy Joseph Borkowski.

During the weeks leading to the end of the war, the cavalry had passed small roving groups of slave laborers, released allied soldiers captured by the Germans, as well as other displaced people. Now these people were seen in the thousands, blown across the countryside like dried leaves in the wind. This put the cavalrymen in a new role. The desperate need for controlled sanitation, order, and discipline required firm measures, but it also had to be carried out as kindly as possible.

The mixture of languages complicated the work of control, and one young officer faced with a looting situation that was getting completely out of hand ordered a .50 caliber machine gun fired overhead. The crowd, including the looters themselves, rushed to the curbstones and cheered, "Oora Americanetz!" The young officer had no idea if his action was about to cause a riot or if he was being cheered, even by the looters, for bringing order.

On May 13, the 116th was ordered to assemble in the vicinity of Lorsch, and once again headed along the autobahn up through Munich, a "motor march" that continued until 5 p.m. on May 14.

"The whole outfit moved into Lorsch and two men were assigned to a house," said Buck Fluharty. "In my case, my tank driver and myself took an upstairs room in a house where a mother and her two daughters lived. All others had similar places. The older daughter, around 20 or so, had a husband missing on the Russian front, younger girl was 16 – they kept our room clean, had outdoor plumbing, little to eat (mostly potatoes dug up from fields around town). We gave them quite a bit to eat from our surplus of rations."

"The German people were hungry," said John Almond. "I remember one little kid coming up to us and wanting scraps from our mess kit he was so hungry."

In a letter home, written on May 22, John Allen wrote:

> Since the time our outfit was on the front line, until the time when the war was over, we were in action all the time. We finally pulled back up the autobahn past Munich to the town of Lorsch, where we enjoyed our first rest. We spearheaded the 12th Armored Division and the 63rd Division and the 4th Division, and some smaller units.
>
> We built up a name for ourselves, and all over the front, everybody knew about the 116th Cavalry. The 101st, which we were a part of, took all the credit, and we did all the work. But the worm has turned now and when anybody speaks about the 101st Cavalry Group, nobody knows about them. They wonder about the 116th. We were up for a presidential citation turned in by the 12th Armored, but our colonel turned it down, since it was only for the 116th, and not for the 101st.
>
> One day we had orders to cross a bridge at all cost and take the town on the other side. We

did and when the 12th got there, they wanted to know where we were – we were gone. They found out we had gone on and taken the next town up the road. When they got there, they found we were five towns up and still advancing. We had the Germans on the run, pushing back a whole army with a few jeeps and armored cars and light tanks.

We had some big guns with us, but we never did see them. We went 20 miles an hour, and they went 20 miles a day. We made good use of our speed, capturing towns, leaving the infantry to clean them up, and moving on to the next town. Sure we got shot at, but we shot back. We lost a few men, but that's war.

Now don't go worrying about me. It's all over and I'm okay. I look the same as I did when I left Ohio. I may be a few pounds thinner, and maybe lost some of my good looks and table manners. I also have picked up a few more cuss words, but will try hard to lose the habit of using them when I get home. I always think about home, and look forward to the letters I get. I'm always glad to hear that all is well with you and Dad and Sis. I did my part and now leave the old biddies who talked about the farmers who were deferred for farm work. Nobody every said anything to me, but I knew it was being thought of me. Maybe some of the boys were in longer than me, but were never on the front lines. Maybe they're hauling supplies or fixing radios or doing this and that. Those were all necessary jobs, but I was there in front of everybody else, helping to spearhead for the 7th Army, which covered half the western front.

When I get back, I'll have a good line to hand them about what the 116th Cavalry Squadron did. There are a bunch of guys here who are really tops, and I'm proud to say I was a part of their battles. True, I came on as a replacement, but they had only been on the line about two weeks when I joined them. I did all right in battle, since several times officers spoke words of praise about my efforts under fire. I was made corporal on May 15. It seems like all the boys like me, and they are glad that I am their leader. I say again, don't worry about me. All is well.

Chaplain Maurice Powers

The following letter was written by Chaplain Maurice Powers at the end of the war. Almost every veteran I met had a copy, and they were happy to share them. Often, when I wrote to men, asking to interview them about their service, they sent me this letter instead of a phone number.

Somewhere in Austria, sixth day of peace, May 1945

I sat in a long armored column of hundreds of vehicles with thousands of troops on Hitler's famed autobahn that stretches from Munich to the Austrian border close to the fortress of Der Fuhrer called Berchtesgaden the night when Germany was surrendering its forces to General Eisenhower. Thousands of once proud

Wehrmacht in stolid gray marched by dejectedly. Forlorn, defeated, they hardly raised their eyes as they filed endlessly in column to a prison cage. War was over, but we did not know it at that hour; we only knew the order was to stand by. A few hours before, I beheld what I know now only from memory: a thousand hills in flame, a dozen villages blazing; a thousand spiraling flares that lighted pathways of death, the whining terror of a screaming "meemee" or the dread curse of a tree-bursting 88 mm.

On we pushed down the Saalach Valley into Austria, far below Salzburg and Berchtesgaden, into the snow-crested mountains that lifted their hoary foreheads into the purple azure and glistened into Chiemsee. Valleys were redolent with beauty: clean wholesome Austrian children waving white flags and tossing flowers; maidens matching their Tyrolean costumes with their glistening blonde hair.

Yes, the war is over, yet I see the faces of my men, their pallor, their hollow eyes who look at me in death.

The tanks and armored cars roll on endlessly under spring cloudless skies, even into the night and early morning at the forming of the dew. There are crystal

Chaplain Maurice Powers
Photo courtesy Jay Leonard.

waters here in the Alps and but some will never drink of them. ... The war is over.

When the sirens sounded over the world for VE Day, they hurled ticker tape from stone cliffs into the canyons of Wall Street, they lifted toasts of champagne along the Champs Elysees, Picadilly Circus in London was in a holiday mood, salvoes of artillery belched forth in Moscow. Commentators in American circles proclaimed the might of marching men across African sands, through Cassino, along Normandy beachheads, the break through of the Siegfried Line (which I witnessed myself) and the drive into a prostrate Germany. Eloquent words! But I was with my men (New York's own 101st Mechanized Cavalry armored Unit), men who fought the SS into their last redoubt and on. They said nothing. They just remembered. ...

They knew the Purple Hearts were on the way and imagined neat white crosses where Mack and Chuck were laid. They knew no glorious drives, no magnificent marches. They know only that it was hell all the way. They were almost silent as I walked over two miles down along that column on Hitler's arterial autobahn. "Heck, Father, why celebrate if it's true it's over. There's still Burma and Tokyo.

They knew only that tomorrow meant more C or K rations, the 92nd day without a break. They were silent and humble, for it was a long way from America, from home, the kids, a bride.

I've watched thousands kneel at my masses aboard a transport on the blue breast of the Atlantic. We have shared the vistas of Wordsworth and Scott in the Lake Region of England. The stone houses and pebbled streets. The Channel crossing in LSTs; the push across France through Joan of Arc's Rouen, Verdun, and Soissons, where we slept in the shadow of the old cathedral; down along the Marne and Moselle rivers that claim memories of blood from other decades;

into the valley of the Saar under the aegis of the gallant 7th Army; and then through the Siegfried on to Munich to Austria on the heels of the swift fleeing SS and Wehrmacht.

A daily change of position, blackout driving at night as we moved forward, sniper fire along lonesome highways, towns burning as we rolled into them to occupy, being pinned down by unknown machine gun nests, the crossing of the Rhine on Pontoon bridge, the sudden abandonment of one's jeep when jets sprayed us with steel from the skies at Tauberbishofsheim or Lauda. The mad scramble for a foxhole when 88s spread their mantle of devastation, the terrible tree bursts that killed men of my unit, the panzerfausts that riddled the flower of my combat armored unit. The sleepless nights along a highway bordering the Danube near Augsburg, and then the dreaded ordeal of facing the insanity of Himmler's madmen, called the SS. I have seen

Bordon Holloman.

Photo courtesy of Edith Holloman.

what the product of warped minds can be: my own men blown to shreds by triple mines in the highway. I have helped gather one of the finest soldiers into a litter, his body riddled in three pieces. Others are broken in body and heart-twisted frames that will never walk or speak again.

This May morning, in a cloud of apple blossoms along a mirror-smooth Neckar River, I drove to an American military cemetery to see those I knew and loved. I found endless rows of white crosses set in perfect diagonals that stretched away endlessly in the morning sunlight, marking a design for eternity. Their valor is enveloped forever in silence: perhaps all too soon forgotten except by some Gold Star mother far away.

Most memorable of all my days was not the crossing of the Rhine, nor that of watching the muddy waters of the Danube under our pontoon bridge, nor of the visit to quaint old Heidelberg; the ride through devastated Munich or my hours in Berchtesgaden on the Austrian border, but rather the Concentration Camp on the Lech River near Landsburg and Munich. We were waiting to cross a bridge that had been under fire, when suddenly one of my soldiers came running: "Father, see those smoldering ruins, come quickly. There is the awfulest sight you've ever seen."

I saw the unbelievable sight of hundreds of huddled nude forms still smoldering from the fires initiated the day before. They had been starved until their gaunt forms at death weighed less than 60 pounds in most cases. Twenty escaped from the atrocity of the day before. I spoke with three of them. They told me the story: "We were called political enemies of Nazism."

Some were from Belgium, Poland, Russia, Holland, England, Italy, Spain, and Slovakia. "We were given one crust of bread and three potatoes a week. We ate grass to live," they told me. "The young Jewish and Catholic pair I spoke with was 25 and 28 years old, Sgt. Friedman, an IPW interpreter, was with me. Both prisoners were men of 170 lbs., who both now weighed less than 80 lbs. They told of special cases where prisoners were poisoned, how some were gassed and the lethal chambers of cremation. It beggars description in words. They even spoke of the staff of the camp who celebrated those executions by a bacchanalian orgy, using even the skulls of victims as cognac flasks. Some were made to dig their own graves, then stand on the edge where they could fall in after being machine gunned. This is not fiction. This was told to me by two prisoners who played dead for five hours under a work bench.

Any chaplain has poignant memories of his work. One cold March day the whistled moan of giant 155s came over, knocked the porch off the house we selected as a medical aid station, the second killed four men eight feet from me. The third ripped the back porch to pieces, knocked us down, and wounded two. I cannot understand why I am alive today.

Tec. 4 A.B. Cantrell
of Chicago, Ill.
Photo courtesy of Clair Becker.

"Will I make it, Padre?" knowing they have 10 minutes left.

These men are spearheads, often the first to enter conquered territory. Fearless, fighting, and at once gracious, smiling, amusing and filled with vivacity that only the American soldier has. I've seen them do coiffeurs in a conquered Fraulein's beauty shop near Munich, watched them clear the crèmes from the shelf, pack them away and then turn them into a chaplain's office. I've seen them laugh when they had a manure pile for a front porch to their nightly rest under the stars.

I've seen them weep when their buddies were announced as dead from sniper fire. For

91 consecutive days I rode in column, went with them day and night, knew their fears their lack of baths, their torn clothing, their best girls in Buffalo, Nashville, or Omaha. They were with me Easter Sunday noon in Hardheim when a jet plane strafed the town and dropped two bombs, 8 feet and 30 feet from the church as they knelt at mass.

I saw their faces in the early morning rain when news came that our great Commander-in-Chief [Franklin Roosevelt] was dead on April 12.

I watched their eager faces when I spoke to them of the history of Augsburg, Heidelburg, Worms, Speyer, Munich, and the Beer-Hall Putsch of 1923, of the Brenner Pass and of Mozart's home in Salzburg. You can't get to know an American soldier from the Pathé News, from an Alan Ladd movie, or the glowing account of Ernie Pyle. You must be with them, eat the same K rations, watch them in the motor pools, catch their humor, and glimpse their reactions when mail is handed out. They are real, sincere, wholesome, fearless, yet kind – a flower of manhood.

Memorial Day 1945

On Memorial Day, May 30, 1945, Chaplain Powers held a Memorial Service in Lorsch for members of the 116th Squadron who had died in battle. Like Major French's report on the capture of Field Marshal Kesselring and the chaplain's letter after the war, his Memorial Day sermon was widely distributed.

The day of the service, many of the men went to the American Military Cemetery in Bensheim. Photos taken that day include one of my father with the rest of his platoon. His face, and the faces of the 10 other men in the photo, reflect the mixed emotions Lt. Col. Leonard wrote about in a letter:

" … for the men of the 101st Cavalry, there was little joy even though the war was over. Too many of their friends lay beneath the white markers in Bensheim, where 2,722 U.S. soldiers are buried."

In his sermon, Father Powers remembered the members of the 101st who had died:

> The sergeant in the Graves Registration Office read the list: wrist watch. Check! Wallet and $14.00. Check! Five snapshots, marksman medal, ring, and crucifix. Check! They were placed in a neat canvas bag and sent home. The fact of the death is as common knowledge and has been duly recorded in the hometown paper. Who was he? He was Chuck, Bob, Red, or Hank. Perhaps you never knew his name, but you saw his grave at Bensheim this morning, neat, trim, and very near to one which might have been your own, but wasn't. You have seen him somewhere.

Memorial Day, Lorsch, Germany, 1945.
Photo courtesy Clair Becker.

Perhaps in a coach on the Santa Fe, New York Central, or Southern lines. He mingled amidst crowds in depots across America and occasionally you brushed shoulders with him as he waited with his girl for tickets in line at the Orpheum. He ate beside you in some restaurant and once he passed you on Wilshire Blvd. or Broadway or Wabash Blvd. or down in Altoona, Dallas, or Cheyenne, and he was often known to purchase sodas at Liggett Drug Store long before he was apprenticed to the Army. Well, anyway, he is dead, and you saw his grave this morning. You knew him. I knew him, too.

A few weeks ago he was with you, a part of that mighty machine to overcome ugly, chaotic war, a war of hardness, sweat, and grind-

At the American cemetery in Bensheim, Germany, Memorial Day 1945. Author's father is front row left; Lt. Borkowski is second from the left.
Photo courtesy Joseph Borkowski.

ing fear, where the whistle of death rode on the night wind, and you both saw one hundred hills aflame; a war which saw warped science labor to make men become heretics of civilization. The war here in Germany is over. Territories are being wrangled over, punishment and guilt conferred, and the ruined devastation policed. Charters will be sealed with wax above the bodies of the dead men, and great oratory will laud the men who crashed the Siegfried Line, the Rhine, and the Danube (as you did). In that gallant sweep, some men fell. You knew them personally. And they were like you. They had dreams, plans, and hearts that loved. We who are left praise them. A high school graduating class remember them; a mother, wife, or girlfriend fingers his latest photograph with moist eyes.

Now, no more sight of ugly panzers, no more blackout driving across uncharted roads and fields, no more deadly night patrols, nor

At the American cemetery in Bensheim, Germany, Memorial Day 1945.
Photo courtesy Joseph Borkowski.

tree-bursting 88s that whine and kill. Now only quiet folded hands as he awaits with still blood-stained face the reveille of morning light. He has bivouacked for the last time. But he has left us a heritage: 'No greater love than this: that a man lay down his life for his friends.'

Sleep on, brave men of the Cavalry whom we honor today. You have fought injustice with heroism and consecrated the soil of an alien land with your blood. You have not died for the empty praise of some orator, nor for some posthumous citation, but for the common people like your

Photo courtesy Seab McPherson.

mother and mine that they might have the security and peace ensured by our Bill of Rights. Your death bestowed an obligation on us today: never to compromise what you fought so valiantly to attain. Out of fresh-made graves where you lie peacefully, we seem to hear your voices.

Lorsch 2006

Lorsch

Buck Fluharty had shared a number of stories and photos with me, including a picture of three women that he took in Lorsch – a mother and her two daughters. He and Ralph Nichols, a member of his tank crew, had been billeted in their home for a short time after the war.

"I wish I knew what happened to them," he said when I called to thank him for the photos. That made me wonder along with him if the daughters were still alive and living in Lorsch. I would love to find out if they were, but it seemed un-likely. Not knowing where else to start, I sent an e-mail to the tourism department of the city, hoping someone in that depart-ment might speak English. It was a lucky day for me, since the letter fell into the hands of Petra Wooden.

Born and raised in Lorsch, Wooden seemed eager to help me. She had also spent 20 years in the U.S. Air Force and spoke perfect English. In just a few days she not only had located the Levasier sisters, now Anna Gutschalk and Regina Brunnen-gräber, but had contacted them on my behalf. They would be willing to see me, she wrote in her reply e-mail. I immediately let Buck Fluharty know, and he sent a letter to the women, re-establishing a friendship that was more than 60 years old. I was looking forward to visiting Lorsch.

Ted and I had parted company in Munich, and he was on his way to Prague. I felt fairly comfortable reading directional signs and getting around train stations, so I wasn't concerned about being on my own.

To go from Munich to Lorsch by train requires a change in Bensheim. Then there is just a short, five-minute ride to complete the trip. My first mistake, once I got as far as Bensheim, was to look at the regional instead of the local train schedule. I could find no train to Lorsch listed there, but because it is a

small station, I could see a bus from where I stood that would take me where I wanted to go. It would leave in 40 minutes, so I relaxed and spent some time browsing in a small gift shop, buying a map of the area, and reading a book over a cup of coffee.

Anna and Regina Levasier and their mother.

Photo courtesy Buck Fluharty.

I studied my new map and decided I could just watch for the train station from the bus and get of there. Easy. The station was right across the street from my hotel and, so far, every city or town I had visited had a bus stop at the train station. My bus to Lorsch left right on time, and as we approached the town, I began to look for anything that looked like a train station. The bus circled through the city, stopping at a number of different locations, mostly unmarked street corners. I saw nothing that looked like railroad tracks or a train station, and, before long, the bus was clearly headed out of town and back to Bensheim. The driver made eye contact with me in his rearview mirror as he pulled onto the main highway. In German, he asked me where I was going.

"Lorsch," I said.

"Where in Lorsch," is what I think he said next.

"Hauptbahnhoff," I said. Train station.

By understanding a few of his words and watching him shake his head back and forth, I realized that this bus did not stop at the train station. I was going back to Bensheim.

"No problem," I said, smiling at the back of his head. Another 40 minutes had passed.

Back at the Bensheim train station, I went to the tourist agency attached to the train station and asked about Lorsch, something I should have done the first time.

"You just missed the train," the woman said in perfect English. "The next one is in an hour." So I spent another hour in Bensheim, waiting for a five-minute train ride. Someday, I thought, this would be funny. But not yet.

Once I finally caught my train, it really did take only minutes to reach Lorsch, and I was happy to see that the train station really was directly across the street from my hotel, the Karolinger-Hof Hotel and Restaurant.

I needed to call Petra Wooden, but there was no phone in the room and my cell phone needed recharging. I asked permission to use the hotel's phone, and it took a meeting of two or three employees before I finally was understood and received permission.

Petra was happy to hear I had made it to town, and we made our appointment for 3:00 p.m. the next day, still early enough that I would be able to reach Heidelberg for a late dinner that evening. I should have felt better once that was settled, but I didn't. Tears were pushing at the back of my eyes, and my head was starting to ache. I sat down at one of the four tables in the hotel's restaurant, took out my journal, and ordered a glass of wine and dinner – jägersnitzel (pork in a dark mushroom sauce). When dinner came, I ordered a second glass of wine. Only two other people were eating that early – it was

Ralph Nichols with the Levasier family in Lorsch.
Photo courtesy of Buck Fluharty.

about 5:00 p.m. by then – an enormous man in a blue work shirt and suspenders and a woman with stringy, cherry-colored hair.

While writing in my journal, which was filled with photos of my father, the stress and loneliness of the day finally caught up with me, and I started to cry. Unwilling to have strangers witness my tears, I raised my book up close to my face. It wasn't so much that I was lonely or that I missed home, as much as that I missed my father.

Bruce Chatwin writes, "Wherever men have trodden they have left a trail of song (of which we may, now and then, catch an echo) ..." I had come to Germany hoping to hear a bit of that echo, which is why I was sitting alone and miserable in this smoke-filled German restaurant. But I didn't hear it; all I heard was American rock and roll blaring on the radio and the screaming trains braking in the station across the street.

The next morning, I stayed in my room until check-out time, and by then I felt I could face Lorsch one-on-one. The clerk let me check my bags behind the counter, and with four hours to kill before I met Petra Wooden, I went to see the town. I found the post office and mailed some postcards, including one to Buck Fluharty, and I stopped at the floral shop to buy flowers for Anna Gutschalk and Regina Brunnengräber. And I took time to see the sights of Lorsch: an audience hall that was built around 800 for Charlemagne and, curiously, a tobacco museum.

It is likely that my father had also been billeted in Lorsch, but I had no idea where. I suppose it was also possible that the family he stayed with still lived in the same house today, just as Anna Gutschalk lived in the house where Buck Fluharty had stayed. Fluharty told me that the entire 101st moved into Lorsch, and men were assigned two to a house. So where and with whom had my father lived? As I passed elderly men and women on the street, I couldn't help but wonder what would happen if I stopped them and showed them my photos of their town in 1945, and asked if they knew my father.

At 3:00 p.m. Wooden picked me up and drove me to Frau Brunnengräber's house to pick her up, and then drove to Frau Gutschalk's house. Frau Gutschalk had just had surgery, so I promised to keep the visit short.

On the outside, the house looked much the same as it had in 1945. It had been updated, but the shape and the windows remained as they had been. Inside, the walls were covered with family photos, icons, and crosses, and the windows were covered with lace curtains.

As I sat across from the two women at their dining room table, I kept seeing the two girls they once were standing with their mother in Fluharty's photo. In that picture, they pose in front of their home with its large vegetable garden, which is only possible because Lorsch was spared much of the destructive bombing of nearby Mannheim. Both girls are smiling, but Anna's smile is more reserved, while Regina's borders on laughter. Their blonde hair frames round cheeks and brushes the collars of their flower-print dresses. Regina and her mother wear aprons over their dress, but Anna has probably taken hers off for the photo.

Anna Gutschalk and Regina Brunnengräber in 2006.

When I met them, the women were 77 and 81 years old. Regina wore her steel gray hair brushed back from her face. She reminded me of my grandmother, even down to the expression on her face. Anna's hair was white, and she appears more frail than her sister, perhaps because of her recent surgery.

For about an hour we sat and talked about the things old women everywhere enjoy talking about: Frau Gutschalk's recent surgery and the high cost of hospitalization and medicine, our children, and the past. Finally, with Petra Wooden's help, we spoke about the war.

Although neither sister spoke English, and I had almost given up on my limited German, I understood the one phrase they repeated over and over: "We never thought of each other as enemies, only as friends."

Frau Brunnengräber told me that Fluharty had tried to get her and her husband to come to America after the war, but they didn't want to leave Germany. Fluharty was, she said, a good man.

"He never chased after the women," translated Petra Wooden. "He wasn't like that."

Fluharty had painted a picture of her, Frau Brunnengräber said, and in it she was standing on the doorstep and holding a broom. Before I left, she promised to look for the painting and maybe send it to him someday.

I took out the album of photos I had brought with me and showed them the photo Fluharty had taken of them as young women, as well as a few others. Frau Gutschalk pointed to a picture of my father and said she recognized him. For just a moment I hoped, but she remembered him as an officer. Finally, she shook her head and said no, she must be mistaken.

Before I left, Frau Gutschalk gave me two crocheted doilies she had made, and thanked me for coming. Petra gave me a tie with the city crest on it, and asked that I send it to Fluharty. She also gave me a packet of information on the city.

When I got home, I e-mailed photos of the women to Flu-harty, who told me later that he had been stunned by how much they had changed; he hadn't expected them to look like old women. Then he laughed and said that he probably didn't look exactly the same either.

Two weeks after I got home, a thick packet of photos arrived from Joseph Borkowski. Among the photos was one of him with several members of his platoon, including my father. They were in Bensheim, the bane of my trip to Germany. For the first time, I learned of the American Military Cemetery there. On the back of the photo Borkowski had written, "Paying respects to the unlucky ones."

Summer 1945

Heidelberg

In June, the 101st was beginning its occupation duties in an area around Heidelberg and Lorsch. Leaves were being granted, and some of the officers spent time on the Riviera or in the United Kingdom. The enlisted men were able to go on leave, too, once they had been "medically inspected for scabies, lice and venereal disease and were found free of same."

Priority was now the defeat of Japan, so there were not enough ships and planes to get the men home as quickly as they hoped. According to Major Sweeney in *Wingfoot*, this led to a breakdown in discipline in the Army. Resentment began to grow in some divisions, and almost daily demonstrations occurred during June and July in Frankfurt, fifty miles north of where the cavalry was stationed. Commanders of the 101st gave credit to the cavalrymen for never losing their morale or their discipline.

"I was always proud of our men," said Borkowski, "I remember one time in Munich, before the war was over, we were turning a tank around and knocked down a wall in front of a nice home. The man came out and he was pretty mad. He said it was a shame that his wall, which he had built, had survived bombings, and then we come and knock it over. My men took up a collection of $40 to pay for his wall. He cried when we gave it to him. That's how we built goodwill with the German people."

Troop B, 116th, arrived in Heidelberg on June 1 to serve as guard troops for the 6th Army Group.

"It was such a pretty place," said Clinton Thompson. "We spent a month in a hotel there right on the river. We were supposed to keep the civilians in line as peacekeepers and help get the city back in operation. Units that had been there before us

A destroyed bridge across the Neckar River in Heidelberg.

Photo courtesy of Joseph Borkowski.

had made a deal with the mayor, who asked them to spare the city in exchange for a promise there would be no sniper fire. So there was hardly any damage to the city, just the rail yard, which had been bombed. It seemed almost like a vacation."

What had been bombed were the bridges across the river. "There was only one bridge that wasn't bombed," said Borkowski. "We stayed at the Hoffbrau, a hotel near that bridge. The tennis court was right outside our hotel. One thing I remember from Heidelberg was this ballroom on top of a big wine barrel."

That wine barrel was still in Heidelberg when I was there. It is located in the castle that sits above the town. I walked up the hill to the castle on my first full day in Heidelberg and looked out over the city. Spared from the bombing, many of the buildings in the old part of town date back centuries, and, if I ignored the Starbucks signs, I could easily imagine what it looked like when my father was here.

In Heidelberg, the men had time for sightseeing and games, like volleyball. They had German beer and waited for passes, sometimes for quick trips to France or to England.

Clinton Gosnell was quartered in a schoolhouse in Heidelberg right after the war and eager to get back to his girlfriend in England.

"One day I was told to hook up a phone line from the school into the German lines so we could turn the radios on," he wrote. "As I hooked up the lines, I heard a colonel talking to F Troop's captain. He was saying that one man from F Troop was going to go back to England on a furlough the next day. Every other outfit got two men on furlough, but F Troop only got one, because we were a smaller troop. When I got back to the school, my sergeant said to me that I was going back to England the next day on a seven-day pass. I couldn't believe my luck. Next morning I took off in a jeep for headquarters where we gathered in one 10-ton truck to cross the German border. We caught a French train and rode to a port city where

In front of the Brauerei Hotel in Heidelberg.
Photo courtesy Joseph Borkowski.

we crossed the channel to Southhampton. We were issued English train passes that we could ride anywhere in the U.K. I headed north. We pulled into the station about 6 p.m. on a Saturday night. As I walked through the village, I felt everyone was looking at me. Just as I was about to knock on Eileen's door, it opened and she and her friend, Dorothy, came out on their way to a dance. The girlfriend disappeared rather fast when she saw me. It seemed as if the whole town knew by that time that the Yank had come back to marry the Windle girl. It didn't happen just then, but it did happen later on, and we've been married 49 years."

Some of the men made attempts to learn German while in Heidlberg, and Borkowski remembers a woman named Margo who was teaching them. Margo's dad was involved in some aspect of the steel mills after the war.

"She wrote to me when I got back to the states, asking for notebook paper," said Borkowski. "I don't remember if I sent it or not."

In Heidelberg, I crossed the Neckar to the side of the river where the men had fought while the city watched, and I climbed to Philosopher's Walk, where I watched the evening sun warm the red stone of Heiliggeistkirche, Holy Ghost

Above: Playing volleyball by the old bridge in Heidelberg. Below: The chaplain enjoys a beer in Heidelberg.

Photos courtesy of Joseph Borkowski.

Church. The war was over for the men of the 101st, and my father and the others would soon return home. The beauty of Heidelberg would at least be something they could talk about.

At 5:15 p.m. on June 25, good news finally came for the 101st. Lt. Col. Leonard received the orders he had been waiting for: "As of 24 June the 116th Cavalry Reconnaissance Squadron is under alert instruction to be prepared for redeployment indirect through Normandy Base Section." All of their equipment would need to be turned in, and a list of distribution centers would come later.

The following day at around 5 p.m., Leonard received a radiogram letter from Headquarters, 7th Army, dated 23 June 1945. It read: "…the 116th Cavalry Reconnaissance Squadron Mechanized is alerted for early movement from the Army area. Action is being initiated to return Troop B, which is attached to 6th Army Group, to parent unit. Unit is being redeployed indirect through Normandy Base Section. Personnel readiness date is 15 July 1945."

The 116th Squadron was going home. The next week was a busy one as the troopers collected equipment and vehicles and prepared to turn them in to the designated depots. Troop B was relieved of its mission with the 6th Army, and on July 1-2, the troop left Heidelberg and arrived at its new assembly area, Reichenbach, at 2 p.m.

On July 4, the 116th left for Duclair, France. At 7 a.m., Major Feagin, Captain Clarence Spill, and Lt. Mann, along with a small group of enlisted men, departed by quarter-ton truck, and at 8 a.m. the various columns of vehicles departed, including two half-ton trucks loaded with equipment to be turned in at the various depots in Germany, France, and Belgium. They were all to meet again at Camp Twenty Grand. Those men not going by vehicle were transported to Mannheim, where they boarded a train for Duclair. The entire train was composed of box cars with 30 men per car. The long, uncomfortable journey ended on July 6 at 5:45 p.m.

Once in France, the men completed their processing by July 10 and were told they would leave for home on July 18. Their hopes were dashed, however, on July 12, when they received word that the squadron had lost its shipping priority. Days and weeks of disappointed inactivity followed.

Lt. Col. Leonard wrote one more letter to his wife, addressing her as "Fifi" in honor of his return to France.

July 14, 1945
Vicinity of Le Havre, France
My dear Fifi,

Well, we weathered Friday the 13th, nothing unusual happened. All of us wish something would, such as getting on a boat for home. All our details are completed and now we have nary a thing to do but eat and sleep. It's hard to suppress anxiety. No orders for movement have been received by us to date. On our arrival here one week ago, we were advised that our stay would be five or six days. Today I checked with headquarters here and they are at a loss for an explanation as to why we have not received shipment orders. Now rumors are plentiful and not pleasant. All the boys have written home about their expected trip home, and now fear that it is all a dream and morale is sinking. Yours truly, however, has high hopes that everything will work out and believe that the delay is just one of those things that happens in the Army. It is possible, but remote, that the War Department has other plans for us. In that event, there will be a lot of "beefing" in this outfit – so here we sit – really "sweating it out." No passes, no mail and nothing to do. I know that you, too, feel about the same way I do and hope something will break soon. In the interim, bear with me and keep courage (I have 119 points). I will keep you posted. At least I

will give you an idea when we are to leave, when
I hear it officially.

Hughie

≈≈≈

Because of the point system, some men of the 101st left
earlier than others. Buck Fluharty must have been one of those
who went home early, since he remembers being in the Atlantic on the Fourth of July. "The Navy crew fired five-inch guns
straight up to celebrate the holiday. It was a 12-day trip home,
and we ended up right where we left from: Fort Dix, N.J. We
were given a ticket to a mess hall, a one-shot deal. Got the largest steak I ever saw with all the trimmings."

Both squadrons were alerted at different times for movement to the Pacific Theater of Operations, and some of those
who had returned in July were sent to Camp Campbell, Kentucky, to prepare for redeployment.

In front of the Hollander Hof in Heidelberg.
Photo courtesy of Joseph Borkowski.

"Us old-timers were going home to train men for the invasion of Japan," said Gorski. "We weren't worried about going ourselves."

The Japanese surrender on August 15, 1945, ended those plans, and the squadrons were de-activated, each man going to the station nearest his home for discharge.

"We had been told we were going to the Pacific after a furlough," Fluharty remembers, "but during my stay at Fort Meade, I went into Baltimore one night with a friend when VJ day was announced. The whole city went crazy, and we were given a tour around town in a convertible by some happy chap."

Carmickle was back in the States attending a lecture on the invasion of Japan, when a man ran in and interrupted the speaker.

"You can shut up now," the man said. "The war is over."

Although my dad left Europe on July 22, arriving in the U.S. on July 23, presumably by plane, many from his troop were still waiting in August. Finally, on August 13, they got the word that they would sail from LeHavre on August 15 on the liberty ship John B. Moorehead. At 11 a.m., August 15, the men boarded trucks and made the trip to LeHavre. According to Sweeney, they were "the happiest men in the world, finally heading for home."

"The Army took up all of our equipment, which we never saw again," said Frederick Altizer. "We left France on August 15, sailing home a good deal less comfortably than we came over, since our conveyance was a slower, smaller vessel known as a victory ship. Ours was named the S.S. John Morehead. I was seasick all the way home. The Navy fixed us a great meal: Spanish olives, sirloin steak, smothered onions, carrots and peas, parsley potatoes, sliced peaches, ice cream. Most of the boys got so sick they couldn't eat it. They took one bite and headed toward the rail."

The John B. Morehead reached New York harbor on August 26 and docked at Pier 13, Staten Island, at 5:45 p.m. Troops began leaving the ship at 6:30 p.m. and immediately boarded a train for Camp Kilmer, New Jersey, arriving at around 11 p.m. After an orientation lecture, the men finally were fed and quartered.

"I never have forgotten the big steak dinner they fed us," said Altizer. "The first food I'd enjoyed for about a week."

August 27 was spent processing and preparing paperwork. The squadron was broken down into their respective separation centers, and at 5 p.m. the first group left for Fort George Meade. The balance of the groups left at various intervals throughout the night. The normal 30-day recuperation leave was extended to 45 days.

Group headquarters and headquarters troop did not leave Germany until later. On October 10, headquarters moved to Camp Heebert, Tarrington, France, then to Le Havre for embar-

Catching the train in Heidelberg. On the back of the photo: "Note smile on face. Going home."

Photo courtesy of Buck Fluharty.

kation to Boston and from there to Camp Miles Standish, Mass. There the unit was de-activated on October 30, 1945. Col. McClelland had been reassigned to headquarters, Seventh Army, in Heidelberg and was the last member of the Group to leave Germany. He recalls standing on a sidewalk in Jugenheim, waving as the last units pulled out.

"Mac had been an aggressive, hard-driving officer who kept continuous pressure on the Germans throughout the campaign," wrote Graydon in his history. "On the fast-moving, ever-changing battle front, his decisions were quickly made and seldom if ever wrong. The 101st Cavalry could not have had a better war-time leader."

The squadron regrouped at Camp Campbell, Kentucky, with the first group reporting October 18 and the last coming in on October 25. The entire squadron did not report back, since many of the enlisted personnel had been discharged directly from the separation centers. Forty officers and 328 enlisted men reported back to duty in Kentucky.

My dad received his discharge at Ashburn General Hospital in McKinney, Texas, on October 25, 1945. It was signed by George O'Grady, Dental Corps, Acting Executive Officer. Mother was in Canadian, Texas, where she had purchased a floral shop, so I have to assume he left quickly for the 400-mile trip home.

In the morning mail of October 30, General Order #553, Headquarters Seventh Army, dated 27 September 1945 arrived at the headquarters of the 101st. It announced that the 116th Squadron's Troop C, as well as the first platoon of Company F and third platoon of Troop E had earned the Presidential Unit Citation for outstanding performance of duty in action on April 18 and 19 in Merkendorf, Germany.

By November 10, the de-activation of the Squadron was complete. At the end of his narrative, *A History of the 101st Cavalry in World War II*, Col. Charles Graydon wrote:

Thus ends the story of the 101st Cavalry's preparation for and tour of Europe, courtesy of Uncle Sam. Those of us there will long remember the Glory Road we followed and the common cause that bonded us together. But we are prone to forget the long hard work to get ready and then the chaos, the uncertainty, and fear on the battlefield with death always just around the comer. And we must never cease to pay tribute to our fellow troopers who left us in that foreign land to make the long journey to 'Fiddler's Green,' the last resting place of all U.S. Cavalrymen young and old. Perhaps sometime we will all meet there again. If this should happen, and God willing it will, may we also meet those faithful horses we once rode when we were proud and feisty young cavalrymen.

The Silent Years

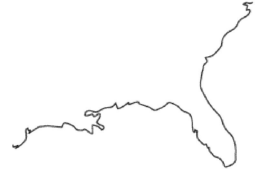

The men of the 101st Cavalry came to the war from many different places – both figuratively and literally. They came as farmers, mechanics, ship builders, and students. None of the men I talked to was much older than 22 when he entered the service; at 34, my father was one of just two or three "old men" in his unit. One of the youngest was Frederick Altizer, who joined at 17. Some were married with families; others were single.

John Almond was drafted at the age of 20. By the time he was discharged at 23, he said he had lived a lifetime.

Joseph Borkowski came into the service straight from college ROTC, and Lou Gergley was a senior in high school facing chemistry and economics exams. In December 1942, a year after the war started, an Army recruiter promised him a GED if he would join. It sounded like a good deal to him at the time.

Bill Hart had been working as an aircraft mechanic, and when I asked if he had enlisted, he said, "I wouldn't have volunteered for a March of Dimes."

Buck Fluharty was 19 years old when he was drafted at the end of 1942. He had been working in a boat yard in Tilghman, Maryland, and riding his Harley.

Richard Stutzman entered the service in 1940, before the war had begun. He was only 17 or 18 years old when he joined, which he did just because his friends were joining. He worked as an arial photographer during the war, interpreting photos of enemy troop movements and where bridges may have been destroyed. He served five years, one month, and twenty-one days.

William Pierce was drafted at the age of 18 on June 17. After training at Fort Knox, he went to Europe where one of his jobs was to meet with the Burgermeister in each town they en-

Buck Fluharty

tered and work with him to accomplish whatever the cavalry's mission might be in that town.

From all over the country the men came, from different cities and towns and different backgrounds. But, like my father, many of the men in the 101st Cavalry came home with one thing in common: they didn't want to talk about the war.

"I came home and talked about how pretty the country was, how clean and well kept," said Clinton Thompson. "People at home couldn't understand how complimentary I was. They didn't want to hear that I found the German people very cordial, that they were just trying to get their lives back to normal. One lady in Germany who spoke English — she was an actress — let us stay in her house at one point, and we slept on feather beds. I remember those things, but no one really wanted to hear about that. And remembering the casualties made it hard for me to talk about the war."

"Borden never talked about his Army experiences until the men began to go to the reunion," said Edith Holloman, whose husband served in Troop A of the 101st Squadron. "It was as if the floodgates were open when they got together. I guess it was bringing closure to something they were a part of 60 years ago. The only thing he told me was that he and his friend Steve were on patrol one time when Steve stepped on a mine and was blown to pieces. Other than that, he didn't tell me anything else, no matter how often I asked him about it. I accidentally found his pictures when I went through his Army trunk after he died. I had never seen them before. I also found his mess kit. Borden was a very private person and a very caring person."

"You just knew there was a line you didn't cross in asking about the war," said Andy Pierce, William Pierce's son, at the 2006 reunion. "And maybe there were things you wouldn't want to hear."

Charles "Duke" Covey was living in Easton, Md., and working at a feed mill when he was drafted. When I asked him about the war, he didn't have much to say. "It was the same thing every day," he said, "fighting and killing one another. You're the first person I ever talked to about it. I just got disgusted, and I didn't talk about it to anyone."

Covey got married after the war and started a chicken business, then the landscaping business. He was a heavy smoker and now is now fighting lung cancer.

Charles Covey

"I started smoking during the war and smoked a couple of packs a day," he said. "I'd smoke when I got a little nervous."

Earl Carmickle went back to Arkansas after the war. He held different jobs, cutting timber for awhile, then working in construction in Ohio. "I worked on some big buildings in Columbus," he said. He tried to stay in touch with his friend, Larry Hayden, but when Carmickle first came home, his mother had cancer. He got Red Cross leave to be with her, and when he returned to base, he had missed everyone. They were gone.

"I had meant to get all their addresses," he said.

Although they lost touch for awhile, he eventually did find Hayden. "Hayden went back to Illinois, and he died in the 1960s," Carmickle said.

In 1957 Carmickle's house burned, along with all his photos, letters and records from the war. "Nothing's left," he said.

Earl Carmickle and Larry Hayden, 1943

Photo courtesy Jeanette Carmickle Walsh.

After the war, Erwin Perkins worked for Archer Daniels Midland Company, now one of the world's largest agricultural processors of soybeans, corn, wheat, and cocoa.

"In 1950 I quit and went to farming," he said. "Wish I'd stayed where I was."

Perkins continued his friendship with Abe Friedman for the rest of his life.

Glenn Eanes was one of 19 men from Danville who ended up in the 101st. As of 2008, only four were still living.

"One buddy from Danville got his leg blown off. After the war I put hand controls on his car for him," said Eanes, who worked as general manager for the Oldsmobile dealership in Danville from 1946 to 1958, then for Pontiac.

Bennie Hawkins said his dad always knew he'd make it home from the war. "But I didn't talk about it unless someone asked," he said. "After the war I got a job at the telephone company, and they transferred me five times. I got tired of that, so I went to work for Dominion Power in Lynchburg (Virginia) and retired in 1985. I met my wife at the phone company, and we've been married for 55 years."

Although Hawkins hurt his knee during the war jumping off an armored car, he didn't have anything done to it for many years. "I just never said anything," he said. "It had bothered me ever since the war, but I didn't have the surgery until after I retired. That made it better."

William Evans lost everything he had saved from the war when the hurricanes Ivan and Jeanne flooded his basement. "The name of the family he stayed with in Germany after the war, photos, letters, all of his papers are gone," wrote his daughter, Sharon Valko.

Hart ended up spending 27 years in the Air Force, retiring in 1970. In Vietnam he worked on Cobra helicopters – "the only helicopter I liked," he said.

After the war Lou Gergley worked in a mill for awhile, then went to Sears & Roebucks, where he worked in the service department for 36 years.

"My father worked on the railroad," said William Pierce, "and I had a summer job there. When I came back [from the war], the job was waiting, but eventually I went to work as a locomotive engineer."

Stutzman went home to Sommerset, Penn., after the war, then to Mt. Morris, N.Y., where he ran a gas station until he went to work for the Juvenile Detention Center.

Fluharty took up flying, but quit after heart surgery in his 70s. After 60 years, he still calls the men by the job they had during the war: "my driver, my bow gunner," and like most of the men, he refers to the others as boys: "This boy was from Pennsylvania," or "That boy was a great storyteller."

Glenn Eanes

Their favorite stories to tell are the ones they can tell on each other, often jokes with heartbreaking punchlines.

"This guy was huge," Fluharty said of a trooper from Rochester, N.Y. "I weighed 145 lbs., and he could pick me up with one hand and set me on a tank. He was hit one day with shrapnel in the thigh and went into shock right away and died. We didn't lose a lot of men, but we lost him."

Fluharty also likes to tell about "Fearless Wilkins," a member of one of the recon groups, who would mount a 50-caliber gun on a tripod on his tank tray — "a brute of a weapon," said Fluharty. "He would stand up out of the tank, waist high, and shoot up the Germans in every town he went into. No regard for himself. Even the Germans heard about him. He had no regard for his own safety at all. He was the only man I ever heard of to do that. Everyone knew of him. Even had 'Fearless Wilkins' emblazoned across the back of his combat jacket."

"Some stories I don't remember," said John Gorski, "and some I don't want to talk about. I was talkative as a soldier, but I'm a quiet civilian."

Gorski said he would talk about the war when he met a buddy who had been in the service, "but I only want to talk about it with other service guys."

"When I got home, I just felt like -- what the hell," he said, "I don't want to talk about this. I'm home with my family and my friends. I'm sleeping good; I'm eating good. I don't want to have to think about the war."

Gorski decided he never wanted to work for anyone else again, so he started a tavern in Hartford, Conn., with a friend from school who had also just gotten out of the service. "We bought it from an old man who was ready to get out," he said. "He'd only sell it to a service man, and we were the lucky ones to get it from him."

Later, Gorski's friend left for Canada, and Gorski went into business with another friend, and they opened a restaurant.

"Later we got a bigger one," he said, "and I did that for 40-some years."

Eugene Tharp came home and married his high school sweetheart. He farmed and ranched, and eventually went into auctioneering and insurance. He still tries to work a little. He started an auctioneering business, which his grandson runs now. "It'll be his when I'm gone," he said.

Tharp said he would try to talk about the war after he came home, but couldn't. "I'd get started talking about it, and I'd just break up," he said. Then, at a visit to the VA, he met a Vietnam veteran who said he had the same problem. He had been to a psychiatrist for help, and he suggested Tharp try that.

"One of my daughters took me, and I was diagnosed with post-traumatic stress disorder," he said, giving credit to the "Vietnam boys" for making it okay to seek help for the problems that are an inevitable part of war.

A number of men I talked to would get tears in their eyes talking about the war, and I wondered if it was the fear of breaking down in front of their families that had kept them silent for so many years.

David Gay returned to farming when he got home, and two years after the war, he married his high school sweetheart.

"I was so glad to be home," he said. "I didn't ever want to talk about the war. I can't explain why; I just didn't. My family never asked very much about it. If they did, I would say I didn't want to talk about it. I didn't want to have to explain it."

John Borotka and Joseph Coccia returned to Baltimore after the war. Borotka went to work for Western Electric and Coccia worked for Bethlehem Steel. They had lived near each other before the war, but didn't know each other then. During the war their mothers became friends.

"John told his mother everything, and I told mine nothing," said Coccia, "so they would get together so my mother could find out what was going on."

Joseph Coccia and John Borotka, 2008

Borotka said it was difficult putting his experience into words. "I can picture Merkendorf in my mind," he said. "I can see six German officers standing in a room getting ready to surrender to me, cutting their insignia off their lapels, but describing it to someone else so it makes sense is hard."

Even though he doesn't talk about it much, Borotka said, it is still on his mind.

"I go to bed with it. I lay in bed and go over it in my mind. It never goes away."

Starting Over

Afterthe war, my father went home to Texas, planning to settle down there with my mother and
raise cattle. Things didn't work out quite that way,
and in 1948 they moved to Oregon. In 1949, after 12 years of
marriage, they had their first child. Me.

I spent long hours as a child, walking in my father's shadow as he irrigated the 40 acres where we lived in Redmond.
We walked through juniper groves and around the piles of
lava rock that were stacked by whoever first cleared this land.
He would tell me that the Indians were really here first, and to
prove it he would show me a hollowed-out rock they once used
to grind corn. I asked if the Indians would have cleared the
rock from the land, and he would just shrug.

In the pasture's hilly places, those not fit for plowing or
grazing, lava rocks lay scattered where they first landed. Flung

out by volcanoes millennia ago, they lay so close together that I could step from stone to stone and never touch the ground.

When the water was down, which means it was flowing from the canal through the main ditches along the boundary of our property, my father would take his shovel and dig out small earthen dams along the ditch. Opening these allowed the water to flow out into our pasture. When it was no longer our turn to have the water, he made the trip again, damming all the places he had opened just a few days before. As he jammed the shovel in the soggy ground, we would talk about water skippers and Indians and cows.

He had about a dozen cows, all shapes and sizes, and one bull. They didn't give us any trouble when I helped bring them in for milking, but they were never in a hurry either. We didn't so much drive them as follow them. I often think they would have gotten to the barn just as fast if all we had done was stand in the barn door and whistle.

When my dad milked, my job was to close the stanchion on each cow's neck as she reached through to a manger filled with hay tossed down

The author and her father in 1954.

from the loft overhead. He would then takes hobbles from a nail by the barn door and attach one end to the left hind leg of the cow and the other end caught the cow's tail and was attached to the right hind leg, to keep the cow from kicking him or swishing him with her tail, he said.

He didn't use a milking stool, which he said were for sissies; he would squat instead on his heels beside each cow, lean his head against her belly, and begin the rhythmic squeeze and pull, squeeze and pull that shot milk into a bucket locked between his knees. When the bucket was full, he poured it into a milk can, which went into a cooler outside the barn. Once each day, a flat-bed truck from Eberhard Creamery came, exchanging empty cans for full ones.

In addition to the few cows he milked, my father worked more than 20 years driving truck for a propane gas company. But his avocation was cooking, a skill he picked up on that Texas ranch. He spent his vacations cooking for trail rides, often along the Pacific Crest Trail in the Cascade Mountains, and for special events like the Potato Festival, Bend Water Pageant, or the opening of Pelton Dam and Lake Billy Chinook. His sourdough biscuits and his pies were legendary. It meant something to get one of Ted Welch's pecan pies at Christmas.

I often accompanied him on his cookouts around the state, and he usually let me take friends. If it required being gone overnight, he'd take the covered wagon he used as a chuck wagon. My friend and I would sleep inside, while he bunked underneath on the ground. When our giggling became unbearable, he'd reach up and bang a pan against the floor of the wagon, and we knew to be quiet.

In all those years, I never asked my father much about the war. Only occasionally, while admiring the swords he brought back or watching a movie about the war, did I ever ask him what it was like.

"Germany is a beautiful country," is all he'd say.

Acknowledgements

It would have been impossible to write this book without all the help and encouragement I received from veterans of the 101st Cavalry, their wives, and their children. I am more grateful than I can ever say for the precious stories and photographs they so willingly shared.

Thank you especially to:

Sheila Ramuar Abshire
Frederick Altizer
Joseph Borkowski
Regina Brunnengräber
Joseph Coccia
Anne Cummings
Murray Dressler
Buck Fluharty
David Gay
John Gorski
Bill Hart
Bill Hurley
Cheryl Kashuba
Robert Klein
David Levitas
Erwin Perkins
Mary Romano
Richard Stutzman
Clinton Thomas
Janet Willemain

John Almond
John Altizer
John Borotka
Earle Carmickle
Charles Covey
Henry Dressler
Glenn Eanes
Lev Friedman
Lou Gergley
Anna Gutschalk
Bennie Hawkins
George Jurand
Lou Kiessler
Jay Leonard
Stan Majcherkiewicz
William Pierce
Maciej Siekierski
Eugene Tharp
Jeannette Carmickle Walsh
Petra Wooden

I also want to thank the staff at the National Archives in College Park, Maryland. They were helpful, courteous, and friendly, making my time there looking for information and photographs not only successful, but a pleasure as well.

The majority of the photos in this book were taken by the men themselves as they served in Germany in World War II. I am still awed by their willingness to send original photos to me, trusting that I would take care of and then return these precious mementos. Thank you. Thank you.

Letters and papers:

Thank you to Jay Leonard for sharing the scrapbooks of his father, Lt. Col. Hubert Leonard. The papers he provided were the skeleton I needed to begin shaping the book. And many thanks to John Altizer, who shared material from his website, including the letters of John Allen and Clint Gosnell.

Written histories:

The following histories were also valuable resources and made for fascinating reading:

Altizer, Frederick. *From a Distance: Memories of My War Experiences.* 2006.
Graydon, Col. Charles. *With the 101st in World War II.* 1945.
Sweeney, Maj. Mercer, ed. *Wingfoot: Rhineland and Central Europe Campaigns. Official history, 101st Cavalry Group* (Mechanized). Printed by Hugo Diesbach, Weinheim/Bergstr., Germany. August 1945.

An update on the 101st Cavalry:

Members of the 101st Cavalry Regiment, New York Army National Guard, are still serving; as of October 2008, they are fighting in Afghanistan.

About the Author

The author and her father in a photo taken in 1952.

To learn more about her father's military service, Melaney Welch Moisan spent four years researching the role of the 101st Cavalry in World War II. She has created a website and a blog related to the 101st Cavalry, and her poetry about the men who served in World War II has earned awards from the Oregon State Poetry Association and Willamette Writers. She has an MFA in Creative Nonfiction from Goucher College and works as a writer in Salem, Oregon.

Index of names: 101st Cavalry

Klein, Robert: 26, 113, 170, 171, 227, 259
Kohnle, Walter: 187
Kornblum, William: 185
Kurth, Preston: 207
Kuzniewski, Joseph: 187
Lakitsky, Andrew: 174
Langridge, Jack: 285
Langton, George: 193
Lanning, Barzillai: 36
Leonard, Clarence: 221, 222
Leonard, Hubert: 16, 20, 26, 53, 67, 68-70, 74-89, 106, 108, 150, 195, 211, 212, 298, 314, 346
Levitas, David: 202, 218, 221, 222, 224
Lewis, Leslie: 30
Littleton, Augustine "Gus": 22, 36, 64, 108, 116
Lolos, Bernard: 28
Lupardus, Olaf: 212
Lusher: 227
Lutchko, John: 197
Mack, Frederick: 94
Mann, Ezra: 94, 116, 226, 346
Matanin, Andrew: 121
Mayes, Louis: 222
McAlister, James: 262
McCarty, Ira: 195, 196
McClelland, Charles: 61, 62, 139, 211, 257
McHatten, Rowell: 195
Mehlich, Charles: 2
Mennel, Walter: 30, 34
Meyer, Harold: 114
Moore, Bauldwin: 27
Moore, Carl: 222
Mortenson, Leo: 62, 67, 83, 87, 311
Moss, Edward: 222
Muckstadt, John: 23
Nawn, Leo: 257
Nichols, Ralph: 28, 37, 291, 333
Noonan, John: 30
Odell, Irving: 67
Olenik, Irwin: 96
Olsen, William: 37
Paquette, Raymond: 96, 195
Patterson, Andre: 174
Peele, Louis: 3, 155, 223
Perkins, Erwin: 86, 143, 193, 208-209, 356
Petras, David: 221
Pierce, Charles: 29, 34
Pierce, William: 38, 66, 106, 140, 168, 172, 214, 301, 354, 355, 357

Pollack: 155
Powers, Maurice: 21, 69, 321-331
Ramuar, Roy: 159-161
Reale, Francis: 222
Rest, Lee: 233
Ritchie, Ralph: 110, 113, 142,
Rodrigue, Eldridge: 36
Rodgers, Morton: 202
Romano, John: 27
Romero, Alvin: 3, 121
Rothengast, John: 193, 194, 195
Schafer, Robert: 30-34, 96, 195
Schnalzer, John: 30, 34, 207, 259, 303
Sleptiza, Alec: 3
Spill, Clarence: 346
Stepp, Joseph: 195
Stolt, Dominic: 37, 145
Strange, Hal: 233
Stutzman, Richard: 308, 354, 357
Sullivan, John: 113
Summers, Herbert: 222
Swanson, Jack: 24, 212
Sweeney, Mercer: 72, 87
Swim, Thurman: 24
Terrell, Frank: 222
Tharp, Eugene: 8, 65, 140, 147, 186, 226, 262, 277, 359
Thomas, Irwin: 196
Thompson, Clinton: 17, 64, 136, 194, 342, 354
Turk, Harold: 222
Ulmschneider, Robert: 112-113, 142, 259
Vacek, Charles: 203
Walsh, Patty: 147
Weaver, Buck: 221
Weaver, Lonnie: 222
Weinheimer, William: 86
Weirick, Dale: 110
Welch, Theodore: 39-47, 57-60, 101-103, 361-363
White, Morris: 186
Wichman, Otto: 21
Willemain, Bernard: 155
Winick, Morris: 222
Wilson, Grover Cleveland: 25, 37, 183
Wilson, Harold: 195
Wood, Harvey: 19, 115
Young, Edward: 36

CPSIA information can be obtained at www.ICGtesting.com
Printed in the USA
BVOW04s0227081016

464525BV00002B/167/P